MANAGING UNCERTAINTY:
ETHNOGRAPHIC STUDIES OF ILLNESS,
RISK AND THE STRUGGLE FOR CONTROL

Critical Anthropology

Volume 2

Edited by Michael Jackson
University of Copenhagen

vol. 1
*Matters of Life and Longing: Female Sterilisation in
Northeast Brazil*
by Anne Line Dalsgaard
2004, 253 pages, illustrated
ISBN 87 7289 901 8

IN PREPARATION:
vol. 3
*Destinies at Play: Angolan Refugees and Divination Baskets
in Northwest Zambia*
by Sónia Silva
2005

Critical Anthropology
explores life on the margins
of the modern world,
and demonstrates
the power of ethnography
to provide new insights
into the human condition.

MANAGING UNCERTAINTY

Ethnographic Studies of Illness,
Risk and the Struggle for Control

edited by

Richard Jenkins, Hanne Jessen and Vibeke Steffen

MUSEUM TUSCULANUM PRESS
UNIVERSITY OF COPENHAGEN
2005

Managing Uncertainty
© 2005 Museum Tusculanum Press and the authors
Edited by: Richard Jenkins, Hanne Jessen and Vibeke Steffen
Cover design by: Veronique van der Neut
Composition by: Narayana Press
Set in: A Jenson Pro
Printed by: Narayana Press, www.narayanapress.dk

ISBN 87 7289 963 8
ISSN 1811 – 0665

Published in the series *Critical Anthropology*
Series editor: Professor Michael Jackson, University of Copenhagen

Cover painting: Kåre Jansbøl, The Blue Painting

Published with support from
The Danish Research Council for the Humanities
Nordea Danmark Fonden

Museum Tusculanum Press
Njalsgade 94
DK – 2300 Copenhagen S

www.mtp.dk

CONTENTS

ACKNOWLEDGEMENTS

This collection of essays is based on papers that were presented at the second Nordic Workshop on Medical Anthropology, held in Denmark in January 2000. The workshop had three main themes: 'Body, senses, and experience', 'Health systems, medicines, and technology', and 'Handicap, rehabilitation, and competence'. During the stimulating discussions which took place in the three days of the workshop, a common theme emerged, addressing the ways in which people seek to control risk and uncertainty in their lives, and the consequences for control and certainty of these attempts. We have selected some of the best papers – all of them based on on-going ethnographic research – that addressed this theme and asked the authors to revise their contribution for this volume.

We wish to acknowledge and thank all of the participants in the workshop for their valuable contributions to these discussions, and for their encouragement and support for this volume. We also thank the Danish Social Science Research Council and the Institute of Anthropology, University of Copenhagen, for generously providing funding for the workshop, and the Danish Humanities Research Council and Nordea Danmark Fonden for subsidising publication of the final collection. Michael Jackson deserves out gratitude for his encouragement and useful comments, and last, but not least, our thanks go to Bettina Hauge, whose administrative and practical skills made everything work so smoothly.

Richard Jenkins
Hanne Jessen
Vibeke Steffen
March 2004

ONE

MATTERS OF LIFE AND DEATH
the control of uncertainty
and the uncertainty of control

Richard Jenkins, Hanne Jessen and Vibeke Steffen

Matters of life and death are self-evidently at the heart of human exist-ence. When sickness calls into question that existence we are confronted by the uncertainties of life. In such situations our concerns are not only with the physical body and experiences of physical pain and fragility, but also with the social and symbolic aspects of life and death. These are aspects of well-being that are no less real than the body and its frailties. Sickness in particular and crisis in general pose questions about our very sense of existence and non-existence, and thus raise questions about how to deal with the uncertainties of living and the means with which we try to manoeuvre when the waters of life are troubled. Whether through scientific information and local knowledge, or the manipulation of social and symbolic resources, we seek a sense of control when faced with crisis. Sometimes, however, submission to or acceptance of a situation may be a relevant and attractive response, and just as much an aspect of human agency. In the last resort, the openness of uncertainty may be preferred to certainty and control, not least when our prospects seem grim.

There is a long-standing anthropological tradition of studies concerned with how humans deal with the uncertainties of life, stretching from clas-sical studies of misfortune (Evans-Pritchard 1937; Turner 1968) to recent studies of risk and uncertainty (Douglas 1993; Whyte 1997). Similarly,

the management of uncertainty has become a significant theme in sociological studies of the 'risk-society' (Beck 1992), as well as in research
about biomedical training, professional socialisation and practice (Fox
2000). In all of this work, however, there is a gap that separates analyses
concerned with structural conditions or political economy, on the one
hand, and work that is concerned with individual agency and the human
capacity to deal with situations of crisis, on the other. Within this gap
there is a need to reconcile the tension between individual capacities and
potentialities.

Within the limits set by the environment, the possibilities that are perceived and acted upon by individuals contribute to the dynamics of social
life that may, eventually, test and transform those limits. Bourdieu's notion
of *illusio*, for example, expresses the human drive to invest in dreams and
hopes – if not materially then symbolically – in even the most apparently
hopeless of situations (Bourdieu 2000). This investment in the future may
sometimes appear to be a struggle for actual or immediate control; it may
also, however, be a matter of adjustments, negotiations or imaginings that
sustain an image or illusion of control rather than its reality. From any
individual point of view, the likelihood of achieving desired outcomes
must be weighed against the perceived instability of the situation, and
the alienation inspired by uncertainty against the value that is attached
to life, and all in this in a chaotic world:

> Continuity is an illusion. Disruption to life is a constant in human
> experience. The only continuity that has staying power is the continuity
> of the body, and even that is vulnerable. But that reality is too unsettling
> for people to live with. Faith in continuity of the body may preserve
> the illusion of a more sweeping continuity. (Becker 1997: 190)

While Becker's pessimism is, doubtless, warranted by individual experience, it misses something important that Bourdieu's notion of *illusio*
seems to capture better. The fact that continuity is imagined does not
mean that it is imaginary: it is very real in its consequences (*cf.* Jenkins
1996). That most people, most of the time, obstinately create and find

some continuity in their lives, in the face of hostile circumstances and their own vulnerability, is perhaps the most significant story.

Paying heed to Foucault's notion of governmentality, which stresses that power is relational rather than objective (Foucault 1988), control and uncertainty are always negotiated within social relations. The ethnographic examples presented in this collection illustrate the micro-politics of negotiation with the circumstances of life within different settings and contexts, and how this is often a matter of adjustment to a situation rather than complete, effective power. In the face of indeterminacy, people everywhere struggle to influence, even if they cannot completely control, their present and future situations.

As Susan Reynolds Whyte reminds us in this collection, Geertz has located this struggle in the notion of small specific things, in the suggestive details that are at the heart of the meaning of life for human beings. Humans are never merely victims of fate: despite the impossibility of complete certainty, we actively attempt to create a degree of security or insurance (Whyte 1997: 18). Fate, in theory irresistible and irrevocable, is in practice taken to be somewhat controllable or at least negotiable. That it is not in the nature of humans to submit blindly to the mysteriously inevitable is eloquently attested to by western science and medicine no less than the attempts of other cultures to intervene in destiny (Fortes 1987).

Economic insecurity, reproductive failure, and threatened health are basic and universal concerns. Our efforts to manage such adversities draw on a range of resources. During crises we look for reasons and explanations, and possible strategies and plans are mediated by and through the meanings and knowledge we share with others. Substances, artefacts and techniques – medicines and technologies, or rituals and magic – offer various means by which we attempt to cope with or control illness and misfortune. With respect to all of these, there are generally alternatives available, which in themselves encourage further uncertainty about which is the correct response to a particular problem.

While insisting on the importance of uncertainty to any 'social' conceptualisation of health and illness, in this collection we intend to expand the framework within which it is understood. First, there is a need to look at how people other than medical practitioners – particularly the sick and the members of their social networks – encounter, experience and deal with uncertainty. Second, modern biomedicine is but one focus of our attention: comparative medical anthropology insists that we pay attention to the broadest possible panorama of health- and illness-related behaviours (Helman 2000). Finally, rather than viewing uncertainty as peculiar to matters of life and death, we offer an argument in favour of re-thinking uncertainty as a generic feature, and indeed definitive of, the human condition in general. From this perspective it is not the gravity of life and death which produces uncertainty, but, rather, their uncertainty that makes life and death matter in the first place.

Matters of life and death

This collection of essays addresses a number of specific matters of life and death that have emerged within medical anthropology and the sociology of health and illness, all of which are in one way or another concerned with uncertainty and its control or mitigation.

The first of our themes starts with the daily struggles of human existence. In response, perhaps, to the comfortable, systemic certainties of structural functionalism, there has developed an important strand of literature which looks at *health- or cure-seeking as an attempt to conjure up a sense of relative order in the midst of the chronic uncertainties of life* (Desjarlais 1997; Lock and Kaufert 1998; Whyte 1997). Here the focus has been shifted from structural studies of social and cultural systems to interpretive studies of sick people or their relatives and social networks. One critique of the existential limits of much existing social anthropology, and of the objectification of human suffering implicit in writings that reduce illness to a social construction, proposes approaches that are more 'experience-near' (Csordas 1994; Jackson 1989). Focusing on the experience of social transactions within local moral worlds has paved the road for analyses that orient themselves towards what is at stake for particular persons in particular situations (Kleinman and Kleinman 1991: 277). Thus the emphasis has changed: first, from systems to people, and second, from the bodily transformation of 'illness' into 'health' to a multi-facetted engagement with meaning and experience. The conventional conceptualisation of, and emphasis on, 'getting better', which derives from biomedicine, has been reoriented towards a more holistic and more complex interpretive framework, at the heart of which lies, among other things, the ways in which actors come to terms with uncertainty. In other words, for particular humans in particular situations reasons for being and for behaviour may differ significantly from the reasons of science.

An enormously influential interpretation of formal and informal knowledge and beliefs about health and illness, and the interventions of formal and informal experts, has focused on narrative (Capps and Ochs 1995; Good 1994; Kleinman 1988; Mattingly 1998a). Encounters between the sick and their companions, and between healers and other specialists, have been recast as occasions within which narratives – engaged with possibilities rather than certainties – are formed, rehearsed and enunciated. This is no less the case for scientific biomedicine than for 'indigenous' medicine, and the narrative model has been deployed in a broad variety of research settings (*e.g.* Price 1987; Mogensen 1997; Steffen 1997).

Some of these analyses emphasise narrative, as a form of *being* as much as a way of *saying*. Mattingly's study of occupational therapy in an American hospital, for example, considers the narrative structure of clinical action and demonstrates the importance of intentionality, motive, and action as key structuring devices during therapy. We act because we intend to get something done, to begin something which we hope will lead us along a desirable route. We try to make our actions cumulative, with a sense of a definite ending (Mattingly 1994: 813). In addition to providing everyday life with beginnings, middles and endings, narrative is also an important component of, and contribution to, the processes of negotiation that are so central to health and illness (Jessen 1997; Steffen 2002). The creation of order and meaning that is stressed in narrative analysis can thus be understood in various ways – through *lived* stories as well as through story-*telling* – as a practical attempt to plot paths through the chaos and flow of life's uncertainties.

This collection's second theme is *the diversity and heterogeneity of responses to illness and disability*. Put in another way, in response to uncertainty and distress people do not just do 'what their culture tells them to do'. This seems to be for at least two reasons. First, looking at local knowledge and rules, what Fredrik Barth (1969) called the *cultural stuff*, there is always diversity and ambiguity. This is so with respect to both diagnosis and subsequent response: there are typically alternatives available. Even allowing for an agreed diagnosis, there is rarely, if ever, just one obvious best thing to do (Whyte 1997: 23). A degree of uncertainty is as intrinsic to these processes as it is to life itself. Communal living and relationships, and the formulation of *any* response to misfortune and illness, might become very difficult indeed in the absence of this flexibility. Second, in as much as individuals are not 'cultural clones', they themselves necessarily bring to these situations a range of their own *individual stuff*, ranging from personal history and experience, to emotional ties and responses, to calculative strategies.

The variety of individual and cultural resources which can be brought to bear on any situation has inspired a series of studies which focus on treatment and treatment-seeking as transactions and negotiations between sufferers, their kin and their friends, on the one hand, and professionals and experts, on the other. This understanding of medicine and curing harmonises with the narrative framework, discussed above, and, as with that model, it applies no less to affluent, urbanised industrialised contexts (Lindenbaum and Lock 1993) than to a wide range of 'third world' or 'less developed' settings (Janzen 1978; Sachs 1989). In all cases, in the absence of a definite 'cultural script' the outcome of the encounter is an uncertain product of contingency, process, resources, and power. In this context the rationalisation attempted by modern biomedicine can be understood as a perpetually thwarted attempt to impose particular cultural scripts, backed by the legitimate authority of science and the professional status and power of experts.

Our third theme focuses on *institutionalised medicine as the ration-*

alised control of uncertainty. Flying somewhat in the face of the trium-phalist modern narrative of medicine as humankind's defence against pain, bodily vulnerability, and an unpredictable environment teeming with aggressively hostile infective organisms, institutionalised medicine and healthcare can also be understood as a powerful set of institutions for bringing under control bodies, minds, and whole people, individually and collectively (Foucault 1975; Gordon 1988). The issues here cluster around the long-term attempt in western industrialised states to create, through massive investment in biomedicine and public health measures, a *social* environment of predictability – actuarial and behavioural – and a rational organisation for maintaining it. Since the state exercises its power over living beings *as* living beings, its politics are necessarily *bio*-politics (Foucault 1988: 160).

While one of Foucault's later concerns was the 'technology of the self' in western society – the various ways in which we have acted upon ourselves, and made ourselves the objects of care and domination – recent medical anthropology has emphasised individual agency and experience as well as the dynamics between structure and agency (Samuelsen and Steffen 2004). Studies of new medical technologies, for example, rather than seeing them as merely alienating and repressive have focused on the prag-matic acceptance or rejection of such technologies by those on whom they are practised (Lock *et al.* 2000). That having been said, the constitution and transformation of physical bodies and individual identities through technology is to a great extent steered by policy-making and clinical practice. Here it is necessary to grasp the range of negotiations that take place between individuals and the institutions of society, the complexity of these intersections of personal agency and 'structural' power, and the relationship between institutional control and existential uncertainties.

As part of, first, colonialism, and, subsequently, globalising science and commerce, the hegemony of biomedicine has extended – whether through various kinds of imposition, or local enthusiasm for something that so manifestly works in many cases – far beyond the political, cul-tural and geographical contexts of its original development (*e.g.* Last and Chavunduka 1986). As a result, the provision of healthcare may become a complex local competition or negotiation between indigenous and international medical knowledge and institutions, with the latter often enjoying the sponsorship of the state and powerful vested interests. The political economy of biomedicine has developed in response to this internationalisation (Baer, Singer and Susser 1997), along with a concern with the general imperialism of medicalisation, as it attempts to include ever wider swathes of human misfortune under its gaze.

An appreciation of the bureaucratisation and professionalisation of the organisation and delivery of healthcare is central to any rounded understanding of medicalisation (Foster 1987). Much like managers within any complex organisation, the managerial interests of doctors and administrators encourage them to produce – as far as they *can* – routine and predictable business-as-usual (*e.g.* Koenig 1988; Stimson 1974). In the case of health-care, however, this may also have a further moral dimension, rooted in the particular, and asymmetrical, relationship between the supplicant sick and curers whose talents are scarce. A well-known example of this is the 'sick role' in western medicine, to which the patient is expected to conform in order to qualify as a 'good patient', worthy of medical attention and treatment (Parsons 1951: 428-54). However, since every local body of knowledge about illness includes notions of appropriate sickness behaviour (Lewis 1981), the role of 'appropriate patient' is neither wholly the creation of modern, institutionalised biomedicine nor monolithic.

Medical knowledge and intervention may be theorised as a species of social control in other respects, too: illness is sometimes categorised as behavioural deviance (Conrad and Schneider 1980). This is intimately connected with, first, the historical development of ever-more prescriptive notions of 'normality' within western science and medicine, and the increasing sophistication and enthusiasm with which they are measured (Hacking 1990; Hanson 1993), and, second, the medicalisation of madness and disability (Foucault 1973; Ingstad and Whyte 1995; Jenkins 1998b). This latter is also related to the institutional imperialism of some medical professions. In the context of ever more ambitious public health education programmes, the 'normal' refusal to live a healthy lifestyle – the most spectacular cases are probably alcohol, smoking or sexual behaviour – has also proved to be readily assimilable to moral notions of deviance (Herzlich and Pierret 1987). All of these can be related back to the modern state's project of generalised, rationalised predictability.

So the anthropological and sociological literature points us towards three senses in which matters of life and death are bound up with uncertainty. *First,* health- or cure-seeking can be seen as an attempt by individuals to create, in narrative, discourse and practice, at least some sense of order in the face of the everyday uncertainty of life. These attempts will of course always be embedded within the social relations of acting and communicating with others. *Second,* there is the diversity and heterogeneity of responses to illness and disability: what individuals do is not, for a number of reasons, culturally determined and predictable. *Finally,* institutionalised biomedicine can be understood as the state-sponsored and organised attempt to control uncertainty and create a predictable social environment through rational treatments and public health.

These themes are not, however, the last word on uncertainty. For example, it is not a new idea to suggest that social control produces deviance, rather than *vice versa.* Whether it be Durkheim's insistence that a certain amount of deviance is not only 'normal' but absolutely necessary (1964), the arguments of the labelling perspective in the sociology of deviance (Becker 1963; Lemert 1972; Matza 1969; Plummer 1979), or Jenkins' argument (1998a) that identity, morality, and normality, on the one hand and deviance in all of its manifestations, on the other, are interdependent, the basic point is well-established. In the context of health and illness this suggests some interesting further possibilities. In particular, there is a fourth sense in which matters of life and death are necessarily bound up with uncertainty, in that *attempts to control, reduce or remove uncertainty may actually lead to the generation of further uncertainty, or the accentuation of existing uncertainty.*

This proposition also suggests further analytical connections, in this case with recent social science debates about risk and modernity. It is, for example, well understood that new knowledge about diseases, or about the risks of certain diseases or illnesses, creates new uncertainties (*e.g.* Adam

1998: 164-91; Beck 1992: 127-38). Calculating the risks of illness is one of a number of ways in which human beings attempt not only to exert some sense of control over their lives, but also to lay open possible ways of manoeuvring. However, new methods of testing for all sorts of ills, and new developments in, for example, genetic screening, combined with the growing demands of increasingly well-informed patients, may have shifted the focus of concern from the actual problems of *specific* diseases towards a concern for the risks of living *in general*. 'At-risk-ness' is no longer merely accepted as a basic human condition, but appears to be seen by many people as a state – something like an illness in its own right – which must be managed through screening, tests, and medicines. In the process, 'healthy' individuals are transformed into 'pre-patients' of non-specific future illnesses (Frankenberg 1993; Vuckovic and Nichter 1997).

While a growing literature has been concerned at the macro level with the modern emergence of a so-called 'risk society' (Beck 1992; Douglas 1986, 1992: 3-121; Douglas and Wildavsky 1982; Giddens 1990), ethnographic analysis of the actual everyday consequences of living with these burgeoning uncertainties is underdeveloped (although, see Armstrong *et al.* 1998). In the rest of this book, we present a number of individual chapters, all of which have a bearing on the theme of control and uncertainty with respect to matters of life and death. These are concerned with *the control of uncertainty, the uncertainty of control*, and *the creation of uncertainty*. We will now look at each of these issues in turn.

The control of uncertainty

As we have already said, one of the central concerns of any modern state and its agencies is the coordination of attempts to foster greater certainty and predictability at the systemic level. Without this, the governance of complex societies as we have come to rely upon it – and all societies today are complex, differences in this respect are simply of degree – would probably not be possible. Central to this with respect to the administration of public health is the forecasting and territorial mapping of problems and needs. As Wenzel Geissler's chapter on Kenya illustrates, the state's gaze and the reach of modern medical science and epidemiology extend far beyond the metropolitan centre.

Medicine has more to contribute to the control of uncertainty than laboratory science and statistical analysis, however. Marita Eastmond's discussion of the problematic integration of refugees into Swedish society, betrays a deep collective anxiety about the new immigrants, and about the whole project, particularly at a time when public resources for 'natives' were under pressure. Here, the vocabulary and diagnostic paraphernalia of expert psycho-medicine have been drafted in to legitimate the state's acceptance of refugees and their apparently privileged placement into a special category of disability, and to enhance official control of the situation in general and individual refugees in particular. Medicalisation is such a logical and effective legitimation because it is underpinned by the pervasive images of the suffering and abnormality of refugees offered by the media and in official policies on asylum. As Eastmond shows, however, many of these people may be more interested in getting a job than in getting a diagnosis.

This is not the only example of the medicalisation of problems of human life and experience to which our contributors draw attention. Pills and potions may have their own special legitimatory authority, through which they work their own, specifically modern magic. In Vibeke Steffen's chapter, the Danish use of Antabuse as a treatment for alcoholism is a good example of an attempt to 'fit people in' to society through recourse to medicines. It also suggests that offering medication may help to mitigate professionals' uncertainties about the nature and appropriateness of what they are doing. The Opus Project described by John Aggergaard Larsen, also in Denmark, exemplifies the attempt to 'fit' people diagnosed as mentally ill into society through a combination of medication to control their sensations and behaviour, and therapy to equip them with acceptable narratives about their lives for consumption by themselves and others. Infertility, however, is neither a sickness nor is it a control problem for the 'rest of society'. To those who are affected by it, it is, nonetheless, definitively a matter of life, and in recent years biomedicine has turned its attention to the uncertainties of human reproduction. However, as Tine

Tjørnhøj-Thomsen discusses in her chapter, the technological contribution that medicine can make to the attempt to become pregnant is in itself uncertain.

Medicalisation is not, however, a monolithic one-way process, nor can it banish the uncertainties of health and illness with a magic bullet. In their respective chapters, Hanne Mogensen and Susan Whyte, each drawing on field research in Uganda, point out that many people have available to them at least two different systems of diagnosis and intervention, neither of which is necessarily any better 'understood' than the other. Which one will be chosen, under which circumstances, is not a matter of which one *works* better – that information is elusive, and any judgement fraught with uncertainty – or of blind obedience to local norms. As Mogensen's material illustrates in detail, this is, rather, the outcome of complex interpersonal processes of negotiation and interpretation.

In Guinea Bissau, the Papel families described by Jónína Einarsdóttir also have available to them local knowledge and some access to biomedical healthcare. When the latter was not available or not effective, however, and the lineage under pressure as children continued not to thrive, the ordeal of infant exposure might be a locally legitimate response to the uncertainties of the situation. The expulsion of a child suspected of being non-human might be preferable to not knowing the meaning of events over which control has been lost. Once again, however, this is not a matter of blindly following a 'cultural script': difficult decisions only emerge after difficult inter-personal negotiations, within families and lineages.

Anne-Line Dalsgaard's ethnography from urban Brazil tells a different story of mothers faced with constricted choices. Having *no* children is not an option, but too many children bring economic costs, and multiply the number of things that can go terribly wrong in the future. A woman's body, her fertility, is one of the very few things over which she can exercise control, and sterilisation is the only certain means of doing so. It is one of a limited array of options that these mothers have available if they are to act, and be *seen* to act, like a responsible human being. Because uncertainty is unavoidable, doesn't mean that one can do nothing.

As Susan Reynolds Whyte suggests in her chapter about Uganda, it is not, however, a matter of accepting uncertainty or not. That is not actually a realistically open option: there *is* uncertainty. What matters in Bunyole are practical and specific responses to deal with uncertainty. This is also a matter of time: an orientation towards the future within which life and death proceed.

The uncertainty of control

It is already clear, if only in the regular use of words such as 'attempt' in the previous section, that although curing, medicine, and health interventions of various kinds may aim to minimise or control uncertainty, the pursuit of reliable predictability is in itself a definitively uncertain project. This is so for a number of reasons.

In the first place, to revisit the notion that control produces deviance, the attempt to reduce or otherwise blunt life's uncertainties frequently encounters resistance. For example, in Wenzel Geissler's account of his participation in a Kenyan epidemiological project, the Luo families involved turned to a vocabulary in which rumours of blood-stealing symbolised their distrust of the central state and the external agents of international biomedicine, and served to trump both the researchers' own explanations of what they were doing, and their sponsorship by members of the local elite.

The resistance offered by the Bosnian refugees about whom Marita Eastmond writes is two-fold. First, the assumption of a generalised pathology is resisted and de-emphasised. Even if not everyone participates, this amounts to collective passive resistance to the Swedish state's attempt to funnel the 'refugee problem' into that particular part of the welfare system where the gates are securely kept by doctors and psychologists. Second, the role of the war in creating distress is refuted because it overlooks the social problems of the present, in the host society. By insisting on ability rather than disability, and by demanding jobs, these refugees resist the host society's explanations of their distress and its proposed interventions for dealing with it.

John Aggergaard Larsen also presents us with a situation in which psychiatric categorisation is resisted by some of those on its receiving end. This, of course, may be a paradoxical and vicious circle, in that non-conformity, if not actual resistance, is arguably among the diagnostic characteristics of their pathology in the eyes of those whose opinions count: doctors, psychiatrists, social workers, and so on. In the case of the alcoholics about whom Vibeke Steffen writes, however, not only is denial arguably a *definitive* feature of their condition, but in the games which she describes them as playing with their Antabuse treatment, resistance to the treatment regime is almost a self-conscious narrative theme. There appears to be an almost deliberate cultivation of uncertainty – in their own eyes and the eyes of others – on the part of alcoholics. What do they want? To give up drinking or just to manage it? And what are they trying to manage: their drinking or their public image? Blurring the edges of these questions is actually intrinsic to their game.

Resisting control is, of course, necessarily an attempt to *assert* control, simply from another direction or point of view. It is always a matter of where one stands, and control is never likely to be consensual, or unproblematically localised in one centre. Deliberate attempts at control and resistance aside, there may, for example, simply be incommensurate things going on in a situation: countervailing factors and forces may be at work against each other. This can be seen very clearly in the chapters by Jónína Einarsdóttir and Hanne Mogensen. In Einarsdóttir's account, conflicting relationships and narratives, each very different with respect to what is the matter with ailing children and what should be done about it, pull against each other, towards different outcomes. Mothers may subvert the demands of lineage, and maternal relatives go behind a mother's back. Control is being exercised in two different directions, each undermining the other. Something analogous can be seen in Mogensen's case. While conflicting relational demands may not result in resistance *per se*, they do generate difficulty and confusion. Knowing what to do for the best becomes very problematic, if not impossible.

Resistance or lack of confidence are not everything, however. Uncertainty may simply be an intrinsic and irremediable characteristic of the situation. This is certainly the case with the involuntarily childless men and women to whom Tine Tjørnhøj-Thomsen's ethnography introduces us. Among the things which are significant in this context are the complexity of the particular matter of life and death in question, and the perceived (in)adequacy of existing expert knowledge about it. The whole relationship between the experts and these men and women is, in fact, constructed out of the inability to predict or control fertility. That is the core substance, the truth of the problem in hand.

Nor is this our only example of things that simply cannot, by definition almost, be brought under satisfactory control. In this respect, Mette Nordahl Svendsen's account of the seeking and finding of knowledge about the risks of inherited predispositions towards cancer is particularly poignant, in that here we encounter women who, once they have confirmed that they are more at risk than the rest of the population, often only have very limited options for ameliorating their situation open to them. The management of uncertainty here is at least as much a matter of morality and of keeping options open as it is anything else. The key motif is responsibility, whether to oneself or to one's family, and to be responsible implies, in the first instance, taking on the uncomfortable burden of knowledge.

As we have already discussed, the exercise of adult responsibility also lies at the heart of the dilemmas and decision-making of the Brazilian women Anne-Line Dalsgaard writes about. Try as they might to order and direct their lives, however, everything other than themselves – everything from the global economy, to the Brazilian social system, to local criminals, to the fear and insecurity of neighbours, even to their own children sometimes – is effectively working to frustrate them. Such is the nature of their lives under the present conditions.

The political economy of certainty and uncertainty should not be underestimated or ignored, either. As Susan Reynolds Whyte insists, in Bunyole there are limits to the ability of many people to control life and its misfortunes, if only because access to the resources which make it easier to do so is uneven and often inadequate. Nor is this solely a problem for the 'developing' nations of the world. Although it is a matter of relativities – often relativities so extreme and stark as to be literally matters of life and death – full equality of access to health care resources remains an aspiration, even in the efficient, social democratic welfare states of northern Europe.

The creation of uncertainty

It is a well-established theme in the literature that medicine and healthcare interventions are a response to uncertainty. As we have suggested above, it is less well remarked that our attempts to render matters of life and death more predictable and amenable to human agency may actually exacerbate or create uncertainty. This is a good example of what Max Weber pointed out many years ago (1948: 323-59): that the unintended consequences of what people do are at least as significant in the construction of the human world as their intentions.

Intentions depend, at least in part, upon knowledge, and a little knowledge is well known to be a dangerous thing. In matters of life and death, knowledge is usually only a little, no matter how much we might like it to be otherwise and despite the undoubted power of western biomedicine. And anyway, more knowledge can easily mean less certainty. Jónína Einarsdóttir's chapter, for example, shows that, with respect to infants who fail to thrive among the Papel, there is *always* ambiguity: with respect to diagnosis – there are alternatives available – and subsequent responses. What is more, the authoritative diagnosis of a child as *iran* massively ups the stakes: it resolves nothing. Individuals interpret the alternatives in the context of their personal history and knowledge, emotions, and rational calculations. Mothers do not just 'do what their culture tells them to do'. They have to decide who to believe – what is the matter with my child? what *is* my child? – and what is the right thing to do, and to negotiate the tensions between different versions of the same fundamental relationship, maternity or the demands of matrilineage.

Greater knowledge can also produce social uncertainty with respect to the genetic risk of cancer. Mette Nordahl Svendsen describes how the role of the person receiving genetic counselling as a messenger, charged with the communication of knowledge about their potential risk to relatives, problematises kinship and notions of social belonging. Who is within the family, and who is without? The answer can just as easily point in the direction of inclusion and new relationships, as the reverse.

There is more to the creation of uncertainty than knowledge, however. Certainty today may mean uncertainty tomorrow. In Anne-Line Dalsgaard's ethnography, the women in the Brazilian *bairro* understand well enough the likelihood of disaster in the social networks and way of life to which they are accustomed and within which they belong. Moving away may be an alternative, but it is not necessarily more certain, and certainly more difficult. Nor does the decision to limit the number of one's children through sterilisation necessarily guarantee long-term certainty. It is in fact an exposure to greater risk: the fewer the children, the easier it is to lose them all and be left alone. For these women, however, sterilisation offers the hope of control over individual lives and the possibility of achieving competence.

Despite its goals and intentions, western biomedicine cannot help but sow the seeds of new uncertainties. As Wenzel Geissler argues, the Luo families participating in the project were ambiguous about biomedicine, locating it within their problematic relationship to the Kenyan state. Their experience of biomedicines has also, however, encouraged uncertainty about their own 'traditional' knowledges. The role of the *kachinja* idiom in addressing both of these uncertainties – it is a traditional-style supernatural idiom, but, according to Geissler's argument, located firmly within modernity – is intriguing and suggestive of the ongoing emergence of new knowledge and interpretive frameworks.

There are new frameworks in the offing in Tine Tjørnhøj-Thomsen's material, too. Here, technological medicine impacts in complicated ways on matters of life and death which are generally taken-for-granted and axiomatic. Uncertainties are generated about nature and procreation. The doctor becomes almost the genitor, if not the father, and reproduction raises a host of new questions, more fundamental perhaps than the 'simple' matter of 'just' having a child. It is not too much to say that the meaning of life is problematised.

The issues may be less profound for the Jop'Adhola families studied by

Hanne Mogensen in eastern Uganda, but there is nonetheless uncertainty and, in the case of sickly infants, probably greater urgency. In a manner that is also reminiscent of Einarsdóttir's ethnography, the issues here are to do with the exercise of choice. Faced with at least some choice between biomedicine and traditional alternatives, each with different perceived costs and benefits, the question is, once again, what to do for the best? Nor is this merely a matter of immediate outcomes. In terms of likely futures, as Susan Whyte argues, the alternatives in the attempt to deal with uncertainty – divination or an AIDS test? – dramatise or recognise some uncertainties and downplay or silence others.

Vibeke Steffen's study of the biomedical response to alcoholism in Denmark, a problem to which other kinds of response are generally found elsewhere, highlights an impressive portfolio of uncertainties. What is the medical profession trying to do here, for example? Cure alcoholics or merely control them? Doctors and nurses are themselves often unsure about these matters. The use of Antabuse – a recognised medicine, after all – may help to manage their uncertainties. However, what *is* Antabuse? Is it really a medicine, is it a punishment, or is it merely a maintenance regime? In some respects, it is clear that the *creation* of uncertainty may be an explicit objective for the protagonists. Alcoholics, for example, may want to blur the outlines of the current state of play, and using Antabuse can be one very successful way of doing it. Doctors, on the other hand, may use Antabuse to muddy the waters and create the impression that they know what they're doing more than they actually do.

Biomedicine is also, as has been remarked earlier, an accomplice in the modern state's project of order and predictability. Attempting to 'fit in' awkward people does not, however, necessarily work in the manner that is intended. In Marita Eastmond's study of Bosnian refugees in Sweden, Swedes – and the Swedish system – are trying to deal with their own uncertainties about who these people are, and how to deal with them, by assimilating them to psychiatric categories that have at least an air about them of 'being understood'. However, for the Bosnians themselves, the effects may be the reverse, leading them to question who they are, or have become. This does not help them to 'fit in'.

That the clients of the Opus Project in Copenhagen do not 'fit in' is a problem to themselves and to others: the experiential 'reality' of their varied conditions, and their unpredictability, is not to be doubted. However, as John Aggergaard Larsen shows in his chapter, the process of participating in the Project – with the re-evaluation of an existing identity or biography, and the attempt, by some patients at least, to construct another – does not guarantee greater certainty about individual futures. Since identity is always a matter of becoming, the future remains unpredictable at the personal level. As indeed it must, despite the best efforts of biomedicine.

Dealing with matters of life and death

In situations of crisis, when the paths traced out in front of us become too difficult and uncertainty threatens to be a dominant feature of quotidian life, we must act as human beings. So we try to change the world or the circumstances under which we live, in order to make things more tolerable. We try to bridge the gap between capacities and potentialities. When this cannot be done successfully we may use our imaginations, and try to live as if the connections between the properties and practicalities of things are ruled by magic and enchantment of one kind or another. Thus human attempts to deal with matters of life and death may be as much an engagement with mysterious or occult possibilities as an effort to assert predictable 'rational' control.

With this collection of papers, we want to challenge the concept of control and uncertainty by documenting, on the one hand, how critical situations in various ethnographic settings are experienced and dealt with by humans, and, on the other hand, by suggesting new ways of how to theorize critical situations within the tradition of medical anthropology. In doing so, we have taken up the tradition of anthropological studies of misfortune and uncertainty and combined it with the perspectives of medical sociology in order to bring everyday meaning and agency into play with policy and structure.

We also want to suggest that matters of life and death are anything but obvious. Heidegger's notion of *Dasein*, 'being-in-the-world' or 'being unto death', suggests that we live in a world mapped out and bounded by time and therefore imagine the inevitability of our own death. Whether that is so or not, this knowledge of our own mortality is certainly one of the reasons why life and death matter. The end of things is not, however, all that we can imagine. A blessing and a curse of human cognition is our talent for the complex imagination of options, alternatives, possibilities, and 'what-ifs'. Confronted by the routine uncertainties of the environment and the actions of other humans, individual and collective decision-making in the attempt to establish some predictable control over immediate matters-at-hand necessarily involves imagining options, alternatives, and so on. The result is at least as likely to be further uncertainty as anything else.

This means that uncertainty and human attempts at control are reciprocally implicated in each other in ways that are neither determined nor unidirectional nor predictable. The sum total of our understanding of these matters should not be limited to the somewhat obvious proposition that the uncertainties of life inspire our attempts to control it. There is more going on than this: not least, as we have already argued, our attempts to control the conditions of our lives actually generate further uncertainty.

The medical assault on uncertainty is part of the modern process of cognitive rationalisation that Weber, borrowing an evocative phrase from Schiller, called 'the disenchantment of the world' (Weber 1948: 129-56, 267-301). In principle, in the face of scientific advances, everything has become knowable (if not actually *known*): mysteries are nothing more than things which are waiting to be properly understood, the world becomes more predictable and life more certain. In principle, biomedicine seems to recognise no constraints on its potential competence, whether to cure or comfort.

The material and arguments presented in this collection, however, suggest very strongly that medical rationalisation and disenchantment are not only uneven – at best – but that the progress of science inevitably produces its own uncertainties, and, indeed, its own new mysteries.

These propositions can usefully be placed in the context of a wider range of arguments: that social control creates deviance (Becker 1963; Lemert 1972; Matza 1969), that discipline engenders resistance (Foucault 1980), that rationalisation has its limits (Brubaker 1984), that formalisation necessarily creates informalisation (Harding and Jenkins 1989: 133-38), and that disenchantment is not a condition to which humans, given their capacity for enchanting the world, can realistically aspire (Jenkins 2000; Schneider 1993).

We do not have to accept postmodernism's alternative grand narrative, or the nihilism and incapacitating relativism that lurk behind its celebrations of diversity and multicentricity, to realise that the notion of progress is, even if not flawed, far from simple, or to acknowledge that the more we know, the more our knowledge generates its own exceptions and limits. In the face of our increasing powers we must also confront their interim character and their uncertainty. Furthermore, humans do not just work to reduce uncertainty, they also routinely generate it – often with good reasons. It may not be pushing the argument too far to suggest that humans need uncertainty no less than they need certainty. We certainly do not seem able to banish it. Not only are uncertainties at the heart of matters of life and death, they are also at the heart of the human condition, of human nature if you like. Otherwise, life and death wouldn't matter at all.

TWO

RESTORATION OF SOCIAL ORDER THROUGH THE EXTINCTION OF NON-HUMAN CHILDREN

Jónína Einarsdóttir

Dealing with deviance is an inevitable part of the human experience. Cross-cultural research demonstrates that responses to dysfunctional human bodies or minds may range from extermination to the attribution of positive capacities (Ingstad and Whyte 1995). In this chapter I will focus on the uncertainties and distress involved when the matrilineal Papel in Guinea-Bissau deal with anomalous children[1]. These children are suspected of being non-humans, *i.e.* children born without a human soul, and considered to be dangerous for the members belonging to the matrilineage. The physical and developmental deviations that characterise these infants vary; nonetheless the main preoccupation of their family members is more with etiology than the severity of the child's impairment. Procedures exist to identify the origin of the observed anomaly and for eradication of the child if it is confirmed to be a non-human. To secure the safety of the matrilineage, elderly family members are eager to have these children identified and extinguished. In practice, this results in negotiations with the mothers, whose persistence may influence the outcome.

The Republic of Guinea-Bissau in West Africa is one of the poorest countries in the world, ranking 169 of 174 countries in the UNDP Human Development Index (UNDP 2000). The Biombo region, the site of my fieldwork, is generally regarded as a backward region within the country, in terms of subsistence and infrastructure. The region has about 62,000 inhabitants, of whom three quarters are Papel. Thus Biombo is frequently referred to as Papelland. The Papel make up about seven percent of Guinea-Bissau's multi-ethnic population of approximately 1.2 million inhabitants.

The Papel divide themselves into seven matrilineages, with each lineage represented by a totem (Einarsdóttir 2004). Children belong to the lineage of their mother, and have the totem of her group. Residence is ideally patrilocal and polygamy is frequent. Inheritance is matrilineal, which means that the eldest sister's son of the deceased is the inheritor of his land, goods and compound. The heir also acquires certain rights and responsibilities in relation to the wives and the children of the deceased. Even though they are primarily agriculturists, the Papel are not able – and probably for centuries have not been able – to sustain themselves (Rodney 1970: 32). Malnutrition among children is prevalent in the Biombo region and child death is a common event, as one third of all children born alive are likely to die before they reach the age of five years (Aaby et al. 1997).

Most Papel people adhere to their own religion, while a few are Christians, Catholics or Protestants. According to the Papel religion human souls circulate through deaths and births between 'this world' and the 'other world.' The God of the Papel decides who is to enter the world of the dead. There are two groups of religious specialists who have influential roles as advisers and helpers in both public and private matters. Divination, called *bota sorti* or 'casting lots', is their main instrument. *Balobeirus* belong to the first group of specialists which includes women and men who are capable of communicating with God, either through the mediation of an ancestral soul (*defuntu*) or through a powerful community-based divination instrument named *kansaré* and materialised in biers. Religious specialists named *djambakus* belong to the second group, and are both women and men who collaborate with *iran* (spirit). *Iran* is a term that refers to a wide range of spiritual beings and forces, but also to the ceremonial places dedicated to these spirits. The *djambakus* combats sorcery through collaboration with *iran*, but at the same time she or he is capable of engaging in sorcery as well. They often specialise in healing, using a wide range of herbal medicines and the spiritual powers of their respective *iran*. An *iran* is sometimes described as 'a child who is sent to run errands', which means that an *iran* obeys orders. However, sometimes an *iran* has a will of its own.

After several months in the Biombo region, I noticed for the first time a comment about a particular child who was said to be an *iran*. I was chatting with Matilde, an elderly woman. During our conversation a boy of about twelve years came and he exchanged a few words with Matilde before he left.

'He is my grandchild,' she explained. Then she told me that when her daughter-in-law gave birth to the boy, some people said that he was not a human child, he was an *iran*.

'Iran?' I asked.

'Yeah, that is what they said. Some people said he was dangerous and he had to die.'

'Why?'

'He was born with a big head.'

Matilde's husband, who is a Catholic, proposed that he and Matilde should foster their grandchild. So they did. 'He is such a nice boy,' Matilde said with warmth in her voice.

Later I encountered more children, each of whom was suspected, more or less seriously, of being an *iran*. I also collected numerous stories about such children from many people. The suspected *iran* children I saw had a wide range of physical anomalies or functional impairments. Two of the children were severely paralysed, and they could not sit, walk or reach for things when they grew older. One child was probably blind; he could not sit or reach for things but thrived physically and appeared to be mentally well. Another child was malnourished and could not walk by the age of two years. Still another child had a normal body, but was born prematurely and thus very small. One girl had epileptic fits and her left arm and leg were partially paralysed and atrophic. I heard still more stories of *iran* children from other people. One child was born somehow long, another had a deformed mouth and no nose. One newborn had reddish skin and its sex could not be determined. Yet another had a complete, healthy body but distorted face and stiff neck.

Many people told me about children that were more or less paralysed but without deformities, evidently the most frequent impairment. General descriptions that were given by people of *iran* children, without reference to a particular child, included characteristics such as a spineless body, pale skin, an apathetic face, bizarre eyes and a foaming mouth. Some infants had peculiar behaviour, even the first days after birth they tended to leave the bed by night or moved under the bed in search of eggs. In addition, some people said *iran* children could survive almost without food. Others stressed that these children suckled their mothers' breast all the time, and little by little they would eat up their mothers.

People agree about what causes some women to give birth to an *iran*. Pregnant women should take care not to be naked when washing themselves close to a spring-water well (man-made wells are not dangerous). They should also wash their body quickly and always wash their laundry wearing underwear. If not, an *iran* with a sexual longing for a woman would penetrate her. Then the *iran* would enter the child she has in her womb and prevent a human soul from entering the child, or expel the human soul if one is already there. That *iran* would finally be born and have more or less the appearance of a child. Despite the mother's role in attracting an *iran*, I never heard anyone blame mothers of *iran* children for their unlucky births. Instead people felt pity for them.

When an *iran* child dies no funeral shrouds should be wrapped around the body and no funeral rites should be performed. In addition, no crying is allowed, but mothers are not expected to follow that proscription. The reason for all these proscriptions is that the *iran*, who occupied the child's body, will be delighted with beautiful shrouds and aggrieved weeping and, consequently, be eager to repeat the whole event. It is important to extinguish the body; thus it is preferable to bury it in an ant heap and burn it. After the child's body has been destroyed the mother will be ritually washed to prevent additional *iran* births.

Obviously, anomalous physical appearance at birth, or later a deficient physical capacity without a previous illness, are the main features that contribute to a situation where a child's human nature may be called into question. Considering the wide range of physical problems and anomalies described, the category *iran* child is ambiguous. Infants are apparently not classified as *iran* only with reference to their anomaly, so more conclusive criteria are required.

Identification of non-human children

People agree that there were more *iran* children born in the old days. At that time, I was told, these children were extinguished. A comment on people's ignorance in those days was common. Both men and women have told me that in the old days *iran* children were burnt in an ant heap. An elderly woman said that in her village, before she got married, there was a woman who gave birth to an *iran* child. The child was like a doll, it was *burmedju* [a Kriol term that means 'red', but is often used to describe the colour of white people] and it was neither a boy nor a girl. 'It was taken to an ant heap and burnt,' she maintained. 'Only in the old days, when people were stupid (*tolu*), did people burn these children like that.'

The suspected *iran* children were also 'taken to the sea' (*levadu mar*) to check their identity, an act that became prohibited by law during the colonial period. Several people have described to me how children were taken to the sea, and all the descriptions are similar[2]. As the child belonged to its mother's lineage, the father and people belonging to any other lineage did not have much to say when it concerned the identification of suspected *iran* children. Therefore, the child was taken to the sea only by its elderly maternal relatives, some informants said only women were present while others named both women and men. The family members would take with them an egg, pounded rice flour, and *kana* (distilled alcohol) and put everything in a calabash. The child and the calabash were put on the beach, close to the sea and those who accompanied it would withdraw behind the trees where they could observe the child. If the child was an *iran* it would look around to discern whether anybody was observing, then it would drink the egg and disappear with the other items into the sea. If the child disappeared into the sea, people said that the *iran* had returned to where it came from, its true home. On the other hand, if the child felt uneasy on the beach and started to cry when the sea came in, it was not an *iran*. The child would be comforted and taken home to its mother. All informants emphasised that if an *iran* child was allowed to live it would harm the members of the mother's lineage. The mother was the person with the highest risk of suffering whatever misfortune befalls, or even death, especially if she did not stop breastfeeding the child. Nevertheless, many said mothers often refused any suggestion that their own child was an *iran*, and they would not easily agree to withhold the breast.

When it concerned *iran* children, the most sensitive issue was the identification procedure used to verify their true nature. Even though people said that *iran* children were less common today than in the old days, they claimed that some women still gave birth to an *iran*. They emphasised that it was necessary to verify the nature of such children and, if they were identified as an *iran*, to do away with them. How could the true nature of a suspected *iran* child be determined today? It was prohibited by law to take them to the sea. The discussion I had with Marta is revealing. One day when I visited her home village we found ourselves alone together. I took the opportunity to ask her about *iran* children.

'I don't know anything about *iran* children,' she responded. 'In my village we don't have any such children.'

'So you have never heard about such children?' I insisted.

'Yes, I have. A man and a woman who had moved to another village had a child who was an *iran*. At two years of age the child could not sit or walk. It only suckled the breast all the time,' Marta told me.

'And, what did they do?' I asked.

'The child was taken to the sea and disappeared into the water,' she assured me.

'When was that?'

'A year ago, more or less.'

'Somebody could just throw the child into the sea, couldn't they?' I asked.

Marta sighed. 'Who would do that? Nobody would throw a child into the sea. Jónína. There are people who are so stupid that they think other people are so stupid that they throw their children into the sea.'

Marta told me that many mothers knew it was against the law to take suspected *iran* children to the sea. Therefore, people were not as willing to take children to the sea any more, or at least they tried to do it secretly.

'Nevertheless, children are still taken to the sea, even without their mothers' consent,' Marta affirmed. 'You understand, when the child is away and its mother has shaved off her hair, everybody in the neighbourhood knows that the family has taken the child to the sea.'

'But somebody would go to the police, wouldn't they?'

'No. Who would do that? People don't go to the police. There is no other solution, the child is not human, it is an *iran*. The mother has to accept it,' Marta argued.

'But what about a visit to a *djambakus*?'

'Yes. Of course it is easier to specify a test period (*pui dias*), then the mother waits to see if her child dies or not. That's better. To take a child to the sea is difficult, at least if the child can only lie on her or his back. It is much better to go to *djambakus* than take the child to the sea.'

'What exactly does it mean to go to *djambakus*?'

'A knowledgeable *djambakus* will make a sacrifice to his *iran* and ask for help, then she or he will specify a trial period. The *djambakus* gives the child water to drink and if it urinates, it is a sign that *iran* [i.e., the *iran* that works with that *djambakus*] agrees to do the work. If the child dies within the specified period of days it is an *iran*, if not it is not an *iran*,' Marta said. 'But the mother is not allowed to breastfeed the child during that period. You have to feed the child with other food.'

'Who is allowed to take the child to *djambakus*?' I asked.

'Only maternal relatives. Nobody would dare to take a child who belongs to another lineage, neither to the sea nor to a *djambakus*,' Marta affirmed. 'It is a problem that when children are taken to the sea only those present know what happens.'

The information given by Marta was confirmed in stories of children who were suspected of being non-human.

Case-stories of non-human children

In the following stories of four children who were suspected of being non-human I will focus on parents', especially mothers', practical and emotional involvement in the identification process. I also want to pay attention to competing alternative interpretations of their aberrant body, or lack of functionality, which results in a variety of healthcare-seeking alternatives. The ambiguity of the *iran* category is evident, and the identification procedure does not always give an absolute answer. Even after the death of a child new interpretations of its nature may emerge.

Clara
Clara, three years old, is taken to a *djambakus* to verify her true nature because her mother's family demanded it. I don't know if her mother accepted it or not. I happened to see Clara during the specified test period. Actually, when I came to her compound her mother sat with her daughter in her arms and caressed her. The mother explained that Clara was born a healthy child but when she was 3-4 months of age, she left her with another woman to go fishing. When she came back home Clara was severely sick and did not take the breast. The baby was taken to the mission hospital and then to the national hospital in Bissau where she was admitted for twenty-five days. Since then she had never been healthy, despite repeated visits to the mission hospital and various healers. I asked Clara's mother if she believed her daughter was an *iran*.

'Yeah, it appears so …,' she whispered and started to cry silently.

'But she was born healthy, and became sick. You told me, right?' I asked.

Clara's mother did not respond, but an elderly man explained that the child did not take the breast during all the twenty-five days in the hospital. She somehow survived only on intravenous fluid (*soru*). 'A normal child wouldn't do that,' he argued. The man belonged to the mother's family and had been sent to see if the child would die as it was the last day of the specified test period. Clara's mother's mother was *balobeiru*, a religious specialist who collaborated with an ancestral spirit (*defuntu*), which implied that it was not possible to have Clara at her home during the test period. Thus the child stayed the whole time with her mother, who stopped breastfeeding as required.

I asked Clara's father if he believed his daughter was an *iran*.

'No, I don't know any *iran* children. Only old people say they exist,' he responded. He told me that the child had been taken to various specialists for divination; one said she was an *iran*, another not. She had not been taken to the sea, he confirmed.

Clara survived the appointed period of time, but she died a couple of weeks later. When I met Clara's neighbours, two adult women, I asked them if they thought Clara was an *iran*, or not. They were not sure, but thought it was anyway likely that she was an *iran*. They began to question the identification procedure performed.

'It is no good to let the child stay with its mother during the test period,' one of them explained. 'But a person who owns *defuntu* can't be involved in *iran*. So there was no choice.'

'It was somewhat mysterious how the girl survived in the hospital … only with *soru* for twenty-five days,' the other argued. 'Further, she was three years old and she could not sit or stand. That girl, she suckled the breast all night long.'

'But she was born healthy,' I emphasised.

'That's true,' the other answered. 'When Clara's mother left her with that woman somebody may have stolen her soul.' They agreed, it was a possibility that she had had the disease 'soul stolen' (*alma furtadu*).

Carlos

Carlos had similar problems to those of Clara. When I saw him for the first time he was eight months old. He was a neatly dressed little boy, and obviously well cared for by his young mother. Carlos could not sit or crawl and his legs were extended and crossed. Carlos' mother told me that he was probably born like that, without any control over his body. She had taken him several times to the mission hospital, but finally the nun said that she could not cure him. Carlos had already been treated for the cat and monkey diseases.

One day I happened to meet a neighbour of Carlos. I had not seen Carlos for a couple of months, so I asked her about his health. She informed me that Carlos was gone.

'He was taken to the sea and disappeared into the water by his own force. You understand, he was already one year old, and he couldn't sit or do anything. It seems that he was born like that,' she affirmed.

'Did Carlos' mother accept that he was taken to the sea?' I asked.

The neighbour woman did not know, but remarked that mothers frequently refused to allow their children to be taken to the sea. 'Nevertheless, in case the family insists the mother has to accept it,' she maintained.

Marcelino

Marcelino, six months, was a fat and well formed boy at first glance. However, when I looked closer at him I noticed that his eyes whirled around and that he had no control over his body. Marcelino did not grasp for things or focus his eyes on anything. But I also noticed that Marcelino was a happy looking boy, he sprawled with his hand and legs and laughed for himself. The mother told me that she had taken him many times to the mission hospital to seek care, without results. Someone had proposed that Marcelino had the ant-bear disease and preparation for a washing ceremony was underway, she explained. A physician who saw him suggested that he might be blind.

Marcelino's father arranged for a consultation for his son at the rehabilitation centre in Bissau but Marcelino's maternal great aunt demanded that he first will be taken to the sea to see if he was an *iran* or not. Marcelino's mother refused to allow him to be taken to the sea and his father's mother expressed her disapproval. Finally, Marcelino was taken to a *djambakus*. His father's mother was allowed to be present, but she was not allowed to say anything, since she did not belong to same lineage as Marcelino. On the other hand, his mother was not permitted to be present. The *djambakus* made his sacrifice and specified a test period of seven days. Marcelino stayed with his maternal great aunt during that period who had arranged food for him, but his mother had to stop breastfeeding him. She was even forbidden to see her son during the trial period. Marcelino died the last night of the appointed period without any indication of illness.

Marcelino's mother was filled with grief after the death of her son. 'She cries and she cries and she cries …' a relative told me. People came to console her, but there was no funeral. 'The body was just buried somewhere,' she said. Then Marcelino's mother went to stay with her father for a period of time, to overcome her remorse. She was not happy with her situation; she had had no luck with her childbearing. After five births she had no child alive. Marcelino's mother wanted to take her aunt before the court for killing Marcelino by withholding food. Her family members advised her to let it be. 'She must understand that Marcelino was an *iran*. That's all. There was nothing else to do. Her aunt did the only right thing for the protection of her lineage,' one of them told me. Marcelino's mother never went to the police.

Three years later a female neighbour told me that Marcelino's mother had given birth to a child that seemed to thrive properly; it had already learned to walk at one year of age. I asked her if everybody was still convinced that Marcelino was an *iran*. She told me that finally, the family had resolved the problem: Marcelino was not an *iran*, his mother's mother, who died several years ago, had killed him. Many years before the mother's mother was jealous of her younger co-wife and killed all her children with sorcery. The co-wife got to know who had killed her children and she responded with a counter sorcery. But a person who responds to sorcery with counter sorcery is always punished by God. Thus, God took the co-wife to the other world. From there she took vengeance on Marcelino's mother's mother and killed her. When the mother's mother in turn came to the other world, she too was punished by God for the killing of her co-wife's children; God obliged her to kill all her own grandchildren, i.e. Marcelino and his siblings. The neighbour assured me that Marcelino's mother's one year old child would not survive, and, for sure, Marcelino was not an *iran*.

Celeste

Celeste's story is somewhat different from that of Clara, Carlos and Marcelino. When I saw Celeste for the first time she was about ten years old. I was told that she had convulsions, or fell (*ta kai*) many times every day. Her left arm and leg were partially paralysed and wasted, but she could drag herself along. Her thin body was marked by massive scars after having fallen into the fire many times. Celeste did not talk, but seemingly she understood a little.

Two years later I came to Celeste's compound and Celeste was in a miserable state: dirty, malnourished and severely burnt. She had fallen into the fire a couple of weeks earlier, I was told. When I suggested to Celeste's parents to take her to the mission hospital for treatment, they gratefully accepted. However, next time I came to the village not everybody was happy with my effort to improve Celeste's condition. In the first compound I visited a woman remarked that it would be better to give her some medicines rather than to throw them away on an *iran*. In the next compound there was a party. A group of people chattered and drank.

'How is Celeste?' the senior wife asked.

'She is well, she is getting treatment for her burns,' I responded.

'The nun will cure her?' she asked.

'That is how it is,' I answered.

'You think she is a human being?' she asked me.

'Yes. For sure,' I said. 'You should see Celeste washed and dressed in nice clothes. She is a nice girl.'

'It would be better to give me some medicines than throw them away on an *iran*,' another elderly woman argued and laughed.

Two more women asked about Celeste without commenting on her being an *iran*. At Celeste's compound people asked about her and they seemed happy to hear that she was getting treatment. I later understood that not only the neighbours but also some of Celeste's relatives maintained that she was an *iran*. One day, a woman who belonged to Celeste's compound commented cynically that Celeste's mother not only spent all her time getting her *iran* cured, but she had also begun to arrange Celeste's hair in braids. Even outside the village people asked me about Celeste and openly expressed their suspicion that she might be an *iran*.

Only one person with whom I discussed Celeste's nature argued that she was not an *iran*: Celeste was born healthy, this person said, thus it was more likely that her problems were caused by sorcery. That was in line with what Celeste's parents said. They did not share the idea that their daughter was an *iran*. They said she was a chubby and healthy child the first year of her life when she suddenly became sick. Celeste's mother remembered that day: it was a party and she was responsible for the arrangements. Celeste had started to walk and she sauntered around on her own. The pig had been just slaughtered and Celeste's mother was busy preparing the food. Suddenly Celeste screamed. She had terrible convulsions. It started like that.

Since then Celeste had been sick. Her parents took her to a *djambakus* who extracted a piece of pork from her body, but she did not become better. She still had repeated convulsive attacks and she could not walk anymore. Celeste's parents took her to the nearest health centre. From there she was sent to the rehabilitation centre in Bissau, where she was trained to walk again with the help of some aids. In addition, a number of ceremonies had been performed, her father said, but he was not willing to explain them in further detail. He argued firmly that Celeste was not an *iran*. Celeste's mother was also sure that her daughter was not an *iran*, she knew Celeste was born healthy. Some people had tried to convince her to leave Celeste to die behind her house, but she refused.

After weeks of treatment at the mission hospital Celeste returned to her village. Her burns were cured, she was well-nourished, her hair was beautiful, she had shoes on and a nice dress. However, most importantly, she took medicines that prevented her from falling. Celeste's mother had stayed with her daughter most of the time, but Celeste longed for her father. Celeste's affection for both of her parents was obvious.

I learnt from these and other stories that mothers were reluctant to accept the suggestion that their own child might be an *iran* and some mothers succeeded in preventing their infants from being diagnosed, while others resisted without success. At the same time, none of the mothers called in question the very existence of *iran* children.

Dealing with deviance

The procedure used to identify the true nature of suspected *iran* children described above corresponds to what in the anthropological literature is commonly referred to as infanticide. The term may be used differently in different disciplines (Barfield 1997). Within criminology, infanticide is frequently limited to mean the killing of a child under one year of age. Sometimes its use is further restricted to mean the killing of a child by one of the parents, or only its mother. Anthropologists have classified infanticide as outright, direct or violent in contrast to indirect or passive forms (Harris 1977; Miller 1987; Scrimshaw 1984). Outright, direct or violent forms of infanticide are committed when something is consciously done that causes the death of a child. On the other hand, indirect or passive forms contribute to death through inaction, for instance by the withholding of food or failure to seek care.

Evolutionary approaches within biology, psychology and anthropology have over the last decades regarded infanticide as a rational, adaptive strategy among most species, including humans (Ball and Hill 1996; Bartlett, Sussman, and Cheverud 1993; Birdsell 1993; Daly and Wilson 1984 and 1988; Hausfater and Hrdy 1984; Hrdy 1990 and 1999; Parmigiani and vom Saal 1990; Schrimshaw 1978). Daly and Wilson, for instance, argue that infanticide is primarily based on rational decision making, and 'whatever the expressed rationale, however, choosing not to raise a deformed child obviously serves the parent's fitness interests' (Daly and Wilson 1984: 492). In a world-wide study of infanticide based on ethnographic data from the Human Relations Area Files (HRAF), Daly and Wilson find that most of 60 randomly selected societies where infanticide was practised can be divided into three categories, based on pre-defined 'cost-benefit questions' (1984: 488-92). The first category includes societies where infants with 'wrong' fathers are the victims of infanticide. In the second group infants born with deformity or some illness are killed, and in the third group are societies with infant killing as a consequence of maternal incapacity to rear the infant.

I wish to propose two categories of infanticide, based on the motives given for the killing of infants by those involved[3]. Such an approach means that the interpretations given by those involved in infanticide must be taken more seriously than they are by Daly and Wilson (1984). An examination of religious and ethical considerations highlights the attribution of statuses such as humanness, personhood, or social membership as crucial if we wish to understand infanticide. Although cross-cultural comparison is complicated by the fact that various authors use these terms without always specifying their content, there is variation in whether or not human nature, personhood and social membership are attributed to newborns. There are also differences among societies concerning which criteria must be satisfied in order to attain these statuses. Sometimes, the achievement of these statuses is taken to be interdependent, or to occur simultaneously.

The first category of infanticide I propose includes elimination of surplus children who are not yet categorised as fully human, lacking personhood or still non-members of their society when they are killed. This is thereby interpreted by the society in question as different from murder. Ethnographic evidence demonstrates that in these cases parents, most often mothers, commit the act. For instance, among the hunter-gatherer group !Kung in the Kalahari desert, the mother's killing of an infant after birth in the forest was accepted in cases of untimely pregnancy, illegitimacy, or deformity (Howell 1979). It was not considered to be a murder, as the infant's life was thought to begin only when it got a name and became accepted as a social member back in the village.

In many societies, naming is the very event that gives an infant social membership or personhood (Alford 1987). Scheper-Hughes (1992) emphasises the display of individual personality and human characteristics such as intentions, preferences, and will, as important for children's achievement of humanness among impoverished mothers in Northeast Brazil. She describes how the shanty town infants gradually gain human nature, and finally fully human status when they have a personal name and the right to the dedicated maternal care that allows them to survive (Scheper-Hughes 1992: 415). For the Punan Bah of Central Borneo the crucial event required for achievement of human status occurs when an ancestor spirit has taken a permanent residence in a child's body (Nicolaisen 1995). Shortly thereafter an infant will be given a name and from then on it is considered to be a person. Before that event, impaired infants were allowed to wither away.

The second category of infanticide I propose covers infanticide to restore the social order. Here the infant is somehow anomalous, and thought of as being without potential for humanity, personhood or social membership. Often these children are considered to be dangerous as well. The infant's parents are sometimes opposed to the eradication of these children, which is often done by some professional specialist. Wrong fatherhood sometimes excludes infants permanently from social member-ship, thus allowing their abandonment or killing (Legesse 1973; Oboler 1985). According to Parkin (1985), the Girama of Kenya traditionally killed a child who was born feet first, or a child whose first two top teeth erupted before his or her bottom ones, as this child was deviant and believed to bring misfortune. The killing was done by an elderly woman, normally unrelated to the child. Parkin maintains that parents opposed the killing of their own children, and clearly 'the Girama understand the conflict between parental love and the danger to the community that such children bring' (ibid.: 226). The eradication of non-human *iran* children in Biombo belongs to this category of infanticide and has certain similarities with the short description given by Parkin.

The question is why should parents, particularly mothers, protect their aberrant children, who are considered to be dangerous. These children do certainly belong to the 'worst bets', those children who are 'listless', and 'wanting to die', as described by Scheper-Hughes (1993), or 'lowered-viability' or 'poor quality' infants, to use the terminology of evolutionary approaches. Nonetheless, Papel mothers (and fathers) try to hinder the performance of identification procedures likely to result in the death of their child. Papel mothers spend emotional and physical energy, their limited resources and reproductive time, keeping their suspected *iran* children alive and finding them a cure. All of this contradicts Hrdy (1999), who argues that women evolved to reproduce in terms of quality not quantity, and Scheper-Hughes (1992), who suggests that mothers in societies with high fertility and child mortality will invest selectively in their children, partly to avoid the destructive consequences of grief, partly to allocate resources to the stronger children.

There are however some similarities between the 'doomed' children of the shanty town, as described by Scheper-Hughes, and the suspected *iran* children in Biombo. The wide range of physical impairments characteristic of suspected *iran* children demonstrates the ambiguity of the *iran* category. Like 'child sickness', the *iran* category is 'impossibly loose, fluid, elastic, and nonspecific' (Scheper-Hughes 1992: 386). The humanness of *iran* children in Biombo and the 'doomed' children of the shanty town is questioned, and they are stigmatised. Scheper-Hughes suggests:

> 'that the rejection of 'failed' babies is the prototype of all stigmatization. Whereas stigma may consign the spurned adult to a life of exclusion and marginality, the stigmatization of a hopelessly dependent neonate or infant is inevitably a death sentence. The sickly, wasted, or congenitally deformed infant challenges the tentative and fragile symbolic boundaries between human and nonhuman, natural and supernatural, normal and abominable. Such infants may fall out of category, and they can be viewed with caution or with revulsion as a source of pollution, disorder, and danger.' (Scheper-Hughes 1992: 375)

However, the reaction of the two groups of mothers of these stigmatised children is different. The dictum that a child is either born an *iran* or it is not an *iran* is a point Papel mothers tend to use when arguing that their child is not an *iran*. When the child is obviously born with a disability, alternative suggestions for its condition may be launched. We see from the descriptions that there are many competing alternative interpretations of the child's anomalous body or impaired abilities. As a result, the suspected *iran* child has to be taken to a wide range of healers, diviners and health personnel before the decision is taken to perform the fearful *iran* identification procedure. The hope for cure is there and it encourages mothers, and sometimes others, actively to a solution.

The identification procedure is not faultless, either, when it concerns the true nature of the child. Sometimes the performance may be questioned, and thus the child's death or survival can be explained differently. A child's death may be attributed to the withholding of food, or to the fact that the child was thrown into the water. Survival may be explained by the mother's presence and eventual breastfeeding of the child during the trial period. Despite a seemingly successful identification procedure, later, new evidence may give rise to new interpretations. We are dealing with conflicting interests where actors interpret events differently to advance their case. Anxious maternal relatives may be more concerned with the extinction of an eventual *iran* child than with a strictly performed verification procedure. This fact is recognised by Marta, who admits that it is a problem that only those who are present know what really happens. Marcelino's great aunt is fearful because of the potential misfortune he may cause to her lineage. She demands an identification procedure and Marcelino dies. Marcelino's mother does not trust her aunt's impartiality.

Many of those with whom I discussed the issue of *iran* children emphasised that fear of these children is an important factor that contributes to their destruction. It is the responsibility of elderly maternal kin to erase *iran* children, otherwise they may bring misfortune to their lineage members. Despite this, mothers' devoted hopes for a cure make them reluctant to stop breastfeeding a weak child that clearly will not survive without the breast. Mothers, and sometimes others, tend to argue for other interpretations of their child's deviation, while remaining within the framework of the Papel religion and ways of interpreting diseases and death[4]. None of the mothers of suspected *iran* children I talked to called into question the very existence of *iran* children. One alternative might be to take a stance from within another tradition and argue that *iran* children do not exist. Many Christians take that position, for example, but not all.

It is misleading to classify the extinction of *iran* children as a rational reproductive strategy, a killing of 'lowered-viability infants', and then dismiss the non-human, dangerous, nature attributed to *iran* children as simply superstition. A few of the children suspected of being an *iran* are anomalous but healthy. At the same time there are still more disabled children who never become suspected of being an *iran*, because their impairment is interpreted differently, and their humanness is never questioned. Truly human children are not killed, despite severe physical deformity. To kill such children would be classified as a murder and would be an immoral and dangerous act. Strictly formulated, *iran* children are not killed either: *iran* children are erased in a fire, or allowed to return to their true home.

In attempting to understand Papel mothers' involvement in the fate of their *iran* children, we are dealing with anomaly and ambiguity at the same time. According to Mary Douglas:

> an anomaly is an element which does not fit a given set of series; ambiguity is a character of statements capable of two interpretations. But reflection on examples shows that there is very little advantage in distinguishing between these two terms in their practical application. (Douglas 1966: 37)

Then Douglas suggests that 'we find in any culture worthy of the name various provisions for dealing with ambiguous or anomalous events' (*ibid.*: 39). Rather than treating ambiguity and anomaly as inseparable I propose to make a distinction between these terms. Douglas is right, the Papel have their ways of acting: an *iran*, the anomaly in question, should return to its true home or be extinguished. However, the ambiguity of the *iran* category makes it practically difficult to identify and deal with children who are possibly *iran*. While it is this ambiguity that gives mothers their chance to act in the case of individual children, it does not necessarily allow mothers to challenge the very idea that *iran* children are dangerous non-humans and must be eliminated.

One cannot ignore the explanatory power of religion when it concerns *iran* children. Events are predicted if certain measures are not taken to control the situation: for instance the mother will die if she does not stop breastfeeding, or else misfortune will befall the lineage if an *iran* is allowed to live. In line with Horton's theory of religion and world view, the Papel religion provides guidelines for explanation, prediction and control of events[5]. Nonetheless, the Papel religion and world view is not a coherent, static, mechanical system offering faultless solutions to any problem. The Papel recognise that there are alternative ways to explain, and act in response to misfortune, each predicting still other events to come. When negotiating the fate of suspected *iran* children both mothers and their maternal relatives responsible for the well-being of the lineage find a base for their point of view within the Papel religion. Being able to construct clear and consistent arguments is important for those mothers who want their theory to guide action when it concerns the suspicion that their child is a non-human.

Susan Reynold Whyte's focus on the pragmatic agency of those who experience misfortune and suffering fits well with my understanding of Papel mothers' reactions to their children's diseases. Whyte emphasises that 'the qualities of purpose, possibility, and hope are central in Nyole dealings with misfortune' (Whyte 1997: 24). Papel mothers' reactions to their children's diseases are also characterised by seeking help among a range of available alternatives, making trials, and keeping up their hope until death is a fact, even for the least viable children who are suspected of being non-human. Papel mothers (and fathers) of suspected *iran* children maintain hope for a cure in an unknown future. Thus they resist the verification procedure of their suspected *iran* child. Mothers also refuse to stop breastfeeding the child, because they know it will not survive without the breast. And despite proscriptions to the contrary, when the child dies its mother grieves.

Notes

1. This chapter is a shortened and revised version of Chapter Five in *Tired of Weeping* (Einarsdóttir 2004; see also Einarsdóttir 2000). It is based on anthropological fieldwork in Biombo region, Republic of Guinea-Bissau, between 1993 and 1998. The fieldwork was made possible by the support of DanChurch Aid (DCA), Copenhagen.

2. A number of authors have described the procedure of taking a deformed child to the sea, even among other ethnic groups in Guinea-Bissau (Carreira 1971; Crowley 1990; Jao 1995; Mølsted 1995). Carreira (1971) argues that as a response to the action of the colonial authorities most groups have stopped killing their deformed and twin children. He refers to the identification procedure for *iran* children as a ritual murder, a view criticised by Jao (1995). Jao emphasizes that the killing of anomalous infants does not have an economic rationale, *i.e.* to eradicate uneconomic infants, rather it contributes to restoration of social security. Jao recognizes this procedure as belonging to the past, however recent.

3. I want to emphasize that these categories of infanticide do not encompass all known cases of infanticide.

4. See Einarsdóttir (2004), Chapter 4, for more details.

5. Horton (1993) argues that religions, like the modern sciences, are primarily concerned with the explanation, prediction and control of everyday events. While I acknowledge the importance of these in the religious practices of the Papel, I do not entirely accept the universal applicability of his theory.

THREE

BIRTH CONTROL, LIFE CONTROL: FEMALE STERILISATION IN NORTHEAST BRAZIL

Anne Line Dalsgaard

Today female sterilisation is the most commonly used method of birth control in the world (United Nations 1998). Highly effective and safe when correctly performed, it is generally considered a fairly uncomplicated means to reduce unwanted fertility. The World Health Organisation thus writes, in a guide to provision of contraceptive services, that 'Female sterilization may be an attractive contraceptive choice for couples who want no more children' (WHO 1992: 1). In this one-dimensional view sterilisation is just one way among others to solve a practical problem. I will argue in the following, though, that for the women in the focus of my study, sterilisation has a much broader significance: it constitutes a hope for control in one's own life, a quest for a sense of competence and security in a lifeworld shaped by violence and social exclusion.[1]

My argument centres on women's motivation for fertility control in a low-income urban area in Northeast Brazil, a neighbourhood where more than a third of all women of reproductive age are sterilised.[2] When asked why they are sterilised, women refer to their low economic status and inability to look after many children. In their own words they are sterilised because they do not have 'the conditions'. But a close look into their situation reveals this lack of conditions to be a matter of more than economy alone. Life in the neighbourhood is highly unpredictable and people have very few means to counteract unpredictability. Only one thing seems to be certain: having many children does not just multiply economic costs, it multiplies the number of things that may turn out wrong. Given this situation, a woman's body, her fertility, is one of the very few things that *can* be controlled, and sterilisation is the only certain means of doing so. The aim of this striving is not economic maximisation; in the everyday struggle, economy is a means rather than an end in itself. What counts is to be a decent, respectable human being in control of one's own life, in the eyes of others as well as one's own.

A discussion of motivation and fertility change

In its conclusions, the present study stands aloof from the demographic transition theory formulated by Frank Notestein and Kingsley Davis in 1945. This theory was, until recently, the dominant paradigm for understanding demographic change. It locates the causes for fertility transition in major forces of modernisation such as urbanisation, industrialisation and education, under which the economic benefits of childbearing are outstripped by its costs. Within this theoretical framework individual actors are seen as rational, maximising individuals, who, when resources are present, deliberately control their fertility in accordance with their own economic interests. In the absence of home-based production in the urban economy, and with the concomitant reduction of children's labour utility, families cannot afford the time spent on childcare by mothers who otherwise could work outside the home, or the expenses related to formal education. Hence, having many children becomes disadvantageous for parents, who consequently opt for birth control.

However, faith in the assumed relationship between fertility decline and measures of social and economic development has been sharply criticised during recent decades, because empirical studies do not support any such relationship (Kertzer 1995). A notion of culture as an independent factor in demographic change has been applied as an alternative to economic variables. In 1987, the demographers Cleland and Wilson wrote, 'The spread of knowledge and ideas seems to offer a better explanation for the observed pattern than structural determinism' (1987: 20). But by stressing the role of ideational systems, 'loosely defined by religion, language or region' (*ibid*.: 24), Cleland and Wilson took people's adherence to cultural norms for granted and did not take into account individual choices and actions. Only recently, inspired by changed notions of culture and agency within anthropology, new modes of demographic analysis have been sought that go beyond the false dualism between, respectively, economy and culture or structure and agency (Faria 1997/1998; see also Greenhalgh 1995; Kertzer and Fricke 1997).

The present study should be seen as a movement in this direction. Not only does it question the primacy of economic interests as an explanation for the demand for birth control in Brazil, it also shows how cultural, social and political forces merge in individual experience and impel actions for reasons far removed from the rationality so often assumed by demographers. Rather than being the result of deliberate consideration by an independent mind, the agency described in this analysis is based on the 'juggling [of] a variety of interdependent concerns' (Carter 1995: 78) undertaken by subjects immersed in the immediacy of life.

The study proposes a view of fertility as far more fundamental and integral to human life than is often assumed in studies of demographic transition. Wanting or not wanting to have children is not an isolated event in this lifeworld, but part of one's view of self and others, and decisions to control fertility are motivated as much by present suffering and pain as by future outcomes. In this analysis emphasis is put on emotion as the factor that turns collective norms and values into personal matters and translates motivation into action. As expressed by Barbalet: 'Emotion is directly implicated in the actors' transformation of their circumstances, as well as the circumstances' transformation of the actors' dispositions to act' (1998: 27). Women's fear and self-blame are both results of an almost impossible social situation, and fuel for the wish to change that motivates sterilisation. Before turning to the central narrative, however, some background information is needed.

Fertility and sterilisation in Brazil

Since the late 1960s Brazil has experienced a decline in fertility in all geographical regions and social sectors. From an average of around 6 children per woman in the early sixties, the rate dropped to below 2.5 in the mid-nineties (Martine *et al.* 1998: 19). This decline has been remarkable in its speed and was unexpected by demographers and political planners in Brazil, as it happened in the absence of any large-scale family planning programmes and during a time of severe economic crisis. Unlike other Third World nations, Brazil did not adopt a population policy during the 1960s and 1970s. Under military rule, from 1964 to 1985, the official position was for years pro-natalist, later effectively passive. Despite opportunist political proclamations in the 1970s, about every couple's right to family planning, people were left to fulfil this right by their own initiative and economy.

Illegal, self-induced abortion has accounted for a relative high proportion of reduced fertility in Brazil. Particularly during the early phase of the decline, low-income women had recourse to induced abortion in the absence of alternatives (Martine 1998: 175-76). Among non-abortive modern methods only the contraceptive pill and female sterilisation have gained a foothold, and they are today the most commonly known and used methods of fertility regulation. The pill is easily obtainable, relatively cheap and sold in any drugstore, but women often experience side-effects such as headaches, bleeding and unwanted pregnancies. Therefore dissatisfaction and irregular use are common. According to the national health survey, 27.3 percent of all Brazilian women between 15 and 49 years of age, regardless of marital status, were sterilised in 1996 (PNDS 1996)[3]. However, regional and social differences are considerable. In the more developed regions, the Southern region and São Paulo, sterilisation rates are lowest and seem to be slightly decreasing, while they remain on the increase in the poorer regions (Martine 1998: 178). Before 1997, sterilisation was not officially legal in Brazil. It was mainly performed under cover of caesarean sections, or justified by an alleged 'risk of health'.

Regret at having undergone sterilisation is a growing matter of concern in Brazil, but, even so, many women see sterilisation either as a necessary evil or an acceptable good in the absence of alternatives (Serruya 1996; Diniz *et al.* 1998; Kaufmann 1998; Dalsgaard 2004).

The present study was conducted in a low-income neighbourhood in the outskirts of the city of Recife in Pernambuco, Northeast Brazil. In this neighbourhood sterilisation was perceived as an obvious aspiration for a woman. Neighbours usually knew who was sterilised in the houses nearby, and word of new achievements was often spread to neighbours, relatives and friends, in the same way as other prestige-giving news. A neighbourhood survey showed that 37 percent of all women of reproductive age had been sterilised, a third of them before the age of 25.[4] As is common in Brazil, men in this neighbourhood generally did not take responsibility for contraception. Childcare and health matters were considered a woman's domain and so was contraception. Besides, condoms, male sterilisation, and interrupted coitus were all – for different reasons – considered unacceptable for men both by women and the men themselves. Condoms are expensive, unreliable and 'without charm' as people said; male sterilisation drains the masculinity from a man, while interrupted coitus weakens him and in the end may harm his health. Burdensome negotiations between the spouses, unwanted pregnancies or economic constraints placed the responsibility with the women.

Everyday violence in a *bairro popular*

I came to the neighbourhood to study women's motivation for sterilisation. Being an anthropologist I looked for the meaning of fertility and birth control on the micro-level, that is, among people in their everyday life. Everyday life is, however, an elusive and diffuse category. As argued by the anthropologist J. Lowell Lewis it cannot be known in itself: it exists only as a background condition, against which particular events stand out (2000: 539). Hence, the 'everyday life' that I came to know was deduced from the extraordinary. Not that I did not chatter, buy food, wash clothes, fetch water and share the lazy midday in the shadow with my neighbours. I did all this, but it was moments of feast and crisis that gave meaning to these everyday activities. Likewise, some violent events which took place while I was around came to be central for my understanding of people's valorisation of controlled fertility.

The neighbourhood was a so-called *bairro popular* – a low-income neighbourhood, like so many others in Brazil. Some families were miserably poor, most were poor in the sense that they earned just enough for physical subsistence, and a few families were a bit better off. The internal social hierarchy was never stable, as conditions for life were always fluctuating. Unemployment, illness, divorce and other misfortunes could change a fairly stable family economy into misery. Nevertheless, despite these fragile family economies several months of living in the neighbourhood had to pass before I fully realised the pain behind the fluid and flexible way of survival that people practised with such skill. Days were full of good company, and there was a sense of competence around in the bright sunlight that made me overlook the defeats. 'There is always a *jeithinho* – a way out', Brazilians use to say with a captivating smile and indeed there was. The *jeitinho* is usually understood as a 'fast, efficient, and last-minute way of accomplishing a goal', by use of one's social network (Barbosa 1995: 36). The competence I found in the neighbourhood seemed to spring from knowing how to get by in this manner. Relatives, friends, neighbours, all strings were pulled in times of necessity and usually a solution to any problem was found. The reverse side of the coin was the dependence on others that this assurance reinforced, and the vulnerability of the individual when networks failed. Looking closer into the apparent strength and viability of the people I came to know, there turned out to be inescapable moments of *fait accompli*, when relationships dissolved and no strings could be pulled. In such moments the margin of social life came threateningly near.

In her book *Death without Weeping*, Nancy Scheper-Hughes describes the fear of violence, 'of being made to vanish', as all-pervading in the neighbourhood Alto do Cruzeiro, where she did her fieldwork (1992: 232). Located in Pernambuco, like Recife, but separated by the years that have passed from her fieldwork to mine, and by the difference in access to urban facilities, Scheper-Hughes' Alto do Cruzeiro does not fully resemble the neighbourhood where I worked. However, one main feature running through her description resonates with my experience: the fear of violence and its social consequences. People on the Alto feared the indifference and violence from the state to which they were subject. At public clinics and hospitals, the civil registry office, the cemetery, everywhere, they were treated as 'nobodies' and the police terror directed towards them, epitomised by the so-called 'disappearances', confirmed their sense of being worthless to society. Furthermore, rumours of organ-theft reinforced their fear of anonymous disappearance (*ibid.*: 216ff).

People that I came to know equally feared violence. They would look into the darkness of the night and to my naive comment on its beauty they would reply, 'Don't you have *violencia* in Denmark?' I learned, however, that *violencia* meant neither police terror nor organ-theft. Their fear was violence due to the drug dealing and related criminal activities that increasingly dominated the neighbourhood. However, what Schepher-Hughes indicates so precisely is not the object of fear as much as the phenomenology of the fear itself. 'Consciousness moves in and out of an acceptance of the state of things as normal and expectable – violence as taken for granted and sudden ruptures whereby one is suddenly thrown into a state of shock' (Scheper-Hughes 1992: 233). The ambivalence, the waiting for things to happen, creates a constant tension in which people experience themselves as fragile and vulnerable, on the Alto as in my area. Rumours, silences and insinuations fuel the 'free floating anxiety' (*ibid.*: 233).

However, the fear had an extra dimension in the neighbourhood where I worked. In contrast to the threat on the Alto do Cruzeiro, the *violencia* of the neighbourhood did not stem from exterior forces, but from elements within. Indeed some of the criminals had moved to the area in order to hide in the biggest squatter settlement, called the *invasão*, but others were sons of well-known local families, young men attracted by the money and excitement available in criminal circles. The threat was thus fostered by people themselves. Or, rather, by some people: the question was whom.

Association with the wrong kind of people was dangerous and parents had to be on guard in order to keep their children away from bad influences. For this reason, the right upbringing was crucial.

Responsible parenthood

The capacity to bring up children was, first and foremost, seen as dependent on the family's economic situation. Parents should be able to provide for their children, feed them, dress them properly, and pay for medicine and school. People generally held that a couple could have as many children as they could afford to bring up. Poor people should only have two. 'Having one is having none, having two is at least having one', people would say to justify why two children were considered the minimum. Having many children, 'filling the house with children', as people would say, was seen as irresponsibility. As one mother said: 'You take it from the television where you see all these hungry children living underneath a bridge. They [their mothers] do not do anything to avoid children. They have children just to let them suffer'.

Having many children meant suffering. A man from the neighbourhood explained to me how lack of planning was the stigma and tragedy of the poor. Sitting on a ragged and dirty sofa in his shack of a house he said:

> The strange thing, I have observed, is that when they [the rich] want to have a child, they plan. For four, five years. They move together and then they prepare themselves for that child to come and then they have more structure to bring it up. I see it this way, you have a lot of children, and then you buy a thing for one, but not for the other. Sometimes even the food, some times you only have little food and have to divide it, and nobody will be able to fill the stomach. Everybody will be hungry. And then the parents will suffer, because they just let the children be born. I see it like that – it is the curse of the weak class.

Women were confronted with this notion of responsible parenthood when they consulted the health care system. Both negatively and positively expressed it pervaded health care providers' attitudes and acts towards the women. Observing a birth at one of the big hospitals in Recife, I overheard an ironic, but casual, remark from a nurse to a woman who had just delivered. The nurse said: 'Oh, your husband doesn't work, he only knows how to make children, eh?' And, when asking the local gynaecologist for sterilisation the women were met with understanding and reinforcement, in their efforts to be 'responsible'. The gynaecologist told me that she herself had only two children: 'It is fine, more than two is expensive and a lot of responsibility in relation to studies, to make them grow up, put them into life...two is enough for me.' She saw the women who sought her help as suffering from unwanted pregnancies and begging to be rescued. She spoke of a state of emergency that did not leave either time or money for further considerations about the appropriateness of sterilisation, which was the rescue she provided.

The parents' emphasis on the responsible adjustment of fertility to their economic circumstances was thus part of a general discourse, and so was their perception of urgency in relation to their children's schooling. Literacy rates have always been low in Brazil, especially in North and Northeast Brazil,[5] but recently school education has become central, both in political planning and in parents' aspirations. While I was around, Pelé, the famous Brazilian football player, promoted schooling for children in a television campaign. And there was a bill board at the roadside reading, 'Out of the sugar into the future', with two children walking hand in hand with their school bags towards the horizon between tall walls of sugar cane. While few children worked in the neighbourhood, and none in the sugar cane, parents nevertheless agreed on the message. They knew by experience that lack of education was a disadvantage, and they firmly believed that schooling was the way forward. Illiteracy had long been associated with poverty in Brazil, and was often understood in terms of ignorance. Old Dona Severina, who lived in the neighbourhood, stated that many 'ignorants' would still die from hunger in Brazil, because they did not study. Others would say that soon you would need to study in order to get even a simple job. Yet others would state the general assumption that if children did not study, and live a regular life between home and school, they would be lost in the street as the street children one sees on television. 'Loose children' as people said, children that did not stay close to their home and their mother, were seen as out of place and dangerous both to themselves and their surroundings. As Tobias Hecht writes in his book about street children in Recife: 'While street children have been used by some to exemplify the vulnerabilities of childhood, they have also been refashioned in another way – as harbingers of the danger posed to society [...] by the unsupervised youth' (1998: 173).

Nurtured children stay at home

In Brazil the 'street' is perceived as the place of commerce, of men and of prostitutes, whereas the 'house' is the place of the family, of wife and children (Da Matta 1997). This distinction was completely taken for granted in the neighbourhood, and it gave structure to everyday practices and gender relations. Women stayed near home as much as possible, and housework, childcare, and ownership of the house was generally ascribed to women. For good and for bad, houses were women's domain. Men were supposed to participate in the life of the 'street', to work, and to provide economically for their families. From early childhood, children were brought up according to these gender roles, and boys were allowed to run around more freely during daytime. However, when violence broke out or when a child misbehaved, parents would agree that even boys ought to stay at home with their mothers.

My friend and neighbour Sonia had troubles with her teenage sons. She said that they were lazy, played too much football and did not learn anything in school. At times when I came to see her, she had locked all doors to make the children stay at home, in order to keep them away from the dangers of the street. On such days she herself would often be furiously pacing around like a lion in a cage. When talking about these situations, she once said: 'If just one of my children would sit down and read a book, oh, it would be so beautiful!' Reading a book seemed to epitomise the behaviour of the well-educated, home-nurtured child. But in Sonia's house I never saw a book, a newspaper or anything else to read, and Sonia herself read only with huge difficulty. Another day she told me that she found it difficult to help the children with their schoolwork. Sometimes the child had written down the exercise with such bad letters that Sonia could not figure out what it was all about. Sometimes, I think, she was just too restless to sit with a child for the time needed. Worries were many and patience difficult to produce.

Quarrels with husbands and economic problems occupied most women and created a tense atmosphere in their homes. Husbands were supposed to show their care for the family by *não deixar faltar as coisas em casa* (not letting things be lacking at home), but this was an almost impossible task in a situation of widespread unemployment and poverty. A woman could never rely on having a husband to provide for herself and her children. Husbands who spent their scarce money on other women, or alcohol, were common, and the women were often desperately stuck. They had to face the children's demands – for interesting food instead of the perpetual cornmeal, for clothes, for a few coins for some sweets to break the monotony, or for notebooks and pencils needed in school.

The ideal of motherly patience was generally expressed with self-criticism, since most mothers felt they could not live up to it. As Rute, who was 25 and a mother of three children, once put it, 'A good mother is one who understands the child, who gives a good education, gives affection. But it is difficult, because children make one lose one's mind. I will not lie. Mine steal my patience too much. At times I cannot take it and I beat them. Afterwards I get that remorse inside … but the boy did not listen! I punished him.'

The lack of patience posed a serious problem for the women in the long run, as the women knew it might have fatal consequences. Sonia used to say that her sons were so difficult, because they were brought up with misery and no affection at all. When they were small, Sonia lived with them in the interior of Pernambuco, under miserable conditions with a violent man. Today she lives with another man with whom she has two other children. But she is still worried: 'What bothers me is this, because, there is no affection, no affection. Nobody says 'let us talk today,' 'let us sit down here, let us play, let us invent a story.' It doesn't exist, it is only ignorance. The child comes, and then 'Go, go!' The way it is today it is only drugs. Boys who leave the house early, they get involved with some who are older, and start doing wrong things. My fear is this'.

In the women's view, a child should not only have proper food, a good school and 'all the best'. It should also have affection from its parents, in order not to be lost. The women felt the need to give all this to their children, but at times it was difficult not to 'heat up the head', as Irene said when everything became too difficult. Irene worked at the local health post, and she was one of the more politically engaged persons in the neighbourhood. One day when we were discussing the subject, she said:

The rich child is not brought up given slaps, no, he is not beaten, no. He is filled with caresses, filled with liking [...] From what I see, it is only the sons of the poor who are brought up with slaps, humiliation, beaten, because they do not have anything! Because look: if you do not have…if I do not have proper food to give to my children, if I do not have a good school to give them, if I do not have good clothes to give them, do not have snacks, do not have leisure, and I even beat them? [...] The children of today from the poor class have this vice of revolt-ing. It is due to the fact that the parents do not have jobs, we do not have a good home, no leisure and no good food, isn't it so? And then the children become what? Rebellious. The parents are unemployed, many children walk without shoes, because they cannot buy a sandal and when they buy, it is the most fragile sandal that only lasts for a week. Somebody steps on the foot and then it breaks. One has to consider that. I cannot bring up my children, because I cannot give all that to them, that I want to give [...] My children, when a notebook [for the school] is missing, it takes me almost a month to be able to buy it, and that is not what I want. I don't want it to be missing.

Even when they saw that they were prey to poverty in a society that did not support them, the women felt that they were the ones who had to do the impossible. They were the ones to love and care for their children in order to keep them away from the dangers of the street. When, as happened, violence and killing suddenly erupted, their worries were further fuelled. The fear of losing one's children, and perhaps oneself, merged with the despair of not being able to educate the children. The force of these mixed emotions was revealed to me, when – as people said – 'the neighbourhood caught fire'. Only then did I understand what was at stake, when women said, 'We don't have the conditions for bringing up children'.

A painful moment in a mother's life

I was in the neighbourhood, on my second field trip, when a state of shock crept over us all. The events started as something fairly distant. One of the central figures in a drug network was shot within the *invasão*. Nobody really knew who or how, and everybody mentioned the murder as little as possible. It was too dangerous to know about it, and it did not directly affect anybody outside the closed circle of criminals. However, a week later in the middle of the night, in a house outside the *invasão*, a young girl was taken by hooded men. They dragged her away in front of her parents, who did not dare to intervene. The next morning, when the rumours went around, people discussed whether the intruders were the police or the bandits. But soon a part of the *invasão* was taken over by 'them'. Shots were fired to scare away the curious. My friend Neide, and others who lived nearby, fled to other houses. The next day the girl was found, thrown on the ground, raped and killed. She had been the girlfriend of the man who was the supposed murderer of the first victim.

From that day a certain atmosphere of fear spread to almost everybody. Houses were closed in the *invasão* – boards saying, 'House For Sale' were seen everywhere, and health workers no longer visited the families there. Then the next murder happened within the *invasão*. A young man was killed in front of his house in the middle of the night. His wife and his mother had screamed when it all began, but they were ordered to be silent and stay indoors, which they did until daybreak. The corpse lay outside the house all day long waiting for the police to take it away in the afternoon. I was told that it was forbidden to move it before their arrival.

Some days later, the police arrested Miriam, the daughter of Tereza, who once was my neighbour. They came – also hooded – and drove Miriam away in a car without further explanation. She was engaged to a man who apparently had something to do with the drug gang. It was on this occasion that I got frightened. Not that I had any objective reason for it. The whole atmosphere was just loaded with fear, and suddenly I felt that I had poked my nose into too much. I was standing in front of Tereza's house, talking with another of her daughters. Tereza had had a heart attack due to the shock and was hospitalised, and she – the daughter – was afraid of being alone in the house with the children. We were discussing the situation, when a man came up the road towards us. He stopped about 10 meters away and delivered a message from the brother, Roberto. I found that a very strange attitude, the distance was hard to understand. Until, that is, I turned around and saw somebody standing further up the lane, watching us. The whole scenario flashed through my mind: the man watching, me being close enough to receive confidential information, the messenger staying at a distance so that he had to speak very loudly, signalling that no secrets were being passed. I was hurtled into the paranoia that gradually overtook us all, a mistrust infecting friendships and otherwise good relations among neighbours.

In this atmosphere, my friend Neide had to pay dearly. She was struggling to keep her two teenage sons, Fernando and Fábio, out of the drug network. Much later I learnt that she had borrowed money and sold her things in order to provide for her sons, so that they should not be attracted to something 'bad'. On top of these worries she quarrelled with her man, who was not the father of the sons, and who no longer wanted them in the house. And then one day it was announced on the radio that, according to an anonymous source, Neide's sons were the only ones involved in the gang who were still around in the neighbourhood. The police, or whoever it was, showed up, but the sons were not at home. They had fled. Neide was now afraid to stay in her house, during the night. 'The police will return', she said, 'and it is better not to be around, for they prefer to kill immediately'. With this turn of events Neide became dangerous company. Her best friend Elizia disappeared. Neide once said about their friendship that she could always count on Elizia: 'She gives me everything. When I need advice she advises me, and when I am weak because of the children, she calms me down, says, 'relax, *rapaz*'. She gives me strength. She is an excellent friend'. But now Elizia was never around anymore; her house was for sale, too. When a family was threatened, everybody else seemed to turn their back on the unfortunates. Nobody wanted to be involved and, hence, the *violencia* signified more than physical and emotional suffering for the people in the neighbourhood, it meant social exclusion for the affected families.

During the following days, when Neide tried to find a safe place for her sons, she was therefore also seeking a solution to her own isolation. She wanted to get them into a home for drug users. To have them out of the house, to have them in a safe place, so that they would not be killed, and so that she could stay with her husband and in her social network. I helped her contact a social worker from the municipality. It was in the meeting with this well-intentioned social worker that I realised the cruelty of individualising the responsibility for children's upbringing, without providing the social and economic basis for it. In short, Neide began to explain how she saw the problem of her sons. She had left them with their grandmother, when she – Neide – moved together with her new husband. This is a common practice, and Neide had told me about it before without reflecting upon the moral aspect of it. Now she said, however, that her mother had been ignorant and not very good at bringing up the children, but that she – Neide – had done everything possible for them, while they grew up. She was proud, when she stated that she had always provided them with food and good clothes. The social worker then said, 'But, Neide, don't you think that children need more than good clothes and food?' And while Neide was outside for a moment she continued with a sigh: 'How could she do it? Doesn't she understand that she has a responsibility?'

When asked, Neide answered, 'Yes': yes, children need more than shoes, clothes and food. Her efforts to provide these things were not recognised in that situation, however, and her responsibility for what had happened was left hanging in the air. When I came to Neide's house two days later, she had left in the middle of the night with her children. I never saw her again. I know where she lives, alone with her children trying to build a new life somewhere else. One of her sons has subsequently been killed.

Sterilisation as life control

For the women in this study, fertility control was not a question of constructing a prosperous future for oneself. Having few children might improve a family's chances in relation to the economy and upward mobility, but for most women the need to stop childbearing was related to their present situation and the risks it entailed. Children needed food, clothes and motherly care. When food and clothes were scarce, and the parents quarrelling, motherly patience was difficult to muster, and the women felt unable to direct their children's lives away from the dangers of the street. Being responsible for their upbringing, but left without the means to do it properly, the mothers feared losing everything that confirmed their worth as persons: their loved ones, their worth as neighbours or friends worthy of recognition and, due to an indirect linking of irresponsibility and violence, their worth as citizens of the modern Brazilian society. It was a fear of being reduced to nothing, as if the corpses lying there, more or less in decay, waiting for the police to take them away – these corpses that everybody, curiously, would hurry to see – represented the essence of the whole thing. They were the anonymous and worthless product of the poor, who could not control themselves. The poor who gave birth to children they could not educate, because they did not have the conditions. Making ends meet economically was only the immediate concern – what was at stake was something more fundamental. Being fertile was an Achilles heel, a weakness that under certain conditions was directly associated with death, whether symbolic, in the form of social exclusion, or undeniably real. Sterilisation had become a means to counteract this weakness.

It would be a mistake to see these mothers as passively adhering to cultural norms or submitting to social structures. They did, indeed, perceive their maternal role in terms of culturally constructed ideas of femininity. And they saw themselves as low status citizens, lacking the socially-distributed, status-giving signs of worth. But they were not passive victims. They sought ways to cope with the present constraints. Obtaining a sterilisation was not just habitual unreflected behaviour, but a meaningful act from its undertaking to its end, motivated by the pursuit of a goal. The women planned and manipulated in order to reach what they wanted. Nevertheless, the future was only relevant in relation to the present. Their aim was attractive and necessary exactly because it represented an escape from present constraints and worries. When everything runs smooth, we may dream and imagine our splendid future, but only when this imagined self with its innate promises is contested and threatened do we act deliberately. As John Dewey writes, 'The present, not the future, is ours [...] The occasion of deliberation, that is of the attempt to find a stimulus to complete overt action in thought of some future object, is confusion and uncertainty in present activities' (1957: 194). The rationality at play is therefore rational in the sense proposed by William James: for the individual actor it provides a feeling of sufficiency in the present and banishes uncertainty from the future (Barbalet 1998: 47). And at the core of it is the force of emotion.

The women in this study wanted to be recognised as responsible mothers by friends, neighbours and authorities, not just out of vanity but in their striving for a sense of control in an uncertain world. A striving not just to *be* in the world of others, but also to define *what* they wanted to be in their world. Nobody wants to be irresponsible, useless or dead. Theories of demographic transition based on the assumption of future economic improvement do not take this striving into consideration. Economists' models cover only one aspect of human life, and cannot describe the basics of sociality: the fundamental human need for recognition by family, friends and society that people possess. In order to base our work on theories that do not contradict our own experience of what it means to be human (Wikan 1992), we must broaden our scope. Birth control is never an isolated event; in the neighbourhood I came to know it was pivotal to life here and now.

Notes

1. The major part of this article has also been published in my book *Matters of Life and Longing* (2004). However, I have added a perspective here which is pertinent to the present context.

2. The presented data were obtained through eleven months fieldwork in the described area. The fieldwork and the subsequent analysis were financed by the Research Council of the Danish International Development Agency (DANIDA).

3. PNDS (National Survey on Demography and Health) 1996 is still the latest obtainable national survey on reproductive health in Brazil.

4. This survey was part of the present study. It was conducted among 1762 women above the age of 12 living in the neighbourhood. The women were visited by the local primary health workers and asked about age, number of children, sterilisation status and, if sterilised, type of birth at last delivery. Out of 1500 houses in the neighbourhood 1130 were visited.

5. In 1995 illiteracy rates for children in Pernambuco between 10 and 14 years old were 21.7%; for children between 15 and 17 they were 14.3%. The same numbers for Brazil in general were 10% and 6.6%, while for the rich Southeast Region they were 2.4% and 2.1% (UNICEF/IBGE 1991-1996).

FOUR

CLOSE ENCOUNTERS WITH INFERTILITY AND PROCREATIVE TECHNOLOGY

Tine Tjørnhøj-Thomsen

The aim of this chapter is to contribute to an understanding and conceptualisation of how people experience and make sense of infertility and the biomedical technology and knowledge which they encounter in order to have a child. How does technological intervention affect people's lives, bodies, and identities? And what perspectives can the study of the encounters of infertile men and women with procreative technology add to the anthropology of health? My discussion of these questions is based on an empirical study of the longings and the experiences of involuntarily childless people in Denmark in the late nineties and their encounters with reproductive technology (Tjørnhøj-Thomsen 1999a, 1999b). This study explores the individual, social and cultural implications of infertility, childlessness and the various uses of procreative technologies, often described as 'assisted' or 'artificial' fertilisation.

The fieldwork on which my analysis is based was conducted in Denmark between 1995 and 1997. It centred on three local groups of a nation-wide organisation for involuntarily childless people[1]. In these local groups, infertile men and women with very different backgrounds and infertility problems, met regularly to support each other by exchanging individual stories, knowledge and experiences of being infertile, being childless, and undergoing treatment. Taking part in their meetings and social gatherings over a period of two years gave me an opportunity to obtain insights into their life-worlds and to recognise how infertility, childlessness and the encounter with the medical profession, medical knowledge, and technology affected their individual stories and lives over a longer period. This fieldwork also included in-depth interviews with childless couples in their homes, as well as participant observation in infertility clinics.

In this article I suggest that men's and women's experiences of fertility treatment and procreative technologies can be understood and conceptualised in terms of the encounter between three 'worlds': *the complex life-worlds of the fertility patients* (their aspirations for children and biological parenthood and authenticity, their knowledge and social living), *the biomedical 'world'* (its epistemologies, paradigms, discourses and understandings of the body and technologies) and, as one of its concrete and local manifestations, *the local clinical setting* (its temporal structures, spaces, agents, social relationships, professional experience and knowledge, and skilled practices and techniques). This tripartite structure is only analytical, insofar as the worlds, the settings and the forms of knowledge they represent are dynamically interrelated and inform each other in various ways. The biomedical world informs 'popular' understandings of bodily processes, and notions of relatedness and identity, and its knowledges and practices are embedded in historical, social and cultural processes. Likewise the sense-making that is going on in the local clinical setting must be 'situated in contexts of other interpretative systems' (Layne 1992: 31). Culture-specific notions of coming into being and relatedness form one such interpretative context.

In order to account for and explore this complex encounter, I will first discuss the concept of technology in general and procreative technology more specifically. I move on to investigate some recurrent themes in the life-worlds of infertile men and women in order to demonstrate how infertility causes health problems. In the succeeding sections I address more specifically the close encounter with the biomedical world and the clinical setting. I discuss how incomplete knowledge and uncertainties in the biomedical world and the social organisation of the clinical setting affect the experiences of infertile men and women. Finally, I argue that individual experiences of infertility and of technological and medical intervention can be analysed with reference to three interrelated and overlapping processes: fragmentation (Martin 1993), transgression and the displacement of boundaries, and disciplining. Technology splits up and fragments what people normally want to keep together – love, sex and reproduction; body, self and soul – and it simultaneously necessitates the transgression and displacement of the boundaries drawn between separate culturally and historically constituted domains in social life; boundaries that are normally protected. Technological intervention also leads to a disciplining of individual bodies and daily lives and, as we shall see, infertile people are themselves actively involved in the disciplining of their lives.

On technologies
There has been a tendency in anthropology to represent technology and society as external to each other (Ingold 1997) and to view technology (with both fear and hope) as an autonomous agent, outside the realm of the social and the cultural. Although I use the concept technology throughout this article, I share Tim Ingold's thesis that technology is 'embedded in social relations, and can only be understood within this relational matrix, as one aspect of human sociality' (Ingold 1997: 107). Technology is a product of human choices and social processes.

Technology in general, and thus also procreative technology, concerns the dynamic relationships between tools, machines and artefacts and the knowledge, skills and subjectivity of the practitioners. A successful fertility treatment depends on 'skilled practice', which – as Ingold argues – is not just the mechanical application of external forces, but involves qualities of care, judgement and dexterity (Ingold 1997: 110). And it also implies individual experimentation, creativity, mistakes, routine and experience. Furthermore, technology is embedded in specific localities (fertility clinics) and forms of social organisation (divisions of labour and specialities), and the coming into being of technologies is due to individual entrepreneurs, scientific communities, and social, political, economic and historical processes. An account of the cultural, political and economic history of reproductive technologies is beyond the scope of this chapter. I will, however, touch on the central theme in such a history, namely the on-going political struggles over the control of reproduction and individual bodies.

The specific aim of procreative technology is to overcome or bypass infertility (Stanworth 1987)[2]. As with any technology, procreative technologies are not neutral ways of doing things. In Michelle Stanworth's words, they:

> ...bear the hallmark of the cultural context in which they emerge. Prevailing social relations are reflected in the nature of technologies, their particular strength and weaknesses, the possibilities they open up, and the avenues they foreclose. (Stanworth 1990: 290)

Kinship is one possible context for considering procreative technology as it offers a comment on its social implications (Strathern 1993: 7). But the emergence of biomedical knowledge and procreative technology also expresses and redefines cultural notions of kinship and gender.

The preoccupation with women's bodies in Western reproductive medicine seems to have excluded men from the 'clinical gaze'. The result is that andrology was never institutionalised as a medical speciality which could attract researchers and therefore compensate for the lack of knowledge of men's reproductive functions and health (Johannisson 1994). In recent years, however, there has been an increasing interest in andrology in Denmark. One physician exposed this recent interest by telling me that, 'At our clinic we also pull off the men's trousers'. The emergence of a new technique such as micro-insemination, which makes it possible for infertile men to 'father their own children', as an advertisement for a private fertility clinic announced, emphasises and even strengthens the cultural importance of genetic relatedness in kinship thinking.

The developments of procreative technologies have been conditioned by the emergence of visualising technologies such as X-ray and ultrasound, which are closely related to the epistemological standpoint of biomedicine – i.e. the close association between knowing and seeing – and the discovery, isolation and synthesis of hormones (Marsh and Ronner 1996).

Both play a dominant part in the stories of coming into being as parents told by infertile men and women, as I will demonstrate.

Stanworth writes that reproductive technologies can be seen as a double-edged sword. On the one hand, they seem to offer women and men reproductive choices and agency, on the other hand they make it possible for the medical profession and the state to exert control over individual lives (Stanworth 1987: 15-16). There are, however, several edges. The choice not to choose technology is not an easy one, and the disciplining imposed by technology is met with a kind of 'technology of the self' (Foucault 1988).

Infertility and the life-world of infertile people

Framing infertility

Men and women with fertility problems do not consider themselves as ill, and they do not conceptualise their infertility as a disease. However, in order to legitimise their sufferings and quest for treatment they often classify infertility as a kind of *physical* disability, which is not self-inflicted. Therefore, as some argue, it should be cared for at public expense in the same way as broken legs, back injuries, etc. This classification is part of what Margarete Sandelowski describes as 'framing' (a concept which makes good sense when it comes to other health-related problems and diseases):

> How infertility is 'framed' determines what social supports, sympathies and resources are available to infertile people and, even more important, the extent to which infertile people are viewed as deserving of them. (Sandelowski 1993: 21)

The framing of infertility was both stimulated and exposed by an intensive public debate in Denmark accompanying the passage into law of the Assisted Reproduction Act (*Loven om kunstig befrugtning*) between 1995 and 1997, and by the ongoing debate about which diseases or health-related problems should be given priority in the public health care system. The infertile men and women in this study felt strongly that their childlessness ranked low, as it was not a serious or life-threatening health problem, but they also felt agony and distress, when people framed their problem as caused by psychological factors, or as a 'luxury problem'.

In the following sections I argue that infertility *causes* health problems such as psychological and emotional pain and distress. In order to understand how and why, I will portray some recurrent and interrelated themes in the life-worlds of involuntarily childless people. The first theme concerns the temporal disruption and disorder which infertility generates in individual lives. The second concerns their experience of being excluded from a variety of social groupings and communities. The third theme concerns their longing for authenticity.

Temporal disruption and disorder
Infertility produces temporal disorder and disruption in personal bodies, life perspectives and social relationships, as the inability to get children threatens the idea that by having children people *progress* and *relate* in time. When the wished-for-child does not arrive as hoped and planned for, people feel betrayed not only by their bodies and by nature, but also by their own careful timing and by the moral ideology of responsible and planned parenthood (Lundin 1996). Infertility generates, in Ingegerd Wirtberg's words, 'a strong sense of personal betrayal or even guilt, when their own bodies deny the possibility of choice and control and prevent what previously was the self-evident, well-planned next stage to life' (Wirtberg 1992: 45). Losing control in our modern society is a painful experience not least because ideas of freedom of choice are important for people's identity-making (Lundin 1996).

With the discovery of infertility, life becomes indeterminate and unpredictable. The main reason for that is, that infertility prevents people from progressing along the culturally and socially expected life-path (Franklin 1997: 134-5). It causes disruptions in the life perspective – a kind of *narrative loss* (Mattingly 1994) – and generates uncertain futures, which often leads to identity disorientation. 'Who' or 'what' shall I become, people ask themselves. People acquire futures by having children, and many find it particularly disturbing to imagine their future old age and death without children.

Becoming parents is a *rite of passage*, which marks an important change in social status, relatedness and identity. A rite of passage is characterised by a stage of liminality, a stage 'betwixt and between all the recognised fixed points in space-time of structural classification' (Turner 1967: 97). Liminality makes good sense as long as there is a transitional progression in the ritual, a process of becoming. Infertile people, however, are trapped in the liminal phase, imprisoned in a temporal gap between biological and irreversible time, age and the temporal structure of the culturally and socially expected lifecycle: obviously getting older, but unable to progress in life and time. Childless men and women expressed this in numerous ways: 'I am living with the pause button pressed down', as a woman phrased her feeling of not being able to move on in life. A man felt that his ageing was speeded up by his childlessness, he said: 'When you are childless, you become older much quicker. People close to you get children, their children grow up, and the clock is ticking'. Several women felt that their own mothers did not consider them as real and responsible adults, because they had not yet made the transition into motherhood.

This temporal disruption thus manifests itself in the lived experience of social relatedness. When age-mates and friends get children, infertile persons feel they cannot keep up with them but are left behind, excluded not only from the generational move, but also from the intra-generational community of age-mates and peergroup. Experiences of infertility and childlessness are mediated by social relationships, as they simultaneously put these social relationships to a test. Relational insecurity[3] and unexpected quarrels and conflicts within families and among friends often accompany infertility.

Thus there is a close connection between the *narrative loss, the liminality,* and the *sufferings* of infertile men and women, which also has wider analytical implications (*cf.* Mattingly 1994, 1998a; Murphy 1988).

Social exclusions

Infertility restricts individual admission to manifold social communities, groupings and social spaces. These social exclusions cause feelings of lack of recognition, incompleteness and inferiority. Infertile men and women are, first of all, excluded from making a family and a home[4] and from reproducing personal identity. They are deprived of the lived experience of social relatedness associated with family life, but they also feel excluded from other social groupings and communities based on specific experiences, knowledges and activities, that only children and parenthood give access to (Tjørnhøj-Thomsen 1999a). To take one example, the act of telling and exchanging stories about pregnancies and children seems to be a socially very important activity, at least from the perspective of infertile women, who feel incompetent and socially inadequate, as they cannot take an active share in these storytelling communities celebrating the virtues of motherhood. Obviously, having children contributes more to sociality than their parents telling stories about them, and the men and women in the study were painfully aware that as active participants in football clubs, schools, rituals and social ceremonies, children establish social relationships and networks between members of different families.

Longing for authenticity

Temporal disruption and social exclusions result in identity problems and disorientation. The prominent identity-theme in the narratives of infertile men and women was the feeling of not being 'real'. The search for authenticity is one strong motive for undergoing fertility treatment.

The idea of 'real-ness' – or the 'ideology of authenticity' (Weston 1995) – seems first and foremost to be associated with the ability to produce your 'own' genetically related child, and thus be able to see yourself and your partner in the child. This is, however, conditioned by the ability to take a part in and contribute to the culturally valued, socially and legally sanctioned story of coming into being. Stories of coming into being specify, among other things, how persons and life come into existence, what it is composed of, what or who the agents are, and how they are related (Delaney 1991: 3). They are answers to questions about individual and collective origin and identity. 'Where do I come from?', children ask their parents.

The indigenous contemporary standard version of the story emphasises the biological process of procreation, and presents the potential parents as the only actors and contributors. It celebrates not only genetic and biological origin and identity, but also the procreative act as one in which heterosexual sexuality, conjugal love, privacy and intimacy are essential unified components. This story also makes explicit that the child should be planned and wished for, and emphasises the moral ideology of planned parenthood mentioned above. In more general terms, then, the story of coming into being answers questions of how specific (gendered) identities, social relations, and notions of relatedness come into existence. The same story is changed radically in the encounter with technology, as I shall demonstrate below, and the compelling question becomes what it means when technology becomes part of the story of coming into being.

Nobody can, however, be sure of having his or her own child. Those who have had to use a donor, or eventually adopt a child, have had to resolve the problems of what has been named a 'genetic' death (Snowden 1990) by playing down the genetic aspects of relatedness, and the emotional and social security which such bio-genetic ties seems to carry with them. They have had to work hard to redefine meanings of 'real' and 'own'.

Most of the infertile couples hope that procreative technology will help them to get their own child, to break the transitional blockade, to delete the liminal dimensions in their life, and to repair the temporal disruption and the narrative losses. My research indicates that technology may solve the childlessness, but the experiences of infertility, childlessness, and the encounter with technology leave their marks in unprecedented ways.

Close encounters with technology

Uncertain diagnoses and incomplete knowledge
Infertility must be considered a reproductive health problem, not only when we consider its causes, but also when we reflect on its consequences.

As to the causes, it is often stated by physicians (*e.g.* Nyboe Andersen *et al.* 1996) that one third of all instances of infertility is caused by 'female' factors and located in the woman's body (for instance blocked or dysfunctional fallopian tubes caused by pelvic infections), another third is caused by 'male' factors (often low sperm count), and the last third cannot be located physically or explained.

This general and rigid model does not always make sense, primarily because the diagnosis can change, as a consequence of new facts brought to light by another medical examination or an unsuccessful fertility treatment. The emergence of new facts means that the narratives which infertile men and women tell themselves and others, in order to make sense of their infertility, change constantly. This may also affect social relationships.

One woman said that she was almost shocked by the news that none of her eggs was fertilised in the laboratory, probably – she was told – due to the incapacity of the sperm-cells. 'I thought it was me who was the problem, but now it seems there might be something wrong with my husband as well', she announced. The change in aetiology implies a reconsidering and a reallocation of responsibility and guilt, which has consequences for the woman's relationship not only to her husband, but in this particular case also to her mother-in-law. Their relationship had been troublesome for years because the mother-in-law repeatedly commented on the infertility of her daughter-in-law and had made her responsible for the lack of grandchildren. Their relationship now called for revision, due to the new knowledge about the infertility.

The stories told by infertile men and women demonstrate that biomedicine is not a monolithic, unequivocal discourse (Good and Good 1993; Tjørnhøj-Thomsen 1999a: 167ff). Several infertile couples in this study have been examined by many different physicians, who have often disagreed with each other, on the course of fertility treatment and on interpretations of new 'facts', often elicited by visualising technologies. What physicians see on X-ray pictures and ultrasound images is not unambiguous. One fertility specialist told me that he often disagreed with his colleagues: 'It is not that I want to criticise them because there are many ways to do this'. He always ordered the X-ray pictures because, as he said: 'It is important to take a look yourself. Radiologist are theorists, they have never had the internal organs in their own hands'.

To the surprise of the infertile men and women, the biomedical world is one of uncertainties and incomplete knowledge. In Sarah Franklin's words:

> One of the problems encountered in the context of achieved conception, both for professionals and for patients, is the problem of making sense of reproduction in context of evidently 'incomplete' knowledge. (Franklin 1997: 146-7)

These uncertainties also affect the close encounter with technology in another way. The majority of the infertile women and men in the study want to feel that they have done what they could do to have a child, within the range of technical and moral possibilities (Sandelowski 1993: 103, Tjørnhøj-Thomsen 1999a: 221-2). As one woman said: 'You have to do something, because what keeps you up is that in any case, even if you don't get a child, you will get peace with yourself. You can say, that at least you tried'[5].

The problem faced by some couples, however, is that it is almost impossible to get to the point when they feel convinced (and can come to an agreement) that they have done what they could. The 'incomplete' knowledge, and the lack of explanation when the treatment fails, means that there is always a space left for hope, interpretations, and action. There is always another physician to consult, another hormonal drug (or drug dosage) or treatment to try out. Thus while medical technology offers both physicians and patients many possible options and hopes, it simultaneously makes it almost impossible *not* to make a choice among them; it generates a feeling that 'one has no choice not to make a choice' (Strathern 1992: 37). The decision to break off treatment is a difficult one.

Painful attention
Being or becoming infertile also means searching for explanations, often followed by senses of guilt, or blaming someone else: 'Maybe it is because I

lead a wild life in my young days', or 'Maybe my infertility is caused by some drugs my mother took during her pregnancy'. Infertility therefore results in painful attention to earlier life events and activities, to biographies, and to the body. It is, first and foremost, an awareness of the woman's body and the menstrual cycle, which, as a cyclical time structure (of hope and downfall), comes to dominate the life of the infertile couple and makes them lose their linear time perspective. Infertility transforms the *lived* body, in which self and body are unified, to an *object* body where the body (and its procreative substances) is a source of constraints, and in opposition to the self (Rhodes *et al.* 1999, Leder 1990). In the close encounter with technology, such painful attention is intensified, and the fragmentation generated and exposed by it sharpened, as the body and its reproductive organs and substances become objects for technological intervention.

Processes of fragmentation and transgression
When people take the chance of having children by technological intervention, they also change the standard version of coming into being in radical ways. The techniques enable conception to take place in the absence of sex and love. Gametes can be extracted from bodies, stored and transferred to other bodies, which means that procreation is not bound to specific individuals' bodies or times. The process of procreation is made more complex, fragmented, less certain, and even more mysterious (Franklin 1992: 79). By means of visualising techniques, people see and acknowledge new biological processes and entities. Reproductive experiences and decision making become public events involving new actors, such as teams of professional experts and gamete donors (*ibid.*). A commercial dimension is added, transforming childless couples into consumers. This new market has met with some ambivalence. Several infertile couples are troubled by the idea that private fertility clinics and medical industries make money out of their infertility. The financial transaction should, at least, not be direct or visible. According to the Danish and Euro-American cultural repertoire, family, parenthood and reproduction do not belong to the market sphere (Cannell 1990; Tjørnhøj-Thomsen 1999a; Ragoné 1999).

Fertility treatment thus leads to the transgression and reconfiguration of boundaries drawn between cultural and social domains which are normally kept separate and protected. The close encounter with technology propels people to transgress boundaries between the public, the private, and the intimate; between the domain of family and love and the market; between the visible and invisible. One could also add the boundaries between biomedicine and magic and between the natural and the artificial. As for the latter, it is interesting that nature is still such a powerful referent in the clinic and in the experiences of infertile men and women. Thus it is natural to desire children. The physician told me that he loved to 'tamper with nature'; it is common to say that nature only needs 'a helping hand'. Some women also fear that nature will punish them for having children by technological intervention (they fear punishments such as miscarriages, premature and difficult deliveries, disabled, deformed or monstrous children, and early infant death).

Procreative technologies intervene in and reconfigure what is considered as natural. These references to nature, however, are not unambiguous. On the one hand, it is sacred, created by God; on the other hand, nature is a legitimate object for human agency. I would suggest that the ambivalence, which people feel, when they think of procreative technology must be understood within the context of these contradictory ideas about nature.

Feelings of awkwardness, vulnerability, discomfort and pain often originate from these transgressions and reconfigurations. As one example of this, a recurrent problem for infertility patients and the clinical staff is how to deal with sexuality, reproductive organs and substances in a relative public place such as the clinic (Cussins 1998).

Divisions of space, time, labour and bodies
The clinical setting is not only the physical background to social interaction, 'it is a space with internal and external social boundaries which [...] is intimately linked to the events which occur within' (Armstrong 1988: 207). The organisation of clinical time and space, as well as the division of labour, reflects the technologically imposed fragmentation of the pro-

cess of procreation which is taking place there. For example, the special consulting rooms for patients (workplaces for nurses and physicians) are strictly separated from the places where reproductive substances, gametes and embryos are nursed and stored (workplaces for biologists and laboratory technicians).

The experiences of the childless couples are thus generated and mediated by the temporal and spatial organisation of the fertility treatment. When an infertile couple enters the fertility clinic they have often been on a waiting list for months and may look back on a long career as involuntarily childless. In the clinical setting, they must comply and negotiate with other time dimensions, time schedules, routines and tempos. To be the object of intensive treatment requires not only a 'total co-ordination of biological clock and the medical routines' (Lundin 1996: 62), but also a cautious co-ordination between the clinical routines and the everyday social life of the fertility patients.

The experiences of infertile men and women are also constituted and mediated by the occupational, hierarchical, and gendered division of labour in the clinical setting. The main job of the physicians (most of whom are male) is to arrive at a proper diagnosis and to examine and treat the female body. The nurses (mostly women) take care – as they emphasise – of the emotional and psychological issues, while the laboratory technicians and the biologists are responsible for the sperm, the eggs and the fertilisations.

This division of labour reflects the fragmentation between body and body-substances, and the physical and the psychological dimensions of fertility treatment and, not least, the priority given to the body: 'They only pay attention to my medical body – not to me', as one woman described her distressing experience of the biomedically imposed split between 'me' and 'my body' to the detriment of the 'me'. 'They look at my sperm, and then they look at my wife and ask her about the course of treatment', as one man phrased the awkward feelings, which stemmed from his exclusion from the story of coming into being, and from the split between 'me' and 'my sperm'. This split, however, could also often lead infertile men to identify with their low-quality sperm, feeling unmanly and incapable.

The infertile men and particularly women nevertheless expressed a strong need to be 'whole' and to unify their fragmented experiences. They often struggled to get the opportunity to discuss not only the *physical*, but also the *emotional* and *psychological*, dimensions of their infertility with the physician. But physicians – whose time is often considered particularly valuable – do not have sufficient time to allow for conversation and the expression of feelings. The physicians I spoke to also made it very clear, that they did not have sufficient training to cope with the emotional dimensions of these encounters with technology (Tjørnhøj-Thomsen 1999a: 202).

The physician is nevertheless the one who comes close to the woman's body and intimate body parts. As Deborah Lupton writes, this 'involves an investment of trust that often contributes to feelings of vulnerability as well as those of love and closeness' (Lupton 1996: 165). The physician is also the one who, hopefully, can bypass infertility and assist pregnancy. This makes him a powerful key figure, the important third part in the story of coming into being, and he becomes related to potential parents and the wished-for child in an almost kin-like fashion. The relatedness the infertile 'act and feel' towards the physician (Carsten 1997: 290) thus often implies feelings of vulnerability, dependency, confidence, joking, love and anger (Lupton 1996). Nurses and laboratory technicians are remembered with warmth and gratitude, and after a successful treatment the clinical staff receive gifts such as chocolate and wine, accompanied by letters with pictures of the children. Every clinic has its own portrait gallery of 'its' children.

Feeling the drugs – seeing the pain
Processes of fragmentation, transgression and disciplining become even more elaborate and detailed in the course of fertility treatments. These processes can be exemplified by referring to the hormonal treatment and the aspiration procedure (the extraction of eggs from the ovaries). The women and men have to comply with a strict time schedule for their hormonal treatment. They have to learn to inject the daily dosage of hormones, and they must ensure that they have sufficient time and private space for the daily and timetabled injections.

Some women are very affected by the hormonal treatment, and they fear the long-term side effects. They feel they lose control over, and knowledge of, their bodies (some women gain weight, some say that they get depressed, and some cannot concentrate on their daily work). The body becomes an object, a stranger and an unpredictable agent, behaving awkwardly and foolishly. Physicians often categorise the side effects as psychological (caused by the stressful situation in general), whereas the women, in order to legitimise how they *feel,* insist that the side effects are due to the drugs: 'It is good to know that it is not me, but something chemical in my body', as one woman said.

The aspiration procedure is another feared hurdle, in the step-by-step fertility treatment, and some women find it painful. A few women remembered 'seeing the pain': 'It did not hurt, but it is more what you see that hurts', as one woman phrased it, when she recalled the ultrasound image of her ovaries being punctured.

In this situation the power of visualising technologies to transgress and redefine boundaries between the visible and invisible body, and to enforce fragmentation between the body and body parts by representing them in new ways, is brought to the forefront. Although the cultural emphasis on the visual and the close association between seeing and knowing is not new, the implications of these new ways of seeing, showing, and perceiving the body are still to be explored (Lundin 1996). One implication of this 'scopic drive as the paradigm of knowledge' (Braidotti 1994: 49), however, is the disembodying of experience in favour of what is seen, or what is shown, to be more precise (Duden 1993). As for instance in the case of seeing the pain, mentioned above, what is seen does not only take precedence over feelings and other senses. What is seen, *i.e.* the highly magnified pictures of gametes and embryos and the ultrasound images of the womens' interiors, takes on a life of its own[6]. So what is *shown* is one thing; what is *seen* is a question of interpretation, depending on the perspectives (the life-worlds, knowledge, desires, hopes) of the spectators. A woman expressed some sort of kinship-informed visual bonding, saying: 'And when I saw my two fertilised eggs, I thought: Those are my twins'. As Janelle S. Taylor writes: 'kinship bonds may form in an entirely new way through *spectatorship* of technologically mediated imagery as well as through physical or social contact (Taylor 1998: 32, original italics). According to Sandelowski (1994) men, too, seem to benefit from this new access to the woman's body and the egg or the foetus. She argues, that foetal ultrasonography has made women's and men's relationship to the foetus more equal, because this visualising technology give men access to and knowledge of a female world from which they previously have been excluded. Sandelowski writes, that this new imagery also enhances not only the father-child bond but also the marital relationship (Sandelowski 1994: 236).

Disciplining selves
It is hard work to undergo fertility treatment, emotionally as well as physically (*cf.* Franklin 1997). Some of the disciplining in the encounter with technology is, however, imposed by people themselves, in order to maintain at least some mastery of their bodies and lives. Women often, for instance, objectify their body and self simultaneously, from the position of yet another 'self': 'I have to think positively otherwise my body will not conceive'. The stressful processes of fragmentation (of selves and bodies) are closely connected to processes of self-objectification and disciplining. The encounter with procreative technology is thus often met with 'technologies of self', which, as Foucault writes,

> ...permit individuals to effect by their own means or with the help of others a certain numbers of operations on their own bodies and souls, thoughts, conducts, and ways of being, so as to transform themselves in order to attain a certain state of happiness, purity, wisdom, perfection, or immortality. (Foucault 1988: 18)

An example might be eating organic food and a variety of vitamin supplements, or receiving reflexology or healing.

The majority of the infertile couples in my study thus combined biomedical fertility treatments with alternative health care. Not all physicians approved of such combinations of treatments, if they came to know about them. One woman told me, that her physician got very angry, when he realised that she had spent at lot of money on a vitamin cure for her infertile husband in order to improve the quality of his sperm (the physician could not, however, explain the fact that the quality of the sperm, according to the laboratory technicians, actually had improved).

Sometimes people even took to prayer or magic in order to cope with the uncertainties of biomedicine and technology. Biomedicine cannot always offer an explanation of what is to be done or what went wrong, and medical explanations leave many pressing questions unanswered. People therefore often combine several interpretative systems in order to makes sense of what is going on and how to act (Layne 1992). While such coping strategies give them, on the one hand, an opportunity to (re)gain control and agency, it also increases the painful and distressing self-disciplining and self-objectification.

Some researchers ask whether the emotional and physical stress which fertility treatments generate may hinder a successful outcome (Boivin and Tafkeman 1996). The relationship between stress caused by medical treatment and bodily processes is still to be explored. It is, however, interesting, also in a much wider perspective, if the encounter with medical technology hinders a positive outcome of the same encounter.

Conclusion: Infertility, technologies and uncertainties

The encounter with technology – between the life-worlds of infertile men and women, the biomedical world, and the clinical setting – is complex. My study demonstrates that the life-worlds of infertile men and women are characterised by loss of control and by uncertainties. Infertile men and women feel betrayed, not only by nature, but also by the moral ideology which says that they should be able and willing to plan life and life events. The loss of control, the uncertain life perspective, and the social exclusions caused by infertility and childlessness, often lead to severe identity problems, and to emotional and physiological pains, agonies and distress. The majority of infertile couples are hopeful and often quite optimistic when they enter the biomedical world and the local clinical setting. They hope strongly that biomedical knowledge, expertise and technology will produce the wished-for-child, so that they can restore the disorders produced by infertility and thus be healed. At least, they are convinced that they will have an unambiguous diagnosis and a sure explanation of their infertility, if not a certain prognosis.

In this chapter I have shown that, contrary to what people hope for and expect, the biomedical world is uncertain and its knowledge incomplete. New facts and new knowledge are constantly brought to light, and different physicians do not always agree on the interpretation on facts and the course of treatment. Thus, there is no unequivocal connection between biomedicine's striving towards more knowledge and its ability to explain. This also makes it almost impossible to break off an unsuccessful treatment.

Fragmentation, transgression and disciplining are analytical keywords in our understanding of how infertile men and women experience the encounter with technology. Technology fragments what people strive to unify and keep together and transgresses the boundaries between separate, culturally valued domains. The effects of fragmentation and transgression are manifold.

As I have also demonstrated, the course of treatment is not only characterised by uncertainty and incomplete knowledge, but also by surveillance and control. Infertile men and women are not, however, passive, victimised patients. They act in many different ways in order to regain some control and to influence the outcome of the treatment in a positive direction. But their manifold strategies of coping, their technologies of the self, also lead to painful attention and the disciplining of bodies and every day lives.

Fertility treatment seldom cures infertility. It bypasses it. To more and more involuntarily childless couples, however, the encounter with procreative technology results in the wished-for-child. There is no doubt that a child will heal some of the wounds and disruptions caused by infertility and childlessness. But the experiences of being infertile and childless, and of the close encounter with technology, leave their marks on people's bodies, thoughts and future lives. The encounter with technology thus produces uncertainties, which people have to cope with in their future life. This can be exemplified by listening to those women who eventually became pregnant. After months of close attention and care at the fertility clinic, it was experienced as an anticlimax to be just a 'normal' pregnant woman, consulting the midwife according to the standard health system schedule. The encounter with technology also 'makes something out of you', as one woman said in Franklin's study (Franklin 1997: 164-5). The infertile women in my study did not feel 'normal', but different from other pregnant women. First and foremost, they were extremely anxious about their pregnancy. Some of them paid private clinics to get an extra ultrasound scan in order to be reassured that the child was alive: 'You just walk around, your body grows, when you see an ultrasound image you have something confirmed. I need to *see* the movements of the child'.

Nor is it just a matter of the ongoing here-and-now. Both during treatment and pregnancy, and after the child was born, some of the infertile men and women would ponder how, when, and what to tell their child about the manner of its coming into being. Some speculated about whether this story would affect their relationship to the child, or challenge its sense of self and identity. On uncertain questions and answers such as this, their 'new' futures depend.

Notes

1. *Landsforeningen af Ufrivilligt Barnløse* (LFUB)
2. In this study the techniques are artificial insemination with husband's or donor semen, *in vitro* fertilisation and micro-insemination.
3. By relational insecurity I refer to a situation, where people suddenly become uncertain of how to act in and encounter relationships previously considered to be familiar and confident (Sandelowski 1993).
4. The childless couples in my study longed to prepare special places and spaces for children in their homes. Home is, as Bob Simpson writes, '..assumed to be the privileged site, in which life, safety, support, pleasure and intimacy associated with the family will be found' (Simpson 1997: 54).
5. For similar findings see Franklin (1997).

6. Duden writes that there is nothing new about depiction of invisible entities, what is new is, 'the disappearance of the frontier between visible things that are visibly represented and invisible things to which representation imputes visibility' (1993: 16). Thus the distinction between what is seen and what is shown.

FIVE

PURSUING KNOWLEDGE ABOUT
A GENETIC RISK OF CANCER

Mette Nordahl Svendsen

The new genetics is an enterprise about the future. Built into the very idea and practice of biotechnology is the hope that knowledge of genes will help developing cures for serious illness. Such 'promised futures' (Franklin and Lock 2003: 13-15) stimulate enthusiasm about the potency of genetic information and often become a heroic story about scientific progress freeing us from disease.

Cancer genetic counselling is a practice that aims to identify genetic risks in order to present preventive actions to individuals 'at risk'. In this setting, therefore, genetic information is seen as the first step in a preventive process, as such incorporating a notion of the potency of genetic information in controlling health dangers. In cancer genetic counselling, clinical geneticists – called in what follows 'genetic counsellors' – offer an assessment of the genetic risk of cancer in healthy people who have a family history of either breast or ovarian cancer or colorectal cancer. With the identification of genes associated with hereditary colon and breast cancer in the 1990s, genetic testing of asymptomatic individuals has become an option, and cancer genetic counselling clinics have become part of public health care in Denmark as elsewhere in Europe. Out of these counselling services emerges a new social category: the healthy person genetically at risk of cancer.

In the two years during which I followed a group of people through cancer genetic counselling in Denmark, my attention was again and again drawn to the existential and moral aspects of pursuing genetic knowledge and the many social relationships with which genetic risk assessment is concerned. Anne[1], who is thirty-seven years old, is no exception. She has recently suffered from skin cancer, and she is afraid that she may have a genetic risk of breast cancer, due to the many cases of breast cancer in her father's family. She has a leading position in a medical firm and lives on her own with her two daughters, age twelve and fourteen. Talking about her motives for seeking genetic counselling, she says:

> There wasn't any taboo surrounding the many cases of breast cancer in the family, but lack of knowledge has meant that conclusions that should have been drawn have not been drawn. Nobody ever suggested that we should do anything about it. I am very much aware that it is my responsibility to prevent a cancer diagnosis. Others are not responsible for my body and, then there is the fact that I have two girls. I could choose to go on with my check-ups and refuse genetic testing, but that wouldn't solve the issue for my kids.

In her book about responses to uncertainty and misfortune in Uganda, Susan Whyte identifies three aspects of misfortune: first, an inquiry arising out of uncertainty; second, a demand for action and an evaluation of consequences; and third, the broader social and moral concerns to which uncertainty, and responses to it, are linked. The latter implies that 'the process of questioning, doubting, and trying out is about social relationships as well as individual disorders' (Whyte 1997: 3).

The uncertainty that dominates Anne's life concerns her potential of being at risk of hereditary cancer. Like most people participating in cancer genetic counselling, Anne's engagement with counselling does not address the question of 'Why me?', but rather the uncertainty of 'Not yet me'. The central issue for her is the second aspect of uncertainty, a demand for action. In her story, Anne implicitly states that someone in the family *should* take action to control illness and she is explicit about her own feeling of responsibility for her health. Hence, moral concerns give shape to her uncertainty and response. Anne's story also reveals to us that she does not perceive her risk to be isolated from social relations, which are at the same time genetic relations. Her response to a risk of cancer is as much about social relationships as it is about an individual disorder.

The demand for action, its moral implications, and the social relations which action invokes, will be explored in this chapter, in which I address three questions: What motivates people to pursue knowledge of genetic risk? To what dilemmas and questions does this pursuit of knowledge lead? To what broader social and moral concerns is the pursuit of knowledge linked?

My analysis draws on a narrative perspective on experience and action. This perspective considers that 'social life is not cultural rule-following or habitual acting so much as a process of becoming' (Mattingly 1998a: 69). That is, actors think towards endings and have imaginations and desires about what to become. They try 'to make certain things happen, to bring about desirable endings, to search for possibilities that lead in hopeful directions' (*ibid.*: 47). Put differently, action is in quest of a narrative, as stated by Paul Ricoeur (McIntyre 1981: 212). I will argue that the thoughts and actions of people who participate in cancer genetic counselling are informed by narratives of becoming responsible individuals by gaining control, and by narratives about transforming existential uncertainty into certainty through genetic knowledge. I will discuss the move towards certainty, control and responsibility which is demonstrated in narratives, in relation to the disjuncture between belief and knowledge in Western civilisation. This disjuncture recasts uncertainty about risks as 'beliefs', and a feeling of control of risk as 'knowledge', making genetic counselling a gateway to certainty, control and responsibility. I also argue that the process of becoming responsible, and controlling a genetic risk of cancer, becomes an exploration of moral and identity-related questions. These questions concern, in particular, the boundary between individual matters and family matters. The involvement of genetic relatives in genetic risk assessment and the attendant visibility of genetic links come to shape family relationships and family belonging.

The data on which this analysis is based mainly come from observations of cancer genetic counselling sessions at three hospitals in Denmark and interviews with a group of 25 counselees[2] who were followed through a process of counselling. These research activities took place between 1999 and 2001.

The importance of knowing and acting

Seeking certainty, creating hope
Most of the people in this study have experienced severe illnesses in their families and fear future illness themselves. Many consider themselves to be 'next in line' and as such view genes as containing a destiny that is difficult to conquer. Yet, as can be seen from Anne's earlier statement, their wish to change this destiny and 'do something' is strong. Conceived as a destiny, genetic dispositions represent what Michael Jackson calls 'forces of otherness'. He writes that:

> In every human society concepts such as fate, history, evolution, God, chance, and even the weather signify forces of otherness that one cannot fully fathom and over which one can expect to exercise little or no ultimate control. These forces are the given; they are in the nature of things. In spite of this human beings countermand and transform these forces by dint of their imagination and will so that, in every society, it is possible to outline a domain of action and understanding in which people expect to be able to grasp, manipulate, and master their own fate. This is the microcosm in which we demand the right to have our voices heard, in which we expect our acts to have some effect, and into which we strive to extend our practical understanding. (1998: 19-20)

To most counselees, science represents a domain of action in which forces of otherness can be transformed. In seeking cancer genetic counselling they hope to create a path to a future without illness. Olivia, who is in the process of having her risk assessed, says: 'What I can do about my risk is to gain knowledge about it. If I come to know that I have a hereditary risk, then it would be just natural to have regular check-ups, which they [counsellors] recommend'. Like many others seeking counselling, Olivia sees biomedical knowledge about her risk as a gateway to a trajectory of rational actions to control disease. And like most counselees she claims that facing the facts about one's possible genetic dispositions will reduce anxiety. One woman, Birthe, whose brothers have died from colon cancer, says, 'I am the kind of person who wants to know everything. The less you know, the more you imagine things'. In talking about the benefits of scientific knowledge, she indirectly refers to images that are painful and anxiety-provoking. A young woman, Ida, whose mother and aunt are ill with ovarian cancer describes her situation as follows:

> It is indeed satisfying to get a lot of answers instead of walking around worrying. I have been really scared...I have been in a panic in such a way that it takes time to calm down again. But I also think that this is what I can use the counselling for...So that I know what it is...So that I have something concrete to stick to. Then there will be less anxiety.

When the fear of the future frames the present, scientific knowledge is seen as a means to reframe the present, to extirpate fear.

Lise, a twenty-four year old woman who is seeking counselling in order to have a genetic test, says, 'I don't want to be nervous. I don't want to spend all my life being uncertain. I don't want to walk about believing, I want to know and then take it from there'. From this perspective, while scientific knowledge is looked upon as truth and certainty, lack of knowledge is associated with uncertainty and belief as well as with anxiety and speculation. Lise defines a culturally specific distinction between belief and knowledge that is a key epistemological[3] distinction in western civilisation (Good 1994: 17). According to this distinction, beliefs connote doubt, uncertainty and error, while knowledge is objective, correct and empirical. This distinction had a profound impact in anthropology during the twentieth century, when 'belief' was (and to some extent still is) a central concept for the study of culture. Religious and illness explanations, in particular, have been analysed as beliefs, as opposed to true knowledge about cause and effect in the natural world (*ibid.*: 20-1). The disjuncture between knowledge and belief is not specific to the scientific world, but has a strong impact in Western societies in general. It also gives shape to the experience of fearing hereditary cancer and seeking cancer genetic counselling. To counselees genetic knowledge is perceived as truth and certainty, while no knowledge is associated with uncertainty and belief. The disjunction between belief and knowledge supports the understanding that scientific knowledge can control illness and reverse fear by conceptualizing and categorizing one's future on a different scale than that of experience.

The genetic knowledge communicated in cancer genetic counselling concerns a risk factor. Like other kinds of biomedical risk information it is based on epidemiological findings and is statistical. Counselees will often get the message that they have a 50 per cent risk of having inherited a mutated gene which in 80-90 percent of cases will cause cancer. Such a risk factor 'has no fixed nor necessary relationship with future illness, it simply opens up a space of possibility' (Armstrong 1995: 401). However, the uncertainty of risk knowledge when it comes to predicting a future disease for a specific individual, is not perceived as problematic by Lise and others in her situation. Rather, the available genetic risk knowledge is considered more certain and more true than the lack of expert knowledge which is their point of departure.

Ida, Birthe, Lise, Olivia and many others I met in counselling feel invaded by thoughts about what might happen to them due to their family history of cancer. These thoughts have the status of imaginations and beliefs, which can be conquered by true biomedical knowledge. In their cases, belief does not refer to a different rationale about health and illness, as it does in anthropological accounts of non-Western medical systems. Rather, belief comes to refer to the uncertainty of not knowing. They feel uncertain and see scientific knowledge as something that can add contours to the diffuse feeling of being at risk, by making uncertainty and imaginings concrete. Ida, like others too, hopes that knowledge will provide the uneasy experience of being at risk with a language of facts, that is, a language which can recontextualize risk experiences by transferring them from the domain of beliefs and uncertainty to the domain of knowledge and certainty. According to Byron Good the opposition between belief and knowledge in Western civilisation is paralleled by other oppositions, among them the opposition between mind and matter (Good 1994: 63). The concretisation which Ida pursues expresses a desire for reaching facts, matter, and getting rid of a mind full of imaginations.

To counselees, cancer genetic counselling is a possibility that allows practical action through which they hope to extend their practical understanding of past, present and future. In seeking genetic counselling, counselees anticipate the forthcoming, the not-yet, as a space in which illness and fear can be controlled, and through which they become survivors. That is, they act with a sense of an ending (see Mattingly 1998a: 46) that lends meaning to their actions.

The moral imperative of knowing

Although going for check-ups is an important goal to reach from counselling, there is also a moral value attached to the pursuit of genetic knowledge. People who attend cancer genetic counselling perceive knowledge as the opposite of ignoring a risk factor, or being passive about their situation. Jane, who is thirty years old, and at risk of breast/ovarian cancer, explains her desire to know about her risk in this way: 'If there is some kind of knowledge somewhere which concerns me, then I want to know about it. I can't just pretend that it isn't there'. She points to the common attitude among people attending counselling that it is good 'to face the facts', and that a choice not to do so would imply that one tries to hide from reality. For Jane and many others in her situation 'to face the facts' is a morally correct way of dealing with life. To refuse expert knowledge is talked about in terms of 'turning my back on it' or 'cheating myself'. In this model of knowledge, science is equated with reality: scientific facts are understood as objects found in nature which are foundational to and distinct from social relations and social beliefs (cf. the conceptual distinction between knowledge and belief). To face this nature becomes a morally correct way of dealing with life.

Exploring Euro-American models of knowledge, Sarah Franklin builds on Marilyn Strathern's argument that 'the quest for facts about how the world works is also part of the Euro-American quest for selfhood' (Strathern, quoted in Franklin 2001: 306). Franklin writes:

Paradoxically, then, it is because scientific knowledge is seen to be objective and universal that it can have such intimate effects. Strathern's argument thus foregrounds Euro-American assumptions about knowing as being: she is intrigued by the fact that what science says exists 'out there' can tell us who we are 'in here'. We are seen to embody scientific knowledges. They describe the very nature of our being. (Franklin 2001: 306-7)

Thus, science (*e.g.* biology/genetics) is conflated with its objects (*e.g.* genes), and biological knowledge comes to be perceived as ontological facts about reality (*ibid.*: 303). This conflation means that genes are considered biological entities that ontologically are in the world – in bodies – independently of the researchers who investigate, analyse and name DNA sequences. This view on scientific knowledge is central to the categorical distinction between the biological and the social in Euro-American societies. Anthropological studies of reproductive medicine and the new genetics have shed further light on how Euro-Americans distinguish between these categories and consider the relationship between them. In her study of the public debate accompanying the Human Fertilisation and Embryology Act in Britain, Strathern suggests that the debate demonstrates that relationships of responsibility and care are considered after the facts of biology; in this view social relationships are described in reference to biological process and natural needs (Strathern 1992: 25). This makes Strathern argue that for Euro-Americans, 'biology is rooted in an order of reality to which social arrangements must attend, not the other way around' (*ibid.*: 26). Biology is regarded as providing the basis for social life: natural facts (*e.g.* biology) are thought to be foundational to social facts (*e.g.* social relations).

Following Strathern's claim that the biological is looked upon as foundational of social relations as well as individuality (1992), the biology that scientific knowledge describes is perceived as the ground of one's very being. Not to know is associated with conducting one's life on false premises. The heroic and moral quest for knowledge points to a conflation between knowing, being and doing in post-Enlightenment secular culture (see Franklin 2001: 303). This conflation directs people towards knowledge and makes them perceive biological knowledge as having value in and of itself. While, from an existential point of view, the need to act and 'do something' is a struggle for control, the need to 'do something' also resonates with the cultural understanding that to seek counselling and articulate family histories of illness (to the counsellor as to the anthropologist) becomes a way of *acting* in order to *know* one's *being*. The anticipatory element of becoming survivors is at once an existential imperative and a process of becoming morally right persons. The pursuit of genetic knowledge *feels* right. This moral orientation is not an external moral standard, but part of an understanding of oneself as moving towards certainty and taking personal responsibility for one's health. This is so because, as Charles Taylor argues (1989), morality and selfhood are intertwined. To live within a moral horizon (a moral space) is constitutive of human agency. Our sense of the good is interwoven with our sense of self (*ibid.*: 40), such that moral orientation is intimately linked to identity.

Mapping a genetic disease

Cancer genetic counselling[4]
Counselees are usually referred to a cancer genetic counselling clinic by their GPs. A cancer genetic counselling session consists of a conversation with a genetic counsellor, through which a risk assessment is produced based on information about the counselee's personal and family medical histories. The first step in a risk assessment is to draw up a family tree on which information about biological relationships is coupled with information about illness among those who appear on the tree. The counsellor uses this information to assess whether there is any hereditary pattern of illness in the family. If there is, the second step is to study the medical files of all the relatives who fell ill in order to obtain knowledge about the particular development and character of illnesses in the family.[5] The third step is mutation screening, a DNA analysis based on a blood sample

from an affected relative. If a mutation associated with hereditary cancer is identified in the blood sample, a possible fourth step is predictive genetic testing, a procedure that can identify whether specific relatives have the mutation identified in the family. In the Danish cancer genetic services the job of providing relevant information about illness in the family lies with the counselee. Thus, the mapping of disease in a family depends on the personal choices and actions of the counselee (Sachs 1998: 63).

Those who in their first counselling session hope to get an immediate assessment of their risk quickly learn that risk assessment is primarily based on family information and not on an individual blood test. In many families it takes months, sometimes years, to provide the relevant information. Just as the individual is located in a web of genetic connections when exploring her risk, her final risk assessment is based on the family tree. Hence, an individual risk assessment conveys information about the risks of all genetic relatives drawn on the map. In Danish counselling, the counsellor outlines the risk of identified relatives and recommends that the counselee inform them of their risk and tell them about the option of counselling and check-ups. Just as the task of providing family information lies with the counselee, so does the task of informing.

What emerges from this short outline of the process of genetic counselling and testing is that genetic risks are viewed in a context of genetic relatives, and that the identification of genetic risks depends on the co-operation and involvement of other relatives. In the following I will discuss two aspects of the involvement of relatives: the process of asking for family information and the process of passing on risk information to family members.

Asking for information

Counselees often find it difficult to contact distant relatives and ask for illness information. One woman, Lone, whose father died from colon cancer, was encouraged to talk to her brother about the result of his last check-up, as this result may shed light on her own risk of cancer. Recalling her conversation with her brother she says:

It is not something easy to talk about. I thought that he might feel pressured to give me information. I felt bad about that. She [the counsellor] said that you don't die from the disease today. But, anyway, if his check-up showed something, I would feel that it was life threatening for him, thinking…now he has to go through that, and how many years will pass in his case?

To raise the issue of a genetic risk of cancer is to address the risk and possible death of the person being asked. It is by no means a neutral matter, but deeply existential and considered a sensitive and private matter. Lone and others experience asking for information of disease as intruding into private affairs and putting pressure on someone else. In many cases, questions of illness are intimately linked to memories of deceased relatives and to painful experiences of illnesses and of loss. 'It evokes old grief', as one woman phrased it. For the person asking, there is always the fear of hurting a relative and of being rejected.

Although most participants in this study find it difficult to ask relatives for illness information, my interview material shows that it stops rarely anyone from doing it[6]. While most people who ask their relatives for information acknowledge the sensitivity of the information, they also say that relatives have an obligation to co-operate. It may be difficult to co-operate, but, according to the risk rationality of knowledge seekers, the other party has a moral obligation to co-operate, and a relative's resentment should not stand in the way of their own personal desire to reveal a genetic risk. Let me give an example. Nanna (aged thirty) has several relatives in her father's family who have died from colon cancer. On that basis, she has enrolled in a control programme, but finds the procedure of colonoscopy very painful and tends to postpone or cancel her appointments. Being dissatisfied with her present situation, she wants to find out if she is carrying a mutation making her susceptible to colon cancer. The search for a mutation can only be initiated based on a blood sample from a person in her family who is affected by cancer. Neither Nanna nor her father has been ill with cancer. Therefore, she is dependent on the co-operation of her father's sister, a woman of 68 years who has had colon cancer several times. This aunt does not want to participate. Nanna accepts that it is difficult for her aunt to participate, because any identification of a mutation will make it possible to conclude that the mutation was the cause of the illness and death of her daughter (Nanna's cousin). However, Nanna does not think that her aunt's unwillingness should hinder the possible identification of a mutation in the family:

> I have to say that at the time when I pressed for a test, I wouldn't have become…I wouldn't have taken offence, but in all decency, she ought to participate. If she refused it would have affected us and my children and so on.

Nanna argues in favour of her aunt's responsibility towards the family ('us and my children'), which, seen from Nanna's perspective, carries greater weight than her aunt's individual desires. In explaining her action to me, Nanna makes an explicit connection between (the pursuit of) genetic information and obligations within family relationships. Her pressure on her aunt and her expression of it in her talk with me can be seen as actions in which she is trying to 'direct [her] actions and the actions of others in ways that will bring about the proper ending' (Mattingly 1998a: 46): obtaining genetic risk information is to the benefit of all healthy members of the family. In this story, a piece of illness information or an aunt's blood sample are but small elements – almost technical matters – which will lead to the final risk assessment. To accept her aunt's resistance would change the story and the moral stance taken in it (that it is good to know genetic risks). That in the end Nanna's aunt agrees to give a blood sample despite her own wishes illustrates the moral imperative of the story. How can one be against helping other family members take an interest in and care of their health? The mutation is identified soon after. While this gives Nanna and her father the possibility of testing, Nanna's aunt suffers from the genetic knowledge. With the identification of a mutation, she feels that everyone comes to know her guilt.

Another young woman, Heidi, needs information about some distant relatives of her mother. Heidi's mother refuses to call them. Being quite desperate, Heidi in the end guides her mother to the telephone and forces her to call them. Heidi is very disappointed that her mother does not want to help her voluntarily. She decides to exclude her mother from future counselling, as she no longer wants to share her risk assessment with her mother.

The situations of Lone, Nanna and Heidi illustrate that the dependency upon relatives is fundamental to genetic risk assessment. Their stories also reveal the struggles they go through in order to reach the final risk assessment. What makes them go through these struggles? And what are the consequences for social relations?

In her work on narrative reasoning among occupational therapists, Cheryl Mattingly argues that, 'action is a judgement rather than an application of general rules to a particular case' (Mattingly 1998b: 289). She states that judging how to act involves deliberation about what an appropriate action would be, as well as requiring capacities to decipher the intentions of actors, to imagine outcomes, and to 'understand the important historical contexts of which any given moment or single act is just one part' (ibid.: 289-90). The basic argument of Mattingly's work is that narratives shape action and experience. Actors think of themselves as part of stories and shape action so that it takes on a narrative form (Mattingly 1998a: 19). Therefore, 'practical judgment requires the actor to answer such questions as: What story am I part of here? How will these stories change if I take this act in this way, rather than that one?' (Mattingly 1998b: 289-90).

In conversations with me, Lone, Nanna and Heidi do consider the appropriateness of their own and other's actions. They consider the consequences of hurting people and putting them under pressure. They consider the obligation of family members to help each other and they take account of their own strong desire to fulfil the project they have started, as well as their felt obligations towards the biomedical professionals who are involved in the project. In this project a mother's telephone call, an aunt's blood sample, and a piece of information delivered over the phone by a brother, are but small elements which will lead to the final risk assessment. Their project of risk assessment and the felt need for acting responsibly and controlling a future disease is the narrative context for understanding their actions.

Nanna knows that her aunt has her reasons to be reluctant, as well as Heidi knows that her mother finds it uncomfortable to call relatives she has never spoken to. However, these obstacles do not, in their minds, qualify as acceptable reasons for refusing to participate in genetic risk assessment. Their deliberations about how to act explore moral positions, for example that relatives have an obligation to help each other, and that it is one's right and responsibility to find out about risks. Such positions inform the stories Lone, Nanna and Heidi are part of, and thus concern their role as actors (Mattingly 1998b: 290). The stand one takes constitutes identity and projects a future being (Taylor 1989: 47). In the case of these women, their actions towards relatives project their quest for reaching what they see as significant qualities: true knowledge, control and responsibility. While the narrative structure of action is present in these women's accounts, their accounts also suggest that action is informed by, and finds legitimacy in, more general values (such as the moral imperative of knowing as well as in ideas about rights and obligations between relatives). In actions towards relatives they explore and enact notions of rights and responsibilities in a new context, a context of genetic risks and shared substance, illustrating that actions are motivated by shared notions, but not rule governed. Actions allow for improvisation as well as shared comprehension (Hastrup 1995: 80).

To put pressure on relatives to co-operate in risk assessment has consequences for social relations. The process of communicating illness information and the positions people take up in relation to genetic mapping, shape social relationships within families. What is also being shaped, contested and negotiated in discussions about people's willingness to participate in genetic mapping, is the borderline between individual matters and family matters. The visibility of this boundary raises questions of appropriate conduct. Body, illness and health risks are considered individual matters. However, obtaining individual knowledge about genetic risks means 'releasing' what is considered individual (a brother's check-result and an aunt's blood) to other relatives.

Put differently, what is considered an *individual responsibility* for one's own body can only be reached if other relatives enact what could be called a *family responsibility*. For people in the situation of asking for family information, this becomes a moral question: is the reluctance of Nanna's aunt more right than other family members' desire to know their risk? The way people act their way through such moral dilemmas (and the way they think about the issue) expresses practical reasoning and define certain values and reasonings as better than others. The reasoning of Nanna, and other people in her situation, is that relatives have an obligation to participate. This is a moral position that contains the idea of the identification of genetic risks as belonging to the family. The visibility of the boundary between individual matters and family matters, and the moral dilemmas it gives rise to when relatives have to be involved in genetic risk assessment, becomes even more pronounced when it comes to sharing risk information.

Sharing information

Becoming responsible
To demonstrate the issue of information sharing I will present the process of genetic counselling and testing as it took shape in the family of Anne, who was introduced in the beginning of this chapter.

Anne takes the initiative to seek genetic counselling in order to get information about her own risk, and the risks for her children. She does not inform any of her relatives about her intention to see a counsellor. When I ask her about it, she says,

> That was my decision. I am fully capable of handling it myself and I don't want any of my relatives to.....they may have an opinion about it, but I don't care. If they have, those opinions belong to their life and they shouldn't influence what I am doing.

The decision to get genetic counselling is perceived as a decision of the autonomous individual *vis á vis* other autonomous individuals, a view held by most people at the beginning of counselling, before genetic mapping has yet become a family issue. From the family information Anne brings to counselling, the counsellor comes up with a very clear conclusion that her family history indicates hereditary breast cancer. The counsellor recommends that Anne has frequent screenings, and tells her that this option is also an option for her relatives at risk. At that time, Anne passes on the information to her nearest relatives (siblings), and to relatives who have been affected by cancer and from whom help is needed (her father's sister's medical record is needed to investigate the risk, and a blood sample from her father's brother's daughter is needed to search for a mutation). These are the people who Anne thinks the risk assessment concerns. Other cousins, whose mothers have died from, or have been ill with breast cancer, are not informed. This exclusion does not seem to be a conscious strategy. Rather, it expresses the fact that these relatives are not, in her mind, involved in the project as persons. In terms of the narrative, they are not part of the story.

A year later, the mutation is identified in a blood sample from her cousin who has breast cancer. This means that all risk persons in the family can be tested for the specific mutation considered responsible for cancer in the family. To know about a mutation in one person seems to require that the information should be shared with all known genetic relatives of the person. This view is strongly articulated by counsellors. In the dialogue between counsellor and counsellee a shared story is created in which genetic risk assessment aims at fighting illness and death. In this fighting the counsellee is the main character. She is given the mission of informing relatives about the genetic risk factor and their possibilities for acting (*i.e.* counselling, genetic testing, regular screenings). The family tree is an important tool in creating this mission and making other relatives persons in the story.[7] In the counselling in which Anne learns that the mutation is identified in her cousin's blood sample, the risk of all identified relatives are discussed as well as possible ways to pass on the knowledge to those relatives. Informing relatives and making them understand the value of counselling and frequent check-ups become in the dialogue not only a shared goal of the counsellor and Anne, but also the responsibility of Anne. Thus, in Anna's case, the identification of the specific mutation changes her perception of her risk from being something that concerns her and her closest relatives, to being something that concerns all genetic relatives (mapped on the family tree) and leaves her with a duty to inform them. Being asked why she feels a responsibility to inform even distant relatives, Anne says,

> I have knowledge which has or may have an impact on their health, and it is my duty to pass on that knowledge. No doubt about that. How they will use it, is up to them. They may become very frightened, but there is nothing to be done about it.

In her essay on the translation of epidemiological findings to clinical practice and lay understandings, Sandra Gifford argues that clinicians transform the epidemiological concept of risk into a physical entity, a sign of a future disease that can be diagnosed and managed by clinicians (Gifford 1986: 215). Her study reveals that lay people speak of risk as a state of being, as a symptom of illness (*ibid.*: 230). Other studies point in a similar way to the transformation of the statistical concept of risk into a menacing thing, when it enters politics or clinical practice (Adelswärd and Sachs 1996; Douglas 1994). According to Adelswärd and Sachs, medical tests play a crucial role in producing evidence that a person has a particular problem (an increased risk) although he or she may feel perfectly well. Test results may for both health personnel and lay people provide justification for intervention (1996: 1180).

The option of genetic testing may also, in Anne's case, explain the moral imperative to inform relatives which is being created in the dialogue between her and the counsellors. The identification of a mutation revealed in test transforms for both parties an abstract statistical percentage into a thing people have or do not have. From being an activity of mind the risk becomes a material fact. As argued by Franklin, scientific knowledge is easily conflated with its objects. Said differently, a metonymic relationship is established between information and a material object in the body. The result is that Anne comes to talk about risk knowledge as a something that defines her own health, as well as the health of her relatives. The information not only concerns the family, but illuminates genetic relatedness. With the identification of a mutation, genetic risks become material 'things' in the body that constitute our very being and a bodily relationship to other people. Anne's statement suggests that the identification of this 'thing' translates into social obligations to pass on information.

Passing on information

At a counselling session one and a half months later, Anne learns from the counsellor that none of her cousins or their children has signed up for genetic counselling and testing. Although, in our previous talk, she said that her relatives' reactions to the knowledge she gives them is not her business, she does become very concerned that none of them has sought genetic counselling. She is afraid that her cousins are worrying a lot about their risk, and she decides to call some of her relatives again, to recommend that they sign up for counselling. However, Anne hesitates to contact a cousin whose mother died from breast cancer. She says:

> There is the respect for other people's integrity. On the other hand, sometimes you need to transgress boundaries, especially when it is about things like these. At the moment I guess that I hope that when she hears about the test results and screenings of other relatives, it will push her forward without me being the one to do it. After all, it is best when people make the decision themselves.

Similar to people's deliberations when asking relatives for illness information, Anne's consideration in this situation is about the boundary between individual and family matters. Is it better to transgress the personal sphere of her cousin, and talk to her about the benefits of counselling, or is it better to respect her integrity and let the decision be her own business?

Mattingly argues that moral ambiguity is created in narratives by devices such as the presence of different moral perspectives and the depiction of time as open to future revision (1998a: 116). In the above quotation, Anne is framing genetic information in different ways, thus making multiple voices present: to recommend counselling even though it implies a transgression of a what she considers a private boundary, to respect personal integrity, or to let time and the test results of other relatives work for her. She also reveals that the position she holds now may be revised in the future. Her deliberations are what Mattingly (1998b) calls 'practical reasoning', exploring the right action in a certain situation. This reasoning process is located in a field of social relations. While Anne finds it perfectly all right to write her brother a weekly e-mail, reminding him of the name and the telephone number of the counsellor he is to contact, she is less sure about how – if at all – she should discuss the option of counselling with her cousin.

What this points to is that the imagined boundary between the world one calls one's own and the world seen to be 'other' is not fixed (Jackson 1998: 18). Rather, boundaries are imagined in relation to what can cross and cannot cross between specific persons. It is not necessarily impossible for Anne to contact her cousin, but the issue of genetic risk makes the world of her cousin other as well as shared. Anne's deliberations about the right moral position (the good) are shaped by the absence of a close relationship with her cousin and notions of links. Is the identified mutation acting as link between herself and her cousin? Does it in itself justify feelings of care and responsibility for, and actions of control towards, relatives who are genetically close but socially distant? In the situation of Anne, the moral ambiguity concerns the juxtaposition of sameness and difference in relationships that are imagined by way of genetic information but not grounded in experiences of social belonging.

With relatives Anne feels closer to, the issue of genetic testing is actively debated and gives rise to personal conversations about the ways in which breast cancer has affected the lives of everyone of the family. Hence, family history and family belonging are being recast in relation to illness experiences and new knowledge about genetic risks. Relatives enact feelings of concern, responsibility and social belonging through tele-phone conversations about illness, counselling, test results and check-ups. Through genetic mapping, Anne comes to feel a stronger sense of social relatedness, to those relatives with whom she shares her own experience of illness, counselling and risk.

Whatever Anne decides to do in relation to her cousin, whom she has not contacted, Anne's considerations show that her responsibility to control her own personal risk becomes a responsibility – or a need – to control the risk situation of her genetic family. Her concern for the ways in which her relatives handle their risk situation does not become less important when she receives her own test result: she does not have the mutation and can stop worrying about her own risk of hereditary breast cancer. What may also be at stake in Anne's attempts to involve her family in cancer genetic counselling is her desire not to stand alone, but to share her moral choices with others. The support of her relatives legitimises the good in knowing. This aspect of her commitment to inform relatives may not be motivated by family belonging, but it has, indeed, consequences for family belonging.

Being informed
Ellen (aged fifty) is Anne's cousin. Since the illness of her mother and her mother's sister, she has felt at risk of breast cancer and has, on her own initiative, had a few mammograms taken during the past twenty years. Like everyone in the family she knows the family history. However, she is not pleased when her mother tells her about the possibility of genetic testing:

> I was annoyed about it. It was like she wanted to confront us with something that we did know, but wanted to hide a bit. Of course, she wanted to help us. When the possibility of a genetic test existed, she thought we should make use of it. But you think, why should I do that? Why do I need to know? If nothing is found in the next mammogram and the one I should have in two year's time, why should I want to know about my susceptibility? For many years you go around living in blissful ignorance of the possibility of testing. Then, suddenly, it is

smacked on the table and you need to make up your mind: what do you want, what don't you want, which possibilities are available, why and so on.

Having been informed about the possibility of a genetic test, Ellen feels a need to consider the possibility of being tested. The information is of such a kind that it cannot be ignored. Its character makes her feel a need to face 'the facts' or make a deliberate choice not to do so. It is exactly because the information itself demands that she makes up of her mind, that she experiences the act of being told as a transgression of her integrity. The context in which she thinks about herself and the future is changed. Ellen does not consider the information she is given to be 'new knowledge'. Rather, what is new is that the possibility of genetic testing is weakening a previously acceptable position, namely to live without knowledge of genetic risks, and it poses the question: Is it right to let one's future health situation stay unknown and undetermined instead of having it scientifically assessed? The position of not knowing is recast as a position of hiding, indicating the moral value that is placed on facing up to information about one's genetic make-up. As we saw earlier, science is taken to reflect 'the facts' of reality, and not to know about this reality is to conduct one's life on false premises. Ellen also feels under pressure from her mother to act. Yet, what in the end calls forth Ellen's decision to be tested is the fact that, shortly after being informed by her mother, she is diagnosed with abnormal cells in one breast, which may or may not develop into cancer. In this new situation of facing the threat of illness, she experiences the possibility of a genetic test as the right thing to do. The positive test result that follows supports her decision to have both her breasts removed. She says:

> Before I was diagnosed with abnormal cells, I kept thinking, one more year has passed [without illness]. Those family members, who have had cancer, they were all younger than I am now when they were diagnosed. Most of them died while young. I had the idea that it was a disease that hit in youth. I thought, one more year has passed and you

are probably the one to escape. You are the one who hasn't got it. After all, it is not that hereditary. [...] Knowing that I had dysplasia and that I had come this far, to decide to have both of my breasts removed, I thought...It just felt right to be tested. And when the result came I was not shocked. The positive test-result was just a natural consequence of all the other things that had happened to me.

Ellen describes a past in which her perception of when cancer strikes, which is again linked to her experience of her own health and her own luck, feeds an understanding of herself as someone who does not get cancer. In this past it is possible and attractive to think of the future as open – as containing the possibility of no disease. This perspective frames her reactions and feelings at the point of receiving the information. In a later conversation with the counsellor, she uses the image of a seesaw when explaining her understanding of her health at the moment of her diagnosis of abnormal cells. She says;

> It is like a seesaw...a balance. On the one hand there is reason. I knew it was in the family and therefore it was very likely that something would be found in the next mammogram. On the other hand, my desire to survive made me think that I am the one who will escape it.

In her story, this latter perspective is challenged and defeated by the diagnosis she receives of abnormal breast cells. She is now no longer the one who will escape it, she says. 'It' not only seems to refer to a certain hereditary line, but to capture a destiny, a force determining her health, though it is outside her control. Knowing her genetic disposition is to know her destiny as one who may very well get cancer, a view that is also emphasized by the medical experts with whom she is in contact. In this situation, a future of no disease can only be reached through genetic testing and surgical intervention. Uncertainty has been turned into knowledge about a risk that needs to be controlled.

The reaction of Anne's sister, Dorthe, is similar to Ellen's first reaction. Dorthe has long ago decided that 'she is not the one to get cancer in the family'. She does not want to have anything to do with sickness and is very frustrated when her sister tells her about her risk and the possibility of a gene test, making no secret of her positive attitude to genetic testing. Nevertheless, a few months later, Dorthe turns up in counselling to have a genetic test taken. At that time she has also had her first mammogram taken, as recommended by her sister (Anne). Dorthe explains to me that she feels pressure from her sister to be tested, but, more importantly, she feels that the knowledge she now has forces her to know more. In spite of the fact that she does not want information about her risk, the information about the possibility of a genetic test demands action. Ellen's diagnosis and surgery also shapes Dorthe's decision about being tested. The risk, as symbolised by illness embodied in one relative, makes other relatives feel vulnerable and informs their actions.

Ellen is very explicit about the change that the coupling of genetic information and a diagnosis of abnormal cells prompted in her in relation to understanding her future health. The 'diagnoses' displace one self-understanding and move her into another context of action and reflection upon her life trajectory. In her story as told to me, genetic information marks the passage from a past in which she understood herself as the one who would escape it to a present in which she knows her dispositions and acts upon her knowledge. With Luhmann, we may also conceptualize this change of perspective as a change from a sphere of danger to one of scientifically calculated risk. Luhmann suggests that attributing an unfortunate future event to forces outside one's own control makes it a danger, whereas attributing accidents to one's own decisions and actions makes them risks. Thus, the moment one could have acted differently by taking a different decision, the possible unfortunate future event becomes a risk (Luhmann 1997: 177-8). Without embarking here on a Luhmannian systemic analysis, we can still suggest that the distinction between danger and risk illustrates the change that Ellen and Dorthe depict as a change from a 'sphere of danger' in which the possibility of future breast cancer is not objectified by science to a 'sphere of risks' in which the possibility of breast cancer is scientifically assessed and decisions about what to do about it are within their reach. Fear of cancer is transformed into a concrete calculable risk (see also Koch 2002: 96).

Knowledge is irreversible. As soon as Ellen and Dorthe have been informed about a possible pre-stage of cancer or a genetic risk of cancer, they have been moved into a context of scientific knowledge and can only take decisions within that context. Their view of the future, which until then was looked on as containing the possibility of being free of cancer, can only be sustained by seeking more knowledge. Furthermore, with access to information about a genetic risk of cancer, personal ideas about 'not being the one who gets cancer' acquire the status of a 'belief', as opposed to true genetic 'knowledge'. As discussed earlier, moral values are attached to these notions, knowledge being more correct and therefore better than belief. Counselees associate hope, control, certainty and responsibility with knowledge. With the possibility of genetic testing, the situation of Ellen and Dorthe becomes recast as a choice between belief and knowledge, between uncertainty and certainty. Thus, new ways of acquiring the values of responsibility, certainty and control are opened up by genetic testing, just as genetic testing closes off other ways of thinking about the future, by contextualizing them as beliefs. In the stories of Ellen and Dorthe, the moral quest for self-knowledge is situated in a story that emphasizes self-knowledge as a means of acquiring responsibility, certainty and control. To find a position from which to refuse genetic information that is already available seems almost impossible.

As seen in the earlier examples, the decision to be tested is not just a matter of gaining more knowledge in relation to oneself. In Dorthe's counselling session she says, 'I also want to be tested in the interest of the others in my family. If I have it they may also like to be tested', and, 'I don't want to be ignorant when everybody else is being tested'. These statements show that she places her action of genetic testing in the context of a family project, that is, in a story in which she as a family member acts in moral obligations towards the common good of the family. In this story about genetic testing as a family project her actions show her commitment to her family and thus concern social relations in the family and are thought to have an impact on these relations. They manifest a responsible identity in which responsibility is thought of as a quality of the individual towards herself and her family. To avoid testing would not only be a sign of non-commitment to the family, it would also leave her with a very unpleasant feeling of having placed herself outside the community of knowers. What this shows is that relatedness is not a constant. It is continuously under construction (Carsten 2000: 18). The making up of one's mind about testing becomes a process in which relatedness is articulated and created.

In public debate, genetic testing is often presented as a decision of the autonomous individual who decides for herself. The ethnography presented here suggests that counselees do not simply experience genetic counselling as opening up choices but as making them take difficult decisions. The story of Ellen and Dorthe voice the perspective that the creation of genetic knowledge happened to them and put them in a new context within which they had to act. In this context, Euro-American models of knowledge provide an important framework for the decisions taken. At the same time decisions are shaped by and shaping ideas about family relations and ways of belonging to the family.

Conclusion

In this chapter, I have discussed the social dramas arising from the desire to control the risk of future disease and from the many questions regarding relations to genetic relatives. These dramas do not just happen alongside genetic mapping, they shape genetic risk assessment and the experience of being at risk.

To gain genetic knowledge and participate in cancer genetic counselling is perceived by counselees as a means to control future disease and anxiety about disease. During the first stage of counselling, the issue of control is thought of as the individual's responsibility towards her own body (individual responsibility) and a responsibility towards her children (family responsibility). This simultaneous conceptualisation of genetic risk assessment, as individual and familial, becomes more pronounced during the course of genetic counselling. The familial is by no means a fixed entity; the involvement of genetic relatives in genetic risk assessment reframes the boundary between what is considered individual and what is considered familial, as well as reframing *who* is considered familial. The immediate thought that genetic risk assessment concerns oneself and one's children is soon challenged when genetic counselling comes to involve more distant relatives and thus becomes a family matter. Notions of family responsibility are explored in the light of mapping a genetic risk of cancer and passing on information about a genetic risk factor. This exploration involves an exploration of moral positions about what to expect from genetic relatives, what to share with them, and what to do in order to control their risks.

To analyse these moral positions I have found it fruitful to use a narrative perspective on experience and action. The quest of a narrative is not a solitary activity. Working out individual narratives and exploring moral positions happens in counsellings, in actions towards other relatives, in intimate relations to those one loves, and in conversations with the anthropologist. It takes place in social relations in which people, by telling their story, 'define the kind of experience they seek and [...] try to shape' (Mattingly 1998a: 20). The working out of stories and the simultaneous exploration of moral positions are shaped by social relations. At the same time, social relations and identities are redefined in these actions. Carrying through a certain moral position may imply putting pressure on other people and challenging and changing the character of relationships. What Whyte says about responses to uncertainty in Uganda applies in Denmark, too: 'There are consequences on a social level – effects on the shared experience of many individuals' (Whyte 1997: 226). The involvement of relatives in genetic risk assessment shapes family belonging and family relationships. The visibility of genetic links gives way to reflections on who belongs to one's family. From knowledge about a genetic disease and the practices related to genetic counselling, feelings of concern, responsibility and control may develop. Genetic links may become a point of departure for creating new social relationships.

What informs the narratives of people who participate in genetic risk assessment is a juxtaposition between belief and knowledge, according to which knowledge is considered 'the good', associated with truth and constituting facts about reality. That genetic knowledge is interpreted as mirroring facts about reality recasts imaginings of the future held before the possibility of a genetic test as 'belief'. In this sense, genetic information seems to impose its own trajectory of actions that have their own logic and inescapability. Yet such an inescapability (*e.g.* informing relatives, being tested and embarking on preventive action) results from the ways in which genetic knowledge is interpreted in specific social relations. Just as interpretive moves express individual agency, the empirical material points to how the direction of the interpretive moves that are made expresses the social conditions for the possibility of interpretation. I suggest that placing genetic knowledge in the context of self and family, as well as contrasting genetic knowledge with belief, reveals the social platform from which counselees act in, and understand, the world. Thus, genetic knowledge is always *practiced* and understood in relation to specific people, social understandings and social relationships. When counselees interpret genetic knowledge in the context of family relationships and the self, new contexts for understanding identity and social relationships are created. In this sense, knowledge becomes irreversible. The interpretive moves of counselees move them into new frameworks for understanding their lives and obligations in social relationships.

Notes

1. All people referred to in this paper are women, the reason being that the majority of people who took part in my study are women. This over-representation of women is related to the fact that the risk of breast cancer is a risk which women face more than men. Patricia Kaufert argues that breast cancer screening programs define the female body as 'an object in constant need of monitoring, evaluation and surveillance' (Kaufert 2000: 67). Such a perception of the female body as a body which 'may feel well, but is a hiding place for disease' (*ibid.*: 70) may also play an important role in the strong representation of women seeking genetic counselling. Also, within the families I have come to know, women more than men take responsibility for the health of the family. Women, thus, tend to be the ones who take the initiative to seek genetic counselling and inform other relatives about a genetic risk of cancer. They 'do the work of kinship', as di Leonardo puts it (1987).

2. Most of those who seek cancer genetic counselling are not ill and do not consider themselves patients. I therefore call them counselees.

3. The distinction between belief and knowledge is epistemological in the sense that knowledge is taken to mirror natural facts while belief refers to culturally determined ideas about empirical knowledge.

4. This short outline does not contain an analysis of the way risks are communicated, the metaphors used when discussing heredity, the moral messages in communication or the power relations which are inscribed in the counselling situations. It only serves to sketch in the process of counselling.

5. Clinically, hereditary cancer does not differ from other cancers, which is why it cannot be diagnosed in a single individual. In studying medical files, counsellors are interested in information about, for instance, the organs in which cancer is manifest, the age of the individuals who have been diagnosed and possible additional cancers.

6. Those who do refuse to ask relatives for illness information are the ones who have obtained from counselling what is considered most important: check-ups and genetic testing. In their cases, additional family information can shed light on the extent of cancer in the family, but it does not add much to their own risk assessment.

7. The counsellor points at the different relatives drawn on the family tree and asks Anne whether she thinks that they know about a risk of cancer. Anne answers what she knows about her relatives and begins to talk about the ways in which the different relatives might react to the information. In this dialogue it is implicit that

Anne is the one to contact her relatives. In other counselling sessions in which the counselee does not accept her role as messenger right away, the counsellor directly asks the counselee to inform relatives, emphasising the value of genetic risk knowledge for other relatives. The breast cancer genetic counselling clinic has the politic of not passing on risk knowledge to relatives, partly due to the fact that there is no scientific documentation demonstrating that so called preventive actions (regular screening or prophylactic surgery) will save lives, although these actions are believed to do so.

SIX

BLOOD-STEALING RUMOURS IN WESTERN KENYA: A LOCAL CRITIQUE OF MEDICAL RESEARCH IN ITS GLOBAL CONTEXT

Paul Wenzel Geissler

The origin of this chapter is tied to a turn in my research biography. As a biologist, I have worked for a number of years in biological-medical research on child health among the Luo in western Kenya, East Africa[1]. The research was in the field of epidemiology in a broad sense: we examined and treated rural school children and followed up the results of treatment by further examinations. Most of these studies could have been done anywhere in the world, in the sense that the social context was not central to the work or to the results. However, during my stay in Kenya I grew interested in the social context, and my involvement with the people whose children's health I studied led me to change my academic interests towards social anthropology.

One experience that triggered my interest in the sociality of my 'study subjects', was being confronted by their responses to me and to the research I took part in. These responses were very varied. On one side of the spectrum, the research was welcomed for the development that people thought it would bring to the community. This was sometimes a bit embarrassing, because, due to its academic nature, our work did not bring many immediate improvements for the local population. At the other extreme, our project vehicles were at times chased away by angry parents, who accused us of trying to kill their children. Between these extremes, there were rumours, debates and concerns, of which I was only partly aware at the time. Our research was thus evaluated, contested and used by the local people in their local social and political practices.

In this chapter, I want to look at one aspect of the encounter between researcher and researched, namely the accusations that associated us with blood-stealing killers, locally referred to as *kachinja*. These rumours, and the action motivated by them, were provoked by the collection of blood-specimens for the medical research project, but the ideas behind them are older and have a broader frame of reference. As I will try to show, they provide a sort of critique of research in the post-colonial context.

The theme of this chapter is the concrete encounter between different people – a team of scientists and members of an African village community – in a specific locality, which results in talk and action. This talk reflects a moment in what the Comaroffs have called the 'long conversation' that resulted from the colonial conquest of Africa: an exchange between coloniser and colonised, between missionary and non-Christian knowledges, between biomedicine and local medical practices. A conversation in which neither side surrendered and, as it were, 'converted', but through which both sides have continuously developed and changed (Comaroff and Comaroff 1997).

However, the local talk that I look at here is not simply determined by these large historically evolved dichotomies. Like all real life talk, it is full of contingency, contradictions, changes. People engage in talk from their specific position in a localised field of social practice, in a home, a village. I will show how people evoke and use the *kachinja* blood-stealing idiom in the construction of their encounter with research, and in other social relations, and eventually abandon it again.

The chapter has two parts. The first tries to capture some aspects of the experience of research and blood-collection and people's responses to it, focusing on the *kachinja* idiom. To illustrate how this idiom is used, I present two cases of responses to the research work and to my person. Then the *kachinja* idiom is discussed more in detail: I look at how *kachinja* relates to wizardry and evil, and to cultural constructions of the relationship between knowledge, power and body. I examine its possible origin and meanings, its ties to colonial history and why biomedicine and blood-taking are perceived in this way. In the end, I look at people's use of this idiom in their concrete social practice, and briefly at how this use reflects upon concepts like domination and resistance in the post-colonial situation.

The idea of studying the concrete contact between researchers and researched, global and local agents, goes back to Meyer Fortes' early article about what then was called 'cultural contact'. Fortes proposed to study 'contact' as a 'continuous process of interaction', which is always partial and specific to a given situation (Fortes 1936: 53-6). He argued that attention should be paid to the 'dynamic process' in which 'individuals and communities react under contact...' and suggested that by treating 'the contact agents... as integrally part of the community, ... the mechanisms by and through which they react upon the community can be observed' (Fortes 1936: 26-7). As particularly suitable 'contact situations' he recommended studying how an administrator, missionary or medical dispenser enters into and affects social relations. Fortes likened the effect of these agents to that of a magnet, which alters the orientations and energy of structures and objects within its field, and which works through its effect on other agents, beyond the range of immediate contact. Fortes himself never engaged in the explicit ethnography of contact he proposed, and indeed seems to have chosen to ignore the 'magnetic' effects of global power in his local Tallensi worlds. This chapter aims to take up his challenge.

I. The encounter of researcher and researched

Yimbo, the rural area of western Kenya where we worked, is inhabited by Luo people, the second largest ethnic group in Kenya. The Luo are a patrilineal people, who mainly live from subsistence agriculture, fishing and, since colonial occupation, wage labour in the central highlands or the larger cities (Cohen and Odhiambo 1989). Economically and politically, the area is on the Kenyan periphery. Economic links to the rest of the country are extractive. Local products like fish or maize are bought by non-local traders, and labour-migration is the main source of cash income. Politically, Luoland was at the time of my fieldwork a stronghold of opposition to the national government. As a result of its marginalisation, Luoland is relatively poor, and people commonly associate their everyday sufferings – *e.g.* malnutrition, illness and child-death – with their marginal, disadvantaged position in Kenya and the wider world.

The events described here occurred in 1994 when I participated as a student in a biomedical intervention study of the interactions between infections, nutrition and child development, which aimed at identifying ways to improve the health of school-age children. As part of this work, school children were examined for various infections and treated, and blood and stool specimens were regularly collected from them.

From the study subjects' perspective, important aspects of the research encounter were intrusion, order, discipline and hierarchy. Children and teachers were interrupted in their school activities by the research team arriving from the city, more than one hour's drive away. The children were enlisted and given individual study numbers, which determined their position in the various physical examinations and served as identifiers for the two-year study period. The children were thus turned into study subjects. In the schools, a ritual order of sorts was created: the examination teams were placed under trees in the school courtyard, the children were lined up in numerical order, and then they proceeded hastily through the different examinations, repeatedly having their names and numbers checked. The children quickly learned to perform according to the rules of research. They formed lines on their own, corrected each other, and seemed eager to perform well. During blood-collection, hardly any child tried to run away, although all of them feared the pain and the sight of their own blood.

The research hierarchy expands the framework within which the children experience the association between bodily discipline and knowledge. The school is in itself a system of bodily order, with parades and corporal punishment as its most obvious expressions. Knowledge is here tied to physical discipline, which at times appears to be more valued by parents and teachers than academic teaching. The teacher employs physical force to convey knowledge to the children, and the children are expected to learn through this painful experience. From the children's perspective, research entails an extension, beyond the limits of the locality, of this nexus between power over bodies and knowledge: a *daktari* (Kiswahili for 'doctor') from the distant university, the apex of academic achievement, arrives in a car and, rescinding the existing regime of bodily discipline and inducing even the teachers to break their routines, accesses the children's bodies, inflicts pain and extracts blood from them[2].

After the examinations, the team checked the lists and identified children who were absent. Siblings or neighbours of the missing children were found, and the homes of the children, which also had been mapped and numbered, identified. Then the specimen collection was extended into the village. The homes were sometimes remote and could only be reached on foot. In the homes, the parents were briefly greeted, and the brevity of the visit was in itself a problematic experience both for parents and the research team, as it is culturally inappropriate to enter and leave a private home in a hurry. When the child was found in or around the home, the missing blood sample or measurement was taken, provided that parents and child agreed. Few parents refused their child's participation at this point, as good manners prevent most people from refusing a visitor's wish and from entering into an open confrontation with him. Only some, who were convinced of the evil nature of the blood-taking, refused and were subsequently excluded from the research. After the samples had been collected, the team quickly disappeared, returned to the laboratory, and only came back if the child needed some medical treatment.

By this work in the village, the hierarchy of power incorporated also the children's families. From a distance, the researchers reached out into the village with their cars, made their way into the family homestead, and penetrated into the mud hut of a mother, who in this situation was likely to feel poor and powerless. Venous blood-collection is, of course, in itself an intrusive experience of severed body boundaries, but in this field-research setting it can be described as but the pointed end of a long intrusive movement. This movement originates, from the community's perspective, from remote sites of power and knowledge, and aims at the essence of community life, children's blood. During the examination in a distant laboratory, scientific knowledge is applied to the blood. Hereby, it is recontextualised, not as a source of life, but as evidence of disease, and new knowledge is produced and brought back to the village, turning the children into diseased bodies requiring medicine. We have thus a long movement back and forth between the enigmatic realm beyond the reach of villagers, and the heart of the family. Furthermore, this knowledge, derived from blood, is in an incomprehensible way valuable to the researchers. The eagerness with which they pursue their data – *i.e.* somebody's children – might, indeed, be alarming for parents.

The obscurity of these activities in the view of the villagers is not easily changed by the researchers' explanations about the 'common benefit' that research is supposed to produce. The experience that research rarely results in direct improvements of local conditions makes people sceptical. The universal morality that in principle motivates biomedicine differs from the contextual morality of the community, and the argument that research, as such, is good is therefore difficult to convey. It provokes the question: good for whom? And, even if the research was beneficial, why would complete strangers wish to come to an African village and do good? These questions, which are much more than problems of information, give rise to suspicions, which in our case focused on the blood-taking exercise.

Reactions and debates in the village

A few parents chose to prevent our access to their children by blocking the way and succeeded thereby in having their school excluded from the research programme. Other parents, whose children attended the same school, came afterwards to the research group and apologised for the 'superstitious villagers', but as the majority of parents in this school seemed to object to the research, the school was not visited again. The objecting parents, I heard later, suspected that we were blood-thieves, *kachinja*, who they feared would take all or a lot of their children's blood and leave them weakened, infertile or dead. These *kachinja* were believed to move fast along the main roads in their cars and to catch people in order to drain their blood. *Kachinja* were known by everybody and considered by many, including educated people, to be a real threat. When the project cars loaded with red jerry cans were seen moving everywhere in the area, crisscrossing the bush until well after sunset, led by a zealous young European, these parents thus took action to defend their children.

Teachers, parents and children had been informed about the study's aims and methods. The parents of all participating children had signed a consent form agreeing with the collection of blood specimens from their children. In fact, this written consent form was a cause of concern for some of the parents. It was interpreted as a contract of sorts, in which the parents signed away the children's vital fluid. In an oral culture, where death certificates and land titles are the only signed documents exchanged between people, a written document about rights in one's child's blood is likely to provoke concerns[3].

However, these direct confrontations were very few, and most responses to the research were expressed in more well-ordered public discussions after these violent events. Here, *kachinja* rumours were mostly evoked indirectly, referring to other people's 'superstitions' or to 'rumours' that one had heard about somewhere. In this indirect, displaced form they were present in every discussion. Hardly anybody stood up and challenged the suspected blood-thieves face to face, and those who did were silenced, marginalised, or even led away by those who took a more positive attitude to the research, or who simply felt embarrassed about the open conflict with the prestigious visitors. Nevertheless, the atmosphere in these meetings was often tense and sometimes hostile.

Direct critique was expressed in these meetings in a more mundane idiom, questioning the inequality of power and exchanges in research, and suspecting the self-interested use of the blood that we collected and the knowledge generated from it. People's suspicions against the researchers, who came from the capital city and from overseas, expressed ethnic tensions between Luo and other groups, widespread mistrust of the Kenyan state, colonial memories of bloodshed and oppression, and perceptions of global economic exploitation, in which Europe and the US were identified as superior sources of power, with all the ambivalence that power contains in the eyes of the powerless. This critical discourse linked distance and difference to power, and power to value and exploitation. Research was definitely not seen as a neutral endeavour for the general good, but as a road to status and wealth for researchers, be they European or Kenyan: a selfish, extractive practice. To my embarrassment, the English abbreviation 'PhD' surfaced in more than one of these debates, and although I then still understood little *Dholuo*, even I could sense the negative connotations that this term could carry.

Interestingly, women often voiced a more concrete concern, namely that their children had too little blood anyway, and that they ought not lose more of it. This was based on their personal experience with anaemia and resulting illnesses, which they had acquired as women and as mothers. The women's comments and complaints underlined the fact that blood is not only the essence of the body in metaphorical speech, but is also central to the experience of the body and its well-being. I will come back to this theme of blood as experience and symbol below.

The political-economic and nutritional arguments and the *kachinja* idiom were evoked interchangeably. They seemed to form a continuum of evaluative idioms, speculative attempts to give meaning to research and blood-collection within the given social and political context. In short, this explanatory complex expressed fears about the extraction of value from bodies, unequal global exchange relations, and being drained by an uncontrollable outside power with superior knowledge. Which dimensions of the idiom were voiced – nocturnal blood-thieves or neocolonial academics – seemed to depend on the situation: public debates evoked the political arguments, while private discussions between the homesteads, in which I only later participated, drew on more immediate fears and more sinister imaginations.

Teachers made explicit commentaries on the research and its wider political context. They traced the origin of the *kachinja* 'problem', as they saw it, back to the World Wars and to the colonial health services. They shared the view, common throughout Luoland, that in colonial times, and especially in times of war, blood had been taken forcefully in the rural areas in order to be given to whites, in particular soldiers. Thus, 'black blood saved white lives' as one teacher put it. This theme was further expanded when the teachers talked about blood-taking in the colonial health system: they found it obvious – given the racist segregation in 'African', 'Asian' and 'European' hospitals – that blood and organs had been removed by white doctors from Africans and given to the patients of 'European hospitals'. Moreover, several of the teachers suggested, only half believingly, that 'in those days, also, medicine was made from blood', which reflected the notion, which still can be met in rural Luoland, that western pharmaceuticals are made from blood or human bodies (Prince et al. 2001).

Thus colonial memories provided, according to the teachers, the origin of the *kachinja* rumours. Contemporary blood-stealing, which the interviewed teachers accepted as a reality, was linked to the fact that certain politicians fed on blood as part of devil-worship, which was a common media topic during 1994, or to the idea that very wealthy people entertained spirits acquired from the Kenyan coast (*jinn*), who had to be fed with blood. Another version had it that blood-stealing had become good business since the privatisation of health care as part of economic 'adjustment' programmes and the resulting decay of the health care system. A very widespread suspicion, that multinational companies traded in African blood and organs on behalf of rich American recipients, was supported by media reports on the illegal trade in organs between Latin America and the USA. Moreover, they linked these exploitative practices to other common rumours about the destructive intervention of outside forces into Luo society: for example, the supposed spread of AIDS in Kenya by Americans, and the suspected attempts of the government to eradicate the Luo by various means, ranging from large crocodiles to poisoned school milk. Many of these criticisms and rumours were expressed in general terms or as kind jokes, but as a whole, these comments displayed a heightened critical awareness of the economic world system, and of the position of research within this global context and within Kenyan centre-periphery relations.

What was interesting about the teacher's comments was that they oscillated between, on the one hand, explanations of what they called 'superstitions' and 'village gossip', which did not consider *kachinja* as real, and, on the other hand, detailed accounts of *kachinja*, which considered them to be a real threat and linked their evil activities to political and economic realities. This shifting between the registers of rumour and facts could be explained by the peculiar interstitial situation of rural teachers, who share the concerns and imaginations of village people, and at the same time partake in wider academic and political worlds. I think, however, that the ambiguity about what is real and unreal – nocturnal vampires, blood eating politicians, genocidal Europeans – is characteristic of idioms like *kachinja*, which are employed not as definite explanations, final truths, but as tools in search of a way of dealing with what is strange, uncertain, and potentially evil in life. These idioms are not 'systems of thought' or 'explanatory models' that provide security, but pragmatic ways of moving across dangerous terrain, and confronting powerful others. Two case stories may illustrate the pragmatic use of the idiom.

Mr Osunga's dilemma[4]

Mr Osunga, a dynamic, young headmaster at one of the study schools befriended us during the early stages of the study and invited us repeatedly to his home, a well-kept compound of concrete houses, the path to which was indicated with enamel signboards from the main road. After a few days, he suggested that we should stay with him and his family and build our house in his compound. He belonged to a dominant clan of the area, and his father had been a colonial chief, which was one of the reasons why he found it appropriate to welcome the overseas visitors, both out of friendliness, to provide his children an educational experience, and to confirm his family's status in the area. During the conflicts described above, he attended community meetings and convinced people of our good intentions, as well as of his own modernity and ties with the outside world.

At some point, he told me about a little boy who suffered from chronic illness and introduced me to the child's father, who was the owner of the local store, a successful, but somewhat secretive and little-liked man in his forties. The child had a swollen liver and spleen and I offered to take a blood slide to our laboratory. A week later, I returned with the (negative) results of the examinations and was met with unusual hostility by the boy's father, who refused my offer to take the boy to the district hospital. Startled, I went away and looked for my acquaintance in the school, hoping to get an explanation. The headmaster met me politely but was less welcoming than he had been previously and declined knowledge of the case of the little boy, when I asked him. Our relationship subsequently declined and reached rock-bottom when he publicly agitated against our team, putting particular emphasis on the collection of blood-specimens.

Several months later, I was given an explanation by another teacher: my relationship with the late colonial chief's son had revived the idiom of *kachinja*, which in this case was applied to the two prominent local men. The shopkeeper, whose child's blood specimen I had taken, was widely believed to entertain *jinn*, which had to be fed on human blood. His son's illness was by some people attributed to his victims' revenge. The headmaster, who stemmed from the clan that since colonial times had ruled the area, was thus suspected of collaborating with the intruders in their ominous tasks. As a result, he had to give public proof of his dissociation from the presumed masters. Hence his uncommon and open rudeness towards me.

This encounter between two modern, economically developed men of the local society and a travelling European researcher shows the variability of the *kachinja* idiom, its multivalence, and its changing impact on social relations. It can designate as blood-stealers people from different geographical origins, educated, political figures and wealthy people. It plays on associations of knowledge and money, colonial history and local politics.

Okoth's homestead

My acquaintance with the family of Mr Okoth provided some insight into the social functioning of the *kachinja* idiom within a family. Okoth's home was not initially involved in the blood collection, so our visits were of a more social nature. Mr Okoth was a proud host, not least because he practised as an injectionist and was generally regarded as a man of modernity. He was a retired public health technician from the local dispensary, in principle entitled to receive a pension, and was a member of the Anglican Church that has been dominant in the area since colonial occupation. The researchers' visits to his 'office' (the modern name of the man's hut at the centre of the homestead) confirmed his reputation in the village. However, his four wives were aware of the *kachinja* rumours and suspicious about the research. They acted as good hosts, but they asked the research assistant hostile questions. Repeated visits to the second of Mr Okoth's wives established a closer relationship. She voiced her concerns and fears and was eventually satisfied by our explanations. This emerging friendship, however, provoked the animosity of her younger co-wives. They now raised *kachinja* accusations against the second wife and us, which reflected long-standing tensions about child health and survival, and accusations of 'evil eye' attacks between the women.

Giving equal attention to all four wives, we restored our relationships, and soon all four women welcomed us to their houses. These friendly interactions with the women, though, seemed to provoke the hostility of Mr Okoth. The reason for his changed attitude could be found in his relationship to his village neighbours. His association with the outside visitors had caused some of his neighbours to turn against him. Under the leadership of a neighbour, some older men accused Mr Okoth himself of being a *kachinja*, collaborating with us to steal the village children's blood. This neighbour, Mr Odhiambo, was an orthodox member of an independent church. He dressed at times in a loincloth and opposed western influence, especially biomedicine. As a neighbour, he had old land conflicts with Mr Okoth's family, which fed into this *kachinja* debate.

Envy about the potential access to outside resources through the visitors might have contributed, too. The thrust of Mr Odhiambo's argument was however, that Mr Okoth was associated with biomedicine – specifically syringes and needles – and with the state that had paid him for many years. These traits made him the ideal middleman, the *kachinja* working on behalf of remote power-holders, who occasionally came to visit and get their share. Issues of wealth, status and education, state and religion, and antagonistic knowledges about the body merged here in the *kachinja* idiom. It was activated by our appearance in the village, but it was used in a long-standing quarrel between two neighbours about land, ideology, and lifestyle.

What the example of our encounter with Mr Okoth's home shows is that the *kachinja* idiom could be used outside the immediate context of research and the conflicts about blood taking. Here it was employed in ongoing conflicts involving various overlapping fields of interest. In shifting constellations – researchers vs. homestead, second wife and researcher vs. younger wives, wives and researcher vs. husband, homestead and researcher vs. village – the researchers' position shifted from being outside the family and a threat to it, to being a part of it vis-à-vis the rest of the village. On each level, the *kachinja* accusation was linked with different social dichotomies: inside-outside, male-female, rich-poor, state-community, tradition-modernity.

These suspicions did not lead to a breakdown of contact or to violence between the accusers and the accused. Serious allegations, concerning life and death, were made, but they remained tied to specific situations and social relations, and thus open to change. If someone was identified by somebody else as a *kachinja*, this occurred in the context of a certain debate; it did not describe his/her essence; s/he was not stigmatised, excluded or attacked. Rather, the term gave momentary shape to a social constellation at a particular time. Calling someone *kachinja* carried greater force than a common pejorative metaphoric address of the kind that people use in quarrels, because it related to an unusual event: the arrival of the researchers in the village. It gained force from other people's talk about yet other people in the same terms. Through the *kachinja* idiom, particular social relations – Mr Okoth and his neighbour, or Mr Osunga and the villagers – became engaged with the event of the research project. These relations were re-shaped by it, and in turn they re-created the event. In interaction with each other, the different evocations of the idiom in various social conflicts – in the two cited cases and probably many others in the same village – created a rumour: a widely known narrative of evil, a tacit belief, which became, for a limited time and within a certain area or group, a threatening reality that compelled people to act.

After some time, the *kachinja* idiom fell in disuse again. Nobody mentioned blood-stealing in relation to our research or any other social interaction that we heard about. Blood collection was not disputed any more and people even brought us children for examinations. The idiom had lost its use-value in this particular situation. The creative space that it had opened up had collapsed. The idiom, in the sense of a shared narrative or cognitive resource, remains, of course, in people's knowledge, and it will re-appear once a change of the local situation renders it useful for social practice, as our appearance in the village had done.

II. The *kachinja* idiom: origins, meanings and use

The term *kachinja* is not original *Dholuo*[5], but derived from the Bantu/Kiswahili root *chinja* (to slaughter), which occasionally is used in Luo (*chinjo*). It relates to Kiswahili *kuchinja* (butcher), but it seems that only in the Luo version of this word are associations of blood-sucking human murderers made. Derived from the same root, *machinjaji* is used for blood-thieves among the Luhya, northern neighbours of the Luo (Alfred Luoba, personal communication). In Mwanza town, and among the Haya people of the Tanzanian shores of Lake Victoria, to the south of Luoland, they are called *chinjachinja* (Weiss 1998); the same term is used in eastern Congo and Burundi (Ceyssens 1975). It seems thus that the *chinja* based terminology is common in central Africa around the great lakes. In Kiswahili-speaking populations on the East African coast, and in Nairobi and Mombasa, blood-stealing people working for powerful, often white employers are also feared, but here, in contrast, they are most commonly called *mumiani* or *wazimamoto*, i.e. fire-fighters, terms which have been documented in the bigger colonial cities (see *e.g.* Baker 1946; White 1990, 1993a; Pels 1992).

The non-Nilotic origin of the term *kachinja* suggests that it is a new phenomenon, and the similarity of the rumours across Eastern, Central and Southern Africa suggests that we are dealing with a recent phenomenon that is tied to the experiences of the colonial period. This is underlined by the fact that I could not find any evidence of blood-stealing fears, or problems with medical research in the historical literature or in archival sources dating from the first years of British occupation. After 1920, however, references to blood-stealing scares and resistance to blood-collection occur frequently in colonial medical reports[6]. Earliest reports of conflicts about blood-collection date from the time between the wars, when colonial extractive policies reached a first peak, and the local population had experienced generalised colonial violence during the war, as well as labour recruitment and punishments.

What is the relation of the *kachinja* idiom to pre-colonial, traditional Luo ideas of evil? The Luo know of many wizards who kill people and often harm children (Ocholla-Ayayo 1976). Some of these do so by reducing the victim's blood, *e.g.* by attacking one's shadow and sucking blood from there. Their deeds are motivated by hatred or envy, but Luo wizards do not seem to appropriate other people's blood for their own immediate benefit, i.e. to get rich or to gain strength (in contrast to some of their West African counterparts; see Friedman 1994; Geschiere 1995)[7]. Wizardry has the primary aim of harming the victim, and its techniques – e.g. blood-sucking – are secondary means to that evil end. Blood-stealing, in contrast, harms the victim as a consequence of exploiting the victim's body. The profitable *use* of blood is here the primary purpose and the detrimental effect on the victim secondary. While wizardry is essentially *evil*, blood-stealing is morally detached *use*. *Kachinja* is the act of an outsider, uninterested in the victim. Wizardry is, in contrast, motivated by social relatedness. *Kachinja* can therefore not be treated as a kind of wizardry, but as an explanatory idiom in its own right.

At the same time there are similarities: both kinds of evil agent destroy bodies through material techniques; these techniques spring from a specific knowledge; and this knowledge is exclusive and stems from an inaccessible outside power. *Kachinja* and wizardry are both idioms which address the detrimental effects of secret knowledge upon human bodies.

Colonial wars and medicine

The unequal distribution of knowledge and the exploitation of bodies are central to the practice and experience of colonial domination. Power and knowledge were applied to bodies in new and often traumatic ways. The *kachinja* idiom expresses concerns about relations of power, bodies and knowledge, emphasising respectively colonial violence and biomedicine.

I mentioned above that the teachers associated the *kachinja* themes of intrusion and extraction with themes from the colonial occupation. Their explanations draw on social, political, and bodily notions of difference. They involve ideas about inside and outside and transgressions of boundaries and power differentials on different levels (body, house, home, village, ethnicity, nation, race). They address the profitable use of these power differences, and the extraction of vital fluid from the very inside of a community (their children's bodies) to the farthest outside (inaccessible overseas powers). The First World War was a deeply traumatic experience for African peoples, and for many it was in fact the first close experience with the colonial occupation. The Luo were heavily affected by forced recruitment to the British Carrier Corps during the war (Hodges 1986). Assisted by local chiefs, men were recruited from almost every home and more than half of the young men were forced to serve. Roughly one third of them died in the campaign. When recruitment for the war commenced in northern Luoland, only ten years had passed since the first thorough exploration of this area, and contact with the occupier had been extremely scanty up to then. Suddenly and with great force, the brutality of occupation came over the Luo and left deep traces in people's collective memory.

Old Luo people with first or second-hand memories of the war recalled bloodshed and brutality, rigid bodily discipline, and not least biomedical research, treatment, vaccinations and blood transfusions (Iliffe 1998). The war provided an extreme, condensed experience of colonial power over African bodies. A less brutal, but no less physical and indeed close experience with colonial power was the encounter with biomedicine.

Until after the Second World War, the study area had very little direct contact with western medical services, as the nearest dispensary was a day's journey away. Men encountered medicine earlier than women through medical examinations in the military and as labourers with the railways and farms. The first local medical experience came through administrative measures concerned with sleeping sickness control. In the 1930s, mass examinations, including blood sampling, and the confinement and treatment of infected individuals, were conducted in Yimbo[8]. People were removed from their ancestral lands in the tsetse-fly infested areas. This introduction to western medical practices through sleeping sickness research and control seems to have been a typical East African experience (Lyons 1992). Sleeping sickness campaigns combined two central, seemingly contradictory aspects of colonialism, and, in fact, of medicine: close body control and a detached, administrative gaze. The experiences of bodily assault, the breaking of life-giving ties with the land, economic expropriation (forcing people into wage labour), and resultant poverty were captured in the *kachinja* idiom, as has been argued by historians in relation to similar rumours in colonial Rhodesia (White 1995b).

The First World War and sleeping sickness policies appear to be long ago, and medicine has, of course, a more complex face today than half a century ago. If this idiom is used by people in today's Kenya, what issues does it address? *Kachinja* stories focus on the use of syringes and needles to take blood specimens. These seem to be the immediate cause of fear, and the rumours could thus be read as anxiety generated by ignorance, as early colonial interpretations suggested (Baker 1946; Trant 1970). However, the case of Mr Okoth's family provides us with a paradox: he and his wives were concerned about blood-sampling, yet he is an active injectionist using syringes to inject western pharmaceuticals. They initially protected their children from the researcher's intrusion, and yet valued injections higher than all other treatments. This contradictory attitude is typical for people's relationship to medicine in Yimbo and other parts of East Africa. How do we account for this ambivalence?

I would suggest that suspicions about blood-collection were not provoked by perceptions of the medical technology concerned in its material sense, but as an aspect of broader structures of external control over bodies, well-being, and knowledge. For people in Yimbo, biomedicine consists of two domains: firstly, a body of knowledge (*medicine*), embodied by experts and institutions, which is linked to a specific epistemology and power-relations; secondly, *materia medica* and material technologies (*medicines*), which more easily escape the formation of knowledge and relations of power that generated them.

The first domain, *medicine*, is controlled by trained medical professionals and institutions, who diagnose diseases, decide about treatments and usually convey little of their knowledge to the patient (Iliffe 1998). Expert knowledge is made to work upon and control individual bodies and the body social. Biomedical research is the cutting edge of this 'technology of knowledge', in Foucault's sense (1975), which continuously advances its exclusive knowledge-base. Sleeping sickness control is a case in point.

The second domain, *medicines*, in contrast, consists of substances and techniques that are traded and accepted all over Africa; injections are especially popular (Van der Geest *et al.* 1996). In Yimbo, most household-heads possess syringes and inject their family members, and biomedical pharmaceuticals are incorporated into a broadly shared folk-practice and stored in every home. These medicines are, in fact, preferably used within the family rather than in suspect, alien medical institutions. Through these domestic practices, the ambivalent powers of medicine, which is perceived as a threat, is kept at bay, while the power of medicines is used (Whyte 1997).

People in Yimbo say they feel uneasy about medical doctors and institutions, because of their secretive knowledge (doctors don't explain things, and they do not share a common knowledge base with their patients, in contrast to communal Luo medical knowledge); their link to the state (the Luo's relation to which is not unproblematic); their separation from ordinary social life (doctors do not speak *Dholuo*, dispensaries are outside villages); and the personal wealth they display. These traits appear in even sharper relief in medical research. Researchers' knowledge is highly specialised and increases through research; their social position is high and connected to overseas power sources; their rituals are more elaborate than hospital routines and employ less familiar technologies; their wealth and the resources employed in data collection are conspicuous and provoke questions about the value that research generates[9]. Research has additional peculiar qualities: it is proactive – researchers follow their subjects actively; it extracts and alienates parts of their bodies; it often denies reciprocity of knowledge and material gain. These traits are perceived by communities exposed to research in various parts of the world. In consequence, since colonial occupation research has been the most contested manifestation of biomedicine (see *e.g.* Arnold 1993, especially pp. 218-23).

The social meanings of blood

Before I turn back to Mr Okoth and the use of the *kachinja* idiom, I want to have a quick look at the substance that is central to *kachinja*: blood. We have seen that the violent, physical articulation of the colonial situation, in war and in medical research, provided material for idioms like *kachinja*. But why were these issues addressed with reference to blood? Blood has of course social meanings. To share blood is central to Luo understandings of kinship, representing both continuity of descent and affinal exchange relations. Kinship is in turn the basis of agricultural production, subsistence and life. Therefore it makes sense to evoke the alienation of blood in idioms about colonial land-alienation and the break-up of families due to labour migration. The symbolic link between blood, kinship, land and life explains the use of the blood-stealing idiom in relation to sleeping sickness policies, which brought together the extraction of body fluids, the splitting up of families and the eviction from ancestral land in one historical event.

But blood is more than a metaphor of fertility, lineage, land and production. It is a part of the body and thus directly experienced, and employed to explain bodily states and processes. Luo associate food intake with the quality of the blood, which determines health, strength and fertility. Women in particular are conscious of the state of their blood and attribute ill-health to 'little blood' (*remo matin*), caused by insufficient food or illness. The foetus in the womb is thought to be made from blood (and referred to as 'blood', *remo*) and the woman is expected to eat well during pregnancy, so that she can produce more blood. Women know about the importance of blood for child health from own experience of anaemia in pregnancy and children's anaemia. Rather than *representing* health by the blood metaphor, they *experience* their own and their children's well-being through blood. Based on these experiences, blood becomes a measure of the effect of changes in food production and social relations on individual health and communal well-being (Weiss 1996).

Blood is thus the essence of bodily well-being, both as symbol and as a physical experience. Moreover, blood represents the principle of equality of needs that underlies human life. Every body needs an approximately equal amount of blood to live. Losing blood endangers one's life and well-being, and the alienation or accumulation of blood is an abomination (similar to, but worse than, the alienation of food, land or labour). Blood lends itself therefore to idioms about colonial and post-colonial exploitation and abuse. The media reports about the international trade in blood products (and illegal organ trade etc.) that are common in Kenya lend it additional credibility. *Kachinja* is thus rooted in bodily experience and pre-colonial meanings of blood, shaped by local, historical experiences of colonial occupation, and integrated into discourses about local-global, south-north relations. It gains its power to mobilise actions from this multiple frame of reference, which is sufficiently open and diffuse to be adapted to many social situations and used within changing social relationships.

The use of an idiom

The *kachinja* idiom provides an analysis of the unequal distribution of (medical) knowledge within the post-colonial situation, and its effects on the lives of Luo people. It is a response to the loss of control over knowledge and resources. This response emerges from a culture in which most knowledge is communally shared and secret knowledge is regarded as potentially dangerous (see Geissler *et al.* 2002). It is shaped by a society in which bodily and social well-being depend on reciprocity, which was challenged by the unequal colonial exchanges of knowledge, labour and goods. Biomedicine brings together these concerns with knowledge and bodies in an exemplary way, and research, as the spearhead of the biomedical endeavour, is the logical target of this critique of the embodied aspects of inequality.

The wide distribution and repeated occurrence of *kachinja* and similar rumours shows that it is a latent idiom, an image that is generally available to people. It is only voiced to address strained social relations if something unforeseen happens, that triggers its use, like our arrival in the villages. Then it is used if the details of the idiom fit a particular social situation (as we saw in Okoth's home: the overlap of evil eye accusations and bloodsucking in relation to child death, Okoth's medical profession and links with the state, and ours). It is also important that significant persons agree with its use. None of these conditions nor the social tensions themselves are stable. This is clear in the case of Mr Okoth's home, where the ascription of *kachinja* and the positions of accuser and accused repeatedly changed, moving further and further away from the immediate interface of researcher and study subjects, and involving more and more local context and history.

This case shows how the idiom is *used*: it is created, changed and disposed of in social practice. *Kachinja* is a speculative, evaluating idiom, one explanation among many in people's continuous struggle against multiple threats to child health and life, which range from neighbours and co-wives to bodies of global finance. It proposes hypotheses to link and explain empirical facts, memories, and experiences within a specific social situation, a particular moment and location, and to act upon these.

Thus *kachinja* is not a permanent social category identifying a person or group as evil blood-thieves, but expresses a temporary relation, which changes as part of social processes. As with all good hypotheses, it is contested and gives way to better ones, as social life and its evaluation progress.

Some older literature on blood-stealing suggests that it is a 'myth of the oppressed' (Ceyssens 1975), or a 'rumour' that expressed discontent with the colonial condition and was eventually replaced by 'political consciousness' that led to independence (Musambachime 1987). This interpretation certainly holds a general truth. However, the image of a neat line of resistance between coloniser and oppressed seems insufficient to describe the uses of the *kachinja* rumours that we looked at above. Particularly under present post-colonial conditions, which simple associations of skin colour and oppressive relations cannot sufficiently capture, the occurrence of blood-stealing concerns must be understood in a more complex field of global and local relations. More recent studies of blood-stealing in colonial history give a more detailed picture, analysing these idioms as articulations of specific colonial experiences in different historical moments (White 1990, 1993a, 1993b, 1995a, 1995b). Adding further complexity, it has been shown how such idioms changed in the historical process, and how their uses vary between different colonial societies in Asia and Africa (Pels 1992), and how different political fractions within colonised societies have employed the rumours in their local conflicts (Jarosz 1994). Each of these studies draws a more differentiated picture of the colonial encounter, of hegemony and resistance as reflected in blood-stealing rumours. They show how lines of social conflict crisscross the bigger lines drawn by colonial antagonisms, and how rumours link colonial confrontations to social processes within the colonial societies.

The material presented here shows how, in a particular situation, in a specific locality, colonial and post-colonial antagonisms are further refracted, reflected and transformed on the micro-level of social interaction. It shows that the line of 'antagonism' (see Balandier 1966) is too simple an image of colonial tensions, which in reality are perceived and articulated in overlapping, and often interdependent social fields. Sources of power, that partly inhere to these fields (such as domestic relations, gender), and partly originate outside them (such as the post-colonial state, medical science), work on people and influence their social practice. Global antagonisms are realised within these different fields in a local practice which is shaped by conflicts that are, to some extent at least, independent of the post-colonial condition: gender, generation, land ownership, religion and lifestyle. These other fields of conflict are temporarily charged and polarised by wider structural tensions. The 'magnetic' effects of individual agents, relations, and structures within local fields, occur in changing, overlapping, unpredictable constellations, and redirect oppositions, reformulate categorisations and create unforeseen relations and movement (Fortes 1936). Through idioms like *kachinja*, global structures of inequality are enacted by local agents, and at the same time global agents (such as the researchers) get entangled in local structures. In their mutual interaction, biomedical research and technology – as global relations of power and knowledge and as localised material practice – are evaluated, criticised and used.

Conclusion: research as encounter

Luo villagers' responses to biomedical research show how historical and personal memories, bodily experiences and concerns, and social relations interact in the encounter of researcher and researched in an African village. Together, they mobilise an evaluative idiom and feed into actions. These encounters are local events, created in people's social practice. At the same time they are generated within, and refer to, global political and economic (and academic) structures. The blood-stealing idiom incorporates elements of both and mediates between global structures and local agency and between global agents entering local structures.

The *kachinja* idiom refers to unequal exchanges of knowledge and wealth in the post-colonial context. But it also shows that oppression and exploitation do not simply polarise society. Instead, they work on social relations within it and create mutative antagonisms that cannot be captured by concepts like resistance or adaptation. International biomedical research in contemporary Africa is objectively positioned within the exploitative and oppressive structures of late capitalism, and it is perceived as such by those under study. However, the ways in which these structures motivate action depend on the specific situation. And it depends not least on the interaction between the involved persons, the agents of local and global range. Thus it is a field of activity, in which changes can take place, and which can be worked upon by those involved.

The *kachinja* idiom thus poses a challenge to *us*, researchers. It addresses difference and reveals conflicting particular interests, where academic ethos and scientific, particularly biomedical, thought vindicates universal truth and absolute morality. It draws attention to the situatedness of (medical) knowledge and research, no less than any other social practice. These reflections of ourselves in the gaze of the other who is constituted as other in the research, of which *kachinja* is only one example among many, should encourage a more self-critical approach to biomedical (and other) research; an approach to research, which would not only add new details to our preconceived biomedical world view, but also, gradually, change biomedical epistemology and practice. Research, also scientific research, ought to be seen as an encounter: an open practice towards one another which acknowledges difference and uncertainty, and situates biomedicine in a material context, as a local practice within global structures.

An encounter begins with mutual questions, curiosity about one another, and doubts about one's own identity. It is an open-ended social process in time, in which both sides should change. In my understanding, *kachinja* is not so much a rejection of, or resistance towards, medical or other research, but a fairly differentiated critique of our current research practices; practices which do not sufficiently reflect on the relationship between researcher and researched in its global context, or allow for sufficient time or space for a localised encounter to take place. If we do not wish to be regarded as bloodsuckers or cannibals by the people with whom we want to collaborate in the pursue of improved knowledge and improved health, we ought to listen to this critique.

Notes

1. This research was conducted as part of the Kenyan-Danish Health Research Project (KEDAHR), a long-term multidisciplinary research project involving ten Kenyan and Danish research institutions, which in its first phase (1994-96) focused on the health of school age children. I would like to thank the family of 'Mr Okoth', who welcomed me (eventually) and taught me about Luo sociality, and my colleagues from the Division of Vector Borne Diseases, my hosts in Kenya, who taught me scientific fieldwork and impressed me with their collegiality, ethos and dedication. Thanks for their advice to: Susan Benson, Reenish Achieng' and Susan R. Whyte, Jens Aagaard-Hansen, John Iliffe, Gilbert Lewis, Alfred Luoba, Kenneth Ombongi, John Ouma and Michael Whyte, and particularly to Ruth Prince.

2. This knowledge-power structure was underlined by the languages involved in the chain of command directing the work: the researchers speaking English, the team members and teachers speaking English and Kiswahili and sometimes *Dholuo*, and the children speaking *Dholuo*.

3. The appropriateness of written informed consent as demanded by ethical guidelines for medical research could be discussed in the light of this experience, which is probably not unique. Whereas the emphasis in projects often is on the written nature of consent, it ought to be shifted to the information conveyed.

4. All personal names have been changed.

5. In the following discussion of *kachinja*, I focus on Eastern Africa, because the profound differences between West and East African societies and between their historical experiences with colonial occupation, which have shaped ideas about blood-stealing, would require a separate, comparative article. Occult economies have also been found in other parts of the modern world (Taussig 1980; Tsing 1993; Wachtel 1994), and wider comparisons might be worthwhile. My aim here is to explore the specific experiences and events in one situation, moment, place, and *not* to abstract a general explanatory pattern for blood-stealing within global political economy (for the latter see *e.g.* Comaroff and Comaroff 1999a and the critique by Moore 1999; see also Comaroff and Comaroff 1999b).

6. For evidence of conflicts between medical researchers and local people about blood-collection, see e.g.: Papers of Dr. Matson, Rhodes House Library, Oxford, MSS. Afr.s.1792, 3/98, box 20; P. A. Clearkin, *Ramblings and Recollections of a Colonial Doctor 1913-1958*, pp. 119-40, Rhodes House Library, Oxford, MSS.Brit.Emp.r.4/1;

Authorised extracts from diaries and letters of Dr. Kendall, pp. 5-7, Rhodes House Library, Oxford, MSS.Afr.s.2032; T. F. Anderson, *Reminiscences*, pp. 28-9, Rhodes House Library, Oxford, MSS.Afr.s.1653; and Medical Department Annual Report 1948, Subsection: Division of Insect Borne Diseases, p. 69 (thanks to Dr. Kenneth Ombongi for sharing the last two references with me: see Ombongi 2000, chapters 3 and 5). For an autobiographical account of such a conflict, see Trant (1970:127-43). In contrast, the diaries of the first medical research expeditions in the area during 1898-1900 not only record no problems, but great eagerness of local people to participate in the research and particularly the blood-collection, which they regard as a treatment (see the diaries of Dr. A.D.P. Hodges, Rhodes House Library, Oxford, MSS.Afr.s.1782). These sources suggest that local attitudes have changed over time, and that suspicions only took over after the First World War.

7. 'Eating' witchcraft in some west African societies seems to have developed an element of feeding and profit from the victim's body much earlier than in East Africa. It might be related to an earlier involvement of these societies in slave trade and thus exploitative global trade relations (Friedman 1994: 87).

8. In 1932, all 11,345 inhabitants of then Kadimo Division were examined for sleeping sickness and special measures recommended which continued throughout the 1930s. Only after the 2nd World War, when sleeping sickness was declared absent from Kadimo Division (1948), the cleared areas were gradually resettled. See Kenya Annual Medical Report 1931, 1932, 1933, 1937, 1938; and Kenya Medical Research Laboratories Annual Report 1934, Rhodes House Library, Oxford, MSS.Afr.753.12. s.8.

9. In public discussions about blood sampling in south-western Uganda, close to our own study area, which were recorded by Lewis, three interrelated questions appeared in response to blood sampling (Lewis 1992: 120). One is concerned with power: Who defines the aims of research? One is interested in exchange and reciprocity: Who benefits from the research? The third turns towards the body: What do you use our blood for? The first two questions relate to political and economic relations and to ethical problems of power and interest in biomedical research. The third is formulated in different terms: 'Is (our blood) being stolen? Used to strengthen the whites? To spread AIDS?' (Lewis 1992: 120). These questions link power and exchange to the body of the subjects – specifically their blood – and the concrete acts of research, the material contact. They integrate thus structural evaluation with bodily experience and practice.

SEVEN

THE DISORDERS OF DISPLACEMENT: BOSNIAN REFUGEES AND THE RECONSTITUTION OF NORMALITY

Marita Eastmond

In Sweden, the reception of refugees from violent conflict areas has spawned a concern with war-related traumatisation and its consequences for the integration of refugees, stimulating a rapidly growing sector of refugee mental health care and the development of specialist concepts and clinical practice. In this sector, traumatisation is given particular focus and expression through the psychiatric diagnosis of PTSD (Post-Traumatic Stress Disorder)[1].

As its medical history shows, 'psychological trauma' is a very episodic illness category, entering the stage of professional discourse at particular times and in particular political contexts, while being displaced, denied, or forgotten in others. It has gained attention in wartime, albeit with varying names and aetiologies over the years, while the tendency in peace time has been to re-classify the effects of traumatic events as problems of individual psychology. With the increase in violent conflict in many parts of the world, concepts of traumatic memory disorders have again re-surfaced and are today gaining increasing application in a range of other existing diagnoses (van der Kolk *et al.* 1996). Thus, the strange history of trauma as a concept mirrors the disorder itself, with its recurrent periods of oblivion – or repression of insights – surfacing again, years later, when aroused anew by similar events. And in each period of re-emergence, social and political forces have, indeed, shaped the way society has responded to sufferers. Whether violence was on a national scale, as in war, or in the micro-contexts of sexual abuse, as in Herman's analysis (1992), such responses have reflected the politically controversial nature of recognising man-made and socially sanctioned forms of violence on human lives[2].

Given that socio-political and cultural contexts shape the emergence and meaning of a particular disorder at a particular time, what is the social significance of psychological trauma as the concept is applied to refugees received in northern host countries today? External acknowledgement of violence and war-related atrocities is essential for the advocacy of social justice, as well as for the healing of those afflicted. Drawing public attention to the problems of the victims of such violence is important. Health professionals working from a human rights perspective were active in doing this for the large numbers of asylum-seekers from the former Yugoslavia who entered Sweden in the early 1990s.

However, in the wake of tightening asylum policies, the 'trauma' identity may become the only currency with which asylum can be secured (Kleinman and Kleinman 1997). As such, it tends to transform varied and complex human experiences of disruption and disorder into a generalised medical condition. While it is a significant gain for the individuals concerned, as asylum-seekers at a crucial point in time, the medicalised image gaining ground in the media, health care and the refugee welfare bureaucracy has implications for the chances of those granted residence to reconstitute normal life in Swedish society. It tends to reinforce other processes of social exclusion of immigrants. In its focus on events in the past, in the war-torn home country, the trauma image tends to mask the problems of power and dependency experienced as asylum-seekers and refugees in the present, in Sweden.

Drawing on my ethnography of Bosnian Muslim refugees in Sweden, this chapter addresses the emergence of a discursive figure of 'the traumatised refugee' in the host society, and its articulation within the policy and practice of the refugee welfare system. As a point of contrast, it explores the problematic reality as defined by the refugee community, struggling to cope with disruption and uncertainty in their new lives. Their interpretations of distress and disorder may be seen as resistance to the medicalisation of their predicament.

The terms of this interplay are found in the context of two powerful systems of classification and intervention which instantiate what Handel-man (1978) refers to as 'bureaucratic logic', in which taxonomy is central to creating order and control. The first pertains to the international refugee regime, an institutional system of legal classification and containment premised on a particular notion of world order, in which the nation state is the 'natural' place of belonging and enjoying exclusive rights as citizens. In this logic, refugees are 'people out of place', aberrations with respect to the national order of things (Bauman 1990; Malkki 1995a). The other is the equally authoritative medical scientific discourse establishing the boundaries between normality and disorder, based on the pervasive scheme of classification of human behaviour outlined in the DSM (the American Psychiatric Association's *Diagnostic and Statistical Manual of Mental Disorders*). Particularly relevant here is the recent attention of the medical profession to the mental health of refugees in Sweden, where it has been active in defining the problematic reality of refugees.

Together, these regimes are instrumental in shaping popular under-standings of refugees as a particular kind of person with specific needs and forms of agency, as echoed in the policies and institutional practices of the welfare bureaucracy (Eastmond 1998; Graham 1999). What are the implications for those who are so classified, when such models are not compatible with their own conceptions of self and reality? A view from the Bosnian refugee community provides a contrasting interpretation of disorder and how to deal with it.

Professional and popular conceptions of refugees and trauma

What are the significant conceptual frames within which 'the traumatised refugee', as a particular kind of social person requiring intervention and control, is being defined?

Displacement as liminality: The essentialisation of the refugee experience
Refugees challenge the conceptual orders and boundaries of a world of

nation states. As reflected in international refugee policy and host states' security concerns (Abiri 2000), refugees, as people disconnected from place, are problematic. In social science, until recently, they have been notably invisible. They constitute an aberration within a world order in which the nation-state is the given basis of identity and culture (Bauman 1990). *Uprooting* has long been a key metaphor of the plight of refugees. It reveals a sedentary bias – also present in anthropology's recent past – in the conceptualisation of culture, identity and community as bounded and localised, which sees displacement as creating disorder, not only social and political, but sometimes also in the mind of the refugee (Malkki 1995a, 1995b). Malkki critiques the resulting essentialisation of 'the refugee experience' promoted by humanitarian organisations, social science and the media. Refugees are portrayed as devoid of cultural or historical specificity. Uprooted and vulnerable, they are seen as an *a priori* mental health risk category. The picture is compounded by the pervasive media image, informing both popular and professional understandings, of refugees as victims of war and violence. 'Refugees' and 'traumatisation' both become discourses about abnormality, conditions which require interventions of correction and control.

Medicalisation and the individualisation of social suffering
'Traumatisation' enters public discourse in many northern host societies in the 1990s. In Sweden at this time it becomes the predominant explanatory model within which the problems of new refugees are represented[3]. As refugees' experiences are transformed into 'trauma stories' delivered to legal authorities, these become symbolic capital in the negotiation for asylum (Kleinman and Kleinman 1997). Its medical model, PTSD, gains particular prominence in such contexts. One may question the ability of any medical model to translate and represent human suffering, including the complex experiences and concerns of victims of violent disruptions (Kleinman 1995a; Young 1995). The diagnosis itself disregards the historical and moral meanings associated with a traumatic event: it makes no distinction between events as diverse as combat, rape, auto accidents, or Hiroshima. Its focus on the afflicted individual poorly accomodates

alternative understandings of the sufferers, the social and cultural forms in which they express and make sense of their predicament. Even though suffering may be medicalised by victims themselves, one also needs to take account of other, collective understandings. The injuries suffered by victims of violence and forced migration may be formulated in moral, legal, political, or spiritual terms, and anchored to religious or political ideologies (Corlin 1990; Eastmond 1989; Obeysekere 1985; Tapp 1988). These rarely involve the individual alone. As the Bosnian refugees in this study show, distress – its meaning as well as its remedy – may, instead, be negotiated during a dynamic process oriented to the reconstitution of 'normal life', in which restoring social relations is a crucial component.

Historicisation: the primacy of the past
Traumatisation, in popular as well as professional discourse, is concerned with events in the past as the causes of trauma, notably 'the war' in the home country. As Young points out:

> PTSD is a disease of time. The disorder's distinctive pathology is that it permits the past [through traumatic memory] to relive itself in the present in the form of intrusive images and thoughts. (Young 1995: 98)

The diagnostic classification relies on this temporal-causal relation between aetiological event and symptoms. For many refugees, the traumatic aetiological event does not conclude with them leaving the scene, because the war may well continue to disrupt their lives, through the loss of relatives and property in their absence. However, the discourse tends to place the traumatic event somewhere else, removed both in time and place from the contingencies of everyday life in the present. When social problems related to their position as refugees are recognised, they are often referred to as 'secondary' traumatisation, factors which disturb or complicate the healing process in relation to the primary trauma. Symptoms are then abstracted from their symbolic and meaningful context. Thus, unemployment, stigmatisation, de-qualification and social invisibility are seen as 'vulnerability factors', not as causes and characteristics of distress in their own right.

The revolving doors of refugee reception

Since the 1980s, the discourse on traumatisation has acquired particular significance within increasingly restrictive refugee policies, in Sweden as in other northern European countries. The large influx of asylum-seekers from the former Yugoslavia during the early 1990s led to visa restrictions to halt new arrivals, while those already in the country were granted permanent residence. At the time, concerned health professionals had argued the case of these asylum-seekers on the basis of their traumatised condition. In 1994, facing large numbers of new residents to be introduced into Swedish society – over 40,000 from Bosnia-Herzegovina alone, the largest refugee population received to date – parliament granted special funds for rehabilitation to facilitate integration. The funds have spawned a growing sector of specialised refugee health care as well as research, with its primary focus on mental health.

By 1998, twenty-two special centres nation-wide had been established for the care of victims of torture and trauma, mostly through referrals from refugee-related social services or other sectors of the health care system. Importantly, these centres are also involved in training and con-sultancies for the other sectors of society working with refugees, and are an authoritative voice shaping policies and popular images of refugees and their problems. Today, most Swedish municipalities employ staff with special psychological and psychiatric competence with respect to traumatised refugees, and large numbers of other health staff receive training in refugee mental health.

The receipt of refugees in the 1990s coincided with a new integration policy, emphasising the primacy of employment and the economic self-suf-ficiency of refugees. This, ironically, coincided with the worst unemploy-ment situation in the country since the 1930s, but it was largely a response to public concern over the costs of refugee reception (Graham 1999). In response to critics from different positions, the new integration policy adopted in 1997 promotes the 'resourceful refugee' as another discursive figure to offset the notion of refugees as an economic burden. As Graham notes, this also reflects new forms of governmentality, emerging in many western industrialised states, stressing the need to create active subjects and to liberate their potential (Graham 1999: 147). The comprehensive rehabilitation programmes for refugees created at this time should be seen in this light.

However, even in the over-heated economy of the preceding decade un-employment among immigrants had been high (Ekberg 1990). Language, culture, and lack of the 'right' skills were often referred to by civil servants and employers as barriers to the employment of refugees (Franzén 1997). In the 1990s, the need for a flexible and retrainable work force, and the pressure to make refugees profitable in the system, led to a comprehensive programme for their introduction to Swedish society. As Handelman has argued, clients in welfare bureaucracies are always defined as lacking something, incomplete persons with diminished agency; however, the kind of person to be 'completed' is rarely arbitrary, but a matter of the kinds of subjects that state bureaucracies are set up to create (Handelman 1976: 234; Graham 1999: 20). The introduction was thus premised on a set of steps and formal criteria of assessment – such as a given level of Swedish language competence, social orientation, and skills training – that would make refugees eligible to seek employment. However, rather than facilitating rapid integration, the programme has reinforced the clientisa-tion of refugees within the welfare system and the notion that they are unemployable. As noted by Faist (1995), special programmes tend to mark off refugees as especially vulnerable categories, making them unattractive in competitive labour markets[4].

The outcome can be likened to a revolving door in which clients are forever turning in a condition of open-ended liminality. Instead of exiting at the labour market, they are obliged to make yet another round of Swed-ish language classes or employment retraining. It is telling that by 1998 only 10 per cent of those who had arrived in Sweden in 1991 had entered employment (Molin 1998). In the 1990s medical experts proposed that screening for mental health should be added as another criterion for the assessment of newcomers' potential for social functioning and integration. Also, in their intense interaction with the authorities in the introductory years, refugees may at any time be referred to specialist health services, by social workers, unemployment officials, language teachers or others now trained to be tuned in to detecting the signs and symptoms of trauma.

Taken together, the perceptions and practices relating to refugees' integration and mental health which evolved in the 1990s reflect a generalised model of the 'refugee social person', a person that appears to warrant State intervention, either in re-training or treatment. Both, however, tend to be counter-productive, often delaying self-sufficiency and social integration. For those refugees who are channelled into the category of 'disability', exclusion from the labour market and dependency is usually permanent and irreversible[5].

PTSD as problematic reality

In the absence of clear-cut definitions of, and systematic data about, the nature and extent of psycho-pathology among refugees, voices from specialist clinical practice are easily generalised and have gained particular currency[6]. However, their descriptions are based on the selective bias of the cases they see. In the foreword to its policy document, one such centre describes the situation thus:

> A great part of the thousands of refugees who annually settle in our County have been exposed to torture and require special care from the health services. (Weman 1997: 3, my translation)

Another declares that,

> [I]njuries of war and torture are among the most common health problems of refugees, creating difficulties in reconstituting a normal everyday life in exile. (EKT 1997: 11, my translation)

Others warn that, due to such exposure, an undefined number of refugees risk developing PTSD as a chronic and disabling psychiatric disorder, with effects on language learning and an impaired ability to work, leading to welfare dependency and marginalisation (Ekblad and Eriksson 1997).

The tendency to assume the homogeneity of the refugee experience and its attendant psycho-pathology is found also in current psychiatric research. A review of the research literature on refugees and mental health claims that, although the evidence is not clear-cut with respect to migrants and psycho-pathology:

> ...refugees, forming a homogeneous category with regard to the motives for migration and traumatic experiences, show considerable similar-ities in the degree and manifestation of psycho-pathology. (Roth and Ekblad 1993:188)

The focus in clinical documentation and research is on PTSD. Ekblad and Eriksson (1997: 15) claim that PTSD constitutes a considerable problem in the refugee population, although conceding that research results are difficult to compare, due to different methodologies and definitions of ill health used (*ibid.*: 16).

As listed in the DSM, PTSD offers a clearly defined and operation-alised psychiatric diagnosis. While the interpretation of an event by the victim is sometimes said to modify the outcome, the DSM listing for the diagnosis has great problems with what is referred to as 'the subjective relation'. Instead, as Young reminds us (1995), the DSM as a system of classification of disorders relies on a strictly empiricist approach in which, as a standardised psychiatric tool, each disorder is to be identified by criteria accessible to empirical observation and measurement. In clinical contexts, as well as in research on PTSD, in Sweden as elsewhere, there has been comparatively little interest in enquiring into the emic under-standings of disorder among the refugee groups studied.

'Traumatisation' is a more composite term, with fuzzier boundaries. It includes PTSD but may also refer to less durable acute stress reactions. Like PTSD, it overlaps with symptoms of depression, anxiety, and panic disorders (Weisaeth and Mehlum 1997). It also overlaps with a range of reactions to grief and crisis – excluded from the PTSD diagnosis – which are considered to be normal responses to the disruption and losses that refugees from war situations suffer. These reactions make up the so-called 'refugee crisis model', which was the predominant explanatory model of refugee responses employed in the Swedish social and medical services before PTSD/traumatisation entered the scene.

With the category of traumatisation, the boundary between normal and pathological reactions is less clear. Hence, although the clinical reality is complex, and 'traumatisation' encompasses a wide range of reactions and overlapping diagnostic categories from grief responses to serious psychiatric disorder, PTSD tends to become the signifier of that complexity. As the most discretely defined of the diagnostic categories involved, PTSD provides legitimacy to clinicians and researchers alike. Given its status as diagnostic tool, PTSD has also opened up an expanding field of research and become a priority for research funding[7]. However, through the tendency to conflate meanings – in which PTSD and traumatisation become synonymous – the category of disorder is expanded, and 'traumatised refugees' are easily associated with pathology.

The result is the construction of a homogeneous and medicalised category of the refugee population, both in research and clinical practice, one which has also gained ground within the refugee welfare bureaucracy. Bureaucratic categorisation is generally an attempt to maximise predictability (Jenkins 1996), part of establishing order and control (Handelman 1978). For clinicians and other practitioners, such categories are probably instrumental in dealing with their own uncertainty as they struggle to make sense of the complex diversity of experiences and cultural backgrounds of their new patients. However, how do such constructions correspond with the understandings that those so classified have of their predicament? The experiences of a local community of Bosnian refugees provide an interesting contrast with the medicalised model.

A view from a Bosnian refugee community

My ethnography is drawn from a community of about 300 Bosnian refu-gees, a category that has been made nearly synonymous with 'traumatised refugees' in the media, policy and clinical practice. From a broad range of backgrounds, these Muslim families were placed in a small Swedish town in 1993-4, most of them after a number of years awaiting an asylum decision. Their experiences of the war range from those who have been exposed to the atrocities of concentration camps, to others who were able to escape early and were not directly exposed to the war. All suffered losses of different kinds in the disruptions following war and exile.

Today, the host society is their immediate problematic reality. Distress has shifted its focus now that the war has ended: during the first few years in Sweden, those left behind were a constant cause of worry. Even so, with the peace agreement, resuming life as people once knew it is no longer possible, whether in exile or in the home country, where conditions contrast sharply with pre-war life. A key term in the Bosnians' attempts to deal with disruptive reality is 'normality', striving to keep the effects of disruption within the bounds of 'the normal'. In her study of life in Sarajevo during the war, Macek (2000) observed how people dealt with the extreme vicissitudes of everday life through a constant renegotiation of normality. In exile, this normality discourse takes on yet another di-mension of meaning, in resisting pathologisation[8].

One aspect of *normality* is sociality: expressed as *druženje*, it refers to the interactions and webs of reciprocity that made up one's social world, particularly in rural areas (Bringa 1995; Macek 1997). Not only kin, but work mates, neighbours and friends were vital components of such worlds, now shattered by war and flight (Eastmond *et al.* 1994). Sociality is also perceived as vital in promoting and restoring health.

Women more often than men express the need to have others to talk to. An older refugee woman, suffering bodily aches and pains and finding no relief in medication, made repeated attempts to be admitted to hospital. Unsuccessful in obtaining a diagnosis and hospital care, she was finally admitted, for some time, to a rest home. She felt a remarkable recovery, being able to spend all her time with other women: 'I get better when I'm around people, when I can talk to other women, to unload my worries when others listen' (Sennemark 1997, my translation).

This coping strategy, also found in Mimica's evaluation of psycho-social interventions with refugees in Croatia (1997), contrasts sharply with the model of individualised suffering and treatment offered by the host society. Rebuilding these social worlds, restoring sociability as one knew it, is difficult even within the Muslim collectivity. The war has created distrust and the local refugee group, through the dispersal policy of the host, is more of an 'accidental community' (Malkki 1995b). Close friends and kin are elsewhere, in other parts of Sweden or the world. This became evident at the funeral of one informant, which drew together people from many parts of Sweden and Scandinavia, but very few from the local Bosnian Muslim community.

Another aspect of *normality* is related to the ethic of hard work, central in the family welfare project described by Eastmond *et al.* (1994)[9]. In contrast to their notion of the functional family roles and responsibilities needed to build a secure base for the family, the majority of the Bosnians in the community remain unemployed, going between short training courses or traineeships to keep off welfare. This work ethic and its relation to moral status, agency, and well-being, was expressed by a male informant as he complained about the way the authorities defined his problems. In Bosnia he was an industrial worker in a small rural town, and he had spent months in a concentration camp during the war. His brother had disappeared at the same time and he worried about his fate. Often suffering nightmares, feeling restless and depressed, he was recommended psycho-therapy. He had repeatedly tried to get a job, any job, but the local labour market was especially reluctant to admit newcomers:

Not strange that one gets nervous, sitting around all day – they may not think I am fit to work, with my experiences. But look at these two hands, there is nothing wrong with them. I want to work and support my family! They sent me to psychiatric therapy, and it provided relief but I don't get better doing nothing for my family and myself.

After six or seven years of striving to get started again with life, many have become disillusioned, some even report feeling depressed and anxious as a result. Being clients in the welfare system has its social costs not only in terms of real dependency and debt, but also a reputational disadvantage, signalling a position outside of the normal scope of business (Handelman 1976; Graham 1999). Thus, in contrast to the focus on the *violence of the war* in the professional health care sector, the refugees themselves are also concerned with *the violations of every day life*, their continuing stressful experience as dependants of the welfare system, at the margin of society. This is the context in which notions of distress, its sources, behavioural expressions and solutions, must be understood.

Violence, suffering and normality

Today there is a widespread agreement among the Bosnian refugees that the war has left its mark on each and everyone, and implicit profound changes on individuals' ways of thinking and acting. However, they rarely talk about these as traumatisation. Despite its increasingly popular usage in Sweden, this term is not part of the way that these Bosnians conceptualise and talk about war-related distress. It is not that the medical or psychological idiom is unfamiliar – although it is often strange to older, rural people – but it simply does not seem to form part of everyday talk.

As with members of other groups exposed to atrocities, the handful of men in the community who were in the concentration camps do not talk about their experiences, often not even with members of their family. Silence may be a coping strategy to maintain close relations and some image of self-respect. Violations such as sexual degradations and rape, that would, if known, disrupt intimate relations, are surrounded by a sense of personal guilt and social shame. It may also be the silence of 'the unspeakable', around which there is tacit agreement (*cf.* Eastmond 1989). Remarks such as 'He was at Omarska', or 'She comes from Srebrenica', often allude to deeply problematic situations, not to be probed into. Atrocities beyond the normal human imagination may not be communicable to others, especially if there is no common frame of reference in which they make sense.

While Chilean refugees (Eastmond 1989) could place their experiences of torture and imprisonment into an ideological framework in which such suffering made political sense (although not without paradoxes for the individual sufferer), most Bosnian Muslims lack meaningful collective ideologies, religious or political, which may enhance resilience. Some have attempted to explain the war and its suffering within a nationalist discourse but in reality, most of these Bosnians have few established ideological convictions and were largely apolitical at home, like most of their countrymen before the war. Perhaps, as a result, silence as a means of 'forgetting' and 'putting the war behind us' becomes the necessary mode of coping, albeit running counter to the ideal therapeutic approach which they encounter, of remembering, speaking out and working through.

However, apart from the silence surrounding the victims of extreme atrocities, in everyday social interaction there is a set of terms commonly used to reflect reactions to loss and disorder. They, again, engage with the notion of normality. Normality of the individual is closely related to normally functioning family roles, but also to social relations beyond family and kin. A common idiom for expressing the effects on the person of such disruptions is *nervozan/nervozna*, i.e. 'nerves' or 'being nervous'. 'Nerves' is a socially acceptable and known idiom of distress for this group of refugees, but one which has taken on new dimensions of meaning after war and exile. Here, *nervozan*, with worry, grief and anger as its aetiological explanation, resembles the kinds of embodied distress noted from other violent contexts, such as Central America, where *nervios* communicates distress about personal, familial, social and political problems (Low 1994).

Nervozan in the Bosnian population refers to a wide range of reactions to external events, such as worry and irritability, 'shouting at one's children or behaving irrationally', loss of sleep and of concentration, other bodily manifestations (heart problems, head aches and other bodily aches and pains), and emotional reactions such as grief, hurt and anger. Many accounts of 'nerves' make no sharp distinction between bodily and emotional pain, and incorporate the social dimensions of distress. As reported by Sennemark (1997), a husband tells the wife's story of illness and explains that her repeated visit to the hospital emergency ward is because,

> ...she suffers grief. Now all those medications they've given her have worn her down... But there are no remedies for nerves, are there?' The woman herself adds: 'All this pain, it won't go away. It's nerves. Especially at night the pain gets bad. Nothing can cure this illness. After what they did to my niece [killed in front of her eyes], I shall never recover. (My translation)

Disrupted normality in the individual can also be referred to as *živcan/ živcana*, a more serious and aggressive state. 'Nerves' are seen as a passing state and do not violate the code of sociality: 'It can happen to anyone'. It is a rational response to external pressure of different kinds. *Živcan* is more asocial behaviour, less acceptable but explicable through external events: 'I have seen it in people who have been through hell', as one informant put it. One man explains that:

> (T)o be *živcan* is not a condition in any way. It is more an expression of despair, one acts irrationally...it is as if frustration and resignation contribute to creating *živcan*.

Like *nervozan*, *živcan* may also be contingent on the circumstances of the present, as explained by another male informant:

> I see it in young people in their twenties and thirties. Those who could do something with their lives but are not given a chance. Many are becoming resigned and bitter. They are frustrated. I meet many of those... It is especially hard for the young men [the social degradation]. Some simply give up. Most of them don't even have jobs as cleaners. But they need some outlet for their energy. Such guys are *živcana*. They are restless, channel their energy into fighting, being aggressive.

There seems to be a continuum rather than a sharp boundary between *nervozan* and *živcan*, with a degree of overlap where one may develop into the other over time: *živcan* may emerge from 'being nervous for too long'. As one woman put it, reflecting a biological, nervous-system energy model, '…if too highly strung, nerves can be cut loose.' *Živcan* is perceived as a more durable and problematic change, which risks coming close to the pathological. Yet it is distinguished from being insane, *lud/luda*: 'If someone's aggression turns into serious violence, such as killing someone, then one would say the person is *lud*'.

Translations between psychiatric diagnoses and emic categories are of course problematic, for a number of well-known reasons (e.g. Littlewood 1990; Obeysekere 1985). Both sets of categories can be understood as cultural constructions of normality and disorder, in which the entities are far less discrete than offical nosology will acknowledge. While their manifestations can be seen to resemble symptoms of 'trauma-related personality changes', a disorder listed in ICD-10[10], *nervozan* and *živcan* differ in important respects. As in Low's analysis of *nervios* (1994), *nervozan* and *zivcan* with their attendant physical symptoms are more than just idioms of distress. As embodiments of social experience, they not only have causes and sensations but also carry *social* meaning. They say something about the relation between self and society, more specifically about the breakdown of a person's normal relations in the social system, reflecting not only the war and the past, but the contradictions and problems encountered in the host country. Thus, they form part of social process and an ongoing negotiation of normality, responding to the uncertainties of the present. In this post-war existence of exile, individuals struggle to find new ways of connecting to the home country and to the war-torn webs of relations left behind; in the immediate present, they also strive to connect to the new society and re-create relations of normal everyday life. However, the need many express for activity (work), social recognition and a sense of control over their lives stands in sharp contrast to the conditions of unemployment and social marginalisation in which they are living.

Resisting medicalisation, renegotiating normality

We have seen that the responses to war and exile are being differently construed by the host society institutions and by the refugee collectivity. The model of the 'traumatised refugee' is not compatible with the way in which these refugees define themselves and their problematic reality. Both *nervozan* and *živčan* can be seen as counter-classifications which keep potentially problematic behaviour within the bounds of normality, as non-pathological responses[11]. On the other hand, victims of atrocities, such as former prisoners of concentration camps or women who have been raped, tend to remain uncategorised, part of a general silence surrounding such experiences.

As already mentioned, the concern with normalcy, as a way of dealing with the aberrations created by disruption, was common in Bosnia during the war. As refugees, however, emphasising normalcy and agency is also an attempt to resist medicalisation, to define themselves and to resume some control over their lives in a system which places them, in several respects, outside the 'normal' scope of business. In other ways, in their interactions with Swedish society, especially the social services, individuals reject the 'victim' identity, resenting not being recognised in their other capacities or social identities, not least as professionals or good workers.

For some refugees, this has meant insisting on being considered for labour market retraining, with economic support retained, rather than being referred to the health services. Relatives, refugees placed in a different municipality, however, found that retaining social security was conditioned on their active participation in mental health screening and follow-up sessions. Nevertheless, as noted by Low (1994), 'nerves' are sometimes medicalised also by sufferers themselves. In the refugee collective that I studied, somatic complaints such as aches and pains are often taken to the doctor. While a somatic diagnosis (but not a psychiatric one) is sometimes welcomed as a more respectable identity than that bestowed by welfare or unemployment, the idea of long-term sickness leave runs counter to the work ethic. Disability pensions appear to be more attractive to refugees at, or near, retirement age.

Interestingly, although the public attention given to the issue has created high awareness of refugee trauma among the host population, there is relatively little openness about it. In meetings with Swedes, as trainees at workplaces, as parents in the schools of their children, and so on, many complain that this awareness acts instead as a barrier to social contact: Swedes seem to fear that asking personal questions may be insensitive and unwittingly elicit difficult trauma stories or reactions of grief. At the same time, they tend to consider that the ideal form of treatment is talking about such experiences, putting them into words. However, again because of the mystique and medicalisation created around 'trauma', seen as something over which the sufferer and his consciousness has little control, talking is believed to be best left to the specialised professions. Such medical categories, and the caution they seem to instil in non-professionals, tend to exclude the more common reactions of grief and sorrow which, being closer to experiences many adult Swedes themselves have had, might potentially elicit recognition and empathy. This was the conclusion drawn by one middle-aged refugee woman, as a result of an occasion that she felt stood out as unusual, in her experience of relating to Swedes:

> When I did an internship at the local library, there was this woman I worked with. She had recently lost her husband who had died of a sudden heart attack. When I heard of this I started talking to her about it and how I felt about losing members of my family in the war and that way we came to establish a closer relationship. But she didn't ask me much about the war.

The stereotypical conceptions of what counts as a deserving client of welfare bureaucracies may also be a resource to clients in particular situations (Handelman 1976). The victim label may thus be activated in some of these contacts. At the point of arrival, of course, it was the very 'war-victim' identity which helped refugees to secure entry and permanent residence on humanitarian grounds: traumatic experiences met political and legal requirements. Later, as welfare clients, this victim identity may be emphasised in particular situations, in a presentation of self, if it justifies access to a particular benefit, usually of a kind that lies outside of the formal entitlements. For example, it may be part of negotiating the provision of economic assistance to a parent returning to Bosnia, or arguing for a residence permit for a relative. But this leaves power relations and dependency unchanged, making it difficult to escape the sense of debt to the host society and the compliance that is required in return.

An important problematic focus for the refugees is the lack of control over one's life and social reputation which welfare dependency entails, and the lack of social recognition, or even stigma, as immigrants. Thus, for many, the remedy for distress, whatever its sources, lies in re-creating a web of 'normal' social and economic roles and the hope of recuperating the family welfare project that has been built over many years, sometimes generations, and destroyed by the war (Eastmond et al. 1994)[12].

For this purpose, and as an escape from the revolving door of short-term training courses, more long-term re-education has become a strategy for some families, in particular those with a professional background. For many, this implies many years to complete another academic degree, in addition to the one from the home country. For many others, children's education takes on special importance.

Another strategy to overcome dependency and escape the control of social services, for a much smaller group, has been that of returning home. For most of these families, returning only after having acquired Swedish citizenship ensures them a chance to keep a foothold in the host society, if the attempt to secure a living at home fails. An alternative opportunity, used by a few families in my sample, has been to set up dual residence, with regular visits to Sweden to secure continued social security benefits. Thus manipulating the systems of security is seen as a means to achieve a definite return. These strategies, in the struggle for normalisation, reflect a situation of distressing uncertainty, in which neither host nor home country appear to have a viable future to offer.

The politics of trauma

Trauma as a medical category gains particular significance in a social and political context characterised by an increasingly restrictive refugee policy and high immigrant unemployment, and feeds into two major areas of public policy and debate. First, as a politico-medical discourse, the authority of the medical profession is vital in the area of refugee policy, as it facilitates and legitimates the acceptance and rehabilitation of refugees coming out of the former Yugoslavia. Second, when the politico-medical discourse is translated into the institutions of the labour market and welfare, and asylum-seekers become settlers to be socially integrated, another dynamic takes over. In the context of a new integration policy, and the promotion of the 'resourceful refugee', traumatisation is a liability that warrants intervention.

In the classificatory practices of these institutions, refugees form a problematic category. Mental disorder provides another criterion, along with insufficient or 'wrong' skills, according to which refugees are seen as 'incomplete' social persons (Handelman 1976). In society at large, and in particular in a labour market reluctant to hire immigrants, 'trauma', like 'culture', becomes a marker of significant difference that feeds into other processes of social exclusion of refugees and immigrants. Thus, ironically, while intended as a means of facilitating the reconstitution of normal social and economic lives, comprehensive rehabilitation structures tend to work against such normalisation. Medicalisation may simply be another form of clientisation in the Swedish welfare system in the 1990s, in which 'disabled' emerges as a significant category along with those of 'unemployed' and 'social welfare recipient'[13].

As Stone points out (1984), broadening the disability category to include difficulties in obtaining, and not only performing, jobs, reflects the predicament of unemployment in societies with a strong collective work ethic. 'Disability', to the state as well as to those placed in that category, offers moral legitimacy, through medical validation, for not participating in the labour market and for continued social dependency. Thus, for the category of 'traumatised refugees', in the absence of viable economic opportunities, the receiving society offers a sick role and a pathologised identity. For some, this role may become part of their self-identification, providing an explanation for failing to resume normal social functions. For the majority in the community studied, however, who represent a broad range of social backgrounds and war experiences, disability is not a solution actively sought.

The pathology-normality discourses explored here may be seen as opposite strategies – adopted by the receiving state and by the refugees – for dealing with the uncertainty generated by the contradictions of integration. For the state, unemployment challenges the work ethic ('everyone should work') and, in the Swedish welfare state in particular, the ideology of full employment ('everyone has the right to work'). This challenge, in addition to the tendency in modern welfare states to medicalise social problems, promotes an *extended disability* category as a response to the moral dilemma of unemployment (Stone 1984). The refugees, sharing the work ethic of the host society, face the contradiction between the integration policy's ideal of the resourceful and self-sufficient refugee and the absence, in practice, of opportunities to live up to that ideal. In response, Bosnians turn the moral argument of exemption inherent in 'disability' on its head: through their own categories of *extended normality*, they claim both the ability and the right to work.

Different perceptions of refugees and their problematic reality have been shown to exist. On the part of the receiving state and its institutions, through the taxonomic control of difference, bureaucratic categories emerge to handle and contain a complex and unprecedented influx of newcomers. As we have seen, the categories which define the 'refugee social person' also form the basis for interventions which aim to increase integration by shaping active and resourceful subjects. To the practitioners in the receiving system and the population at large, such categorical understandings of refugees also feed into their own attempts at making sense of who the newcomers are and how to deal with them.

Power relations are always active in classifications of normality and disorder. Refugees, as people out of place, are often seen as inherently powerless. However, unlike the 'matter out of place' in Mary Douglas's culture theory, people out of place can creatively act upon and even subvert the categories of abnormality ascribed to them (Malkki 1995b). The Bosnians' renegotiation of normality in response to social disorder, rather than accepting pathology and psychological disorder, is an attempt to contest medicalisation, a rejection of the notion of the 'traumatised refugee'. As an assertion of ability as opposed to disability, it is a way of confronting the profound uncertainty of their position, one in which they themselves, in the aftermath of war, struggle to define who they are, and how they should live 'normal' lives.

Notes

1. As it appeared in the *Diagnostic and Statistical Manual of Mental Disorders* (DSM) of the American Psychiatric Association in 1980, in the aftermath of the Vietnam war, PTSD is unique among the listed disorders in recognising the relation between external events and mental disorder. Its first diagnostic criteria is exposure to a traumatic event that is outside the range of normal human experience and would be markedly distressing to almost anyone. Others are intrusive re-experiencing of the event; avoidance of stimuli associated with the event or numbing of general responsiveness; and increased autonomic arousal (DSM-III-R 1987).
2. Freud's influential trauma neurosis theory is a case in point: Establishing early sexual traumas as the root of hysteric reactions in many young female patients, in *The Aetiology of Hysteria* (1896), only a year, but much controversy, later, his revised theory transformed the patients into the victims of their own sexual fantasies (Herman 1992).
3. This late emergence in the 1990s of the trauma discourse was not solely a result of new kinds of refugees – large numbers from organised violence in Latin America were admitted in the 1970s, but trauma was not defined as their primary problem by the host society.
4. Faist, in a study of immigrant employment in Germany and the U.S., found that employers did not perceive official programmes of educational support and additional training as qualifications but rather as signals that they are 'hard to train' and that, as employees, they would need special support (Faist 1995 cited in Franzén 1997).

5. Disability pensions may offer a legitimate means for tight municipal budgets to shift costs of local social services to that of the State. Also, as Stone (1984) has shown, 'disability' is a flexible category which, although eligibility is based on medical validation, also takes 'vocational limitation factors' into account. In times of high unemployment in many welfare states, disability may thus rest less on the inability to perform jobs than on the inability to obtain jobs. In Sweden, for instance, pension rates for the municipalities are significantly correlated with local unemployment rates (Berglind 1978, cited in Stone 1984).

6. By contrast, primary health care practitioners in Rinkeby, a multi-ethnic, immigrant suburb of Stockholm, report seeing very few PTSD cases in actual practice and in a screening of their patients (Monica Löfvander, personal communication)

7. As reports from medical and social research councils show, there is a growing sector of research in 'minority health' (Hjern 1995), with a clear focus on the mental health of refugees and PTSD (SFR 1994).

8. In a kind of counter-discourse to traumatisation as abnormality, people emphasise normality when commenting on themselves or others: 'Despite all the hardships – (he/she) is remarkably normal', or 'Indeed, most of us are normal, we have managed to pull through'. One said jokingly, 'It's not normal how normal I am!'

9. The work ethic has of course class-based variations in emphasis. For those with an industrial /farming background, it was largely physical, with rewards of respectability and material well-being; for my middle-class informants, work centred on intellectual tasks and promoted status and affluence.

10. Symptoms listed are hostility, vigilance and irritability, but also a sense of emptiness and/or hopelessness (Weisaeith 1997).

11. Cf. Gerholm's (1995) findings on local constructions of schizophrenia in northernmost Sweden.

12. There seem to be no collectively organised strategies for contesting their predicament. The ideological mistrust of such forms from the home country is reinforced by the competition which the host system engenders, in which entitlements, whether economic, vocational, or medical, are based on the qualifications of individuals or, in some cases, families.

13. Although statistics on this particular trend are lacking as yet, available figures indicate that immigrants are over-represented for permanent disability pensions.

EIGHT

CHALLENGING CONTROL: ANTABUSE MEDICATION IN DENMARK

Vibeke Steffen

'Do you live here all by yourself?'
'Oh no', Pippi said. 'Mr. Nilsson and the horse live here as well.'
'Yes, but I mean, don't you have a mother and a father here?'
'No, none at all,' said Pippi cheerfully.
'But who tells you when to go to bed at night then?' asked Annika.
'I do,' said Pippi. 'The first time I say it very gently. And if I disobey, I say it again, very firmly. And if I still disobey, I am in for a thrashing, you see.'

(Lindgren 1995: 15-6, my translation)

In relation to a follow-up study of patients who went through Minnesota Model treatment for alcoholism ten years ago[1], I recently talked to a driving instructor in his early forties. He told me that he had not touched alcohol for the past eight years: that is, until last year when he started suffering from fits of dizziness and related anxiety, which in the end prevented him from doing his work. Since he remembered all too well the pleasant experience of calming down with a cold beer or two, he could not resist the temptation. But one became many and after a few weeks of excessive drinking, he ended up in hospital for detoxification and was offered Antabuse, the standard treatment for alcoholism in Denmark. Antabuse is a medicine that interferes with the breakdown of alcohol in the body by producing very unpleasant symtoms almost immediately after intake. The drug does not treat alcoholism as such, but is taken as a preventive medicine in order to support the patient's will to stop drinking by providing an automatic physical punishment. This man had used Antabuse as a way of controlling his drinking in critical situations many times before, but this time he refused for the following reasons:

> I don't like taking Antabuse anymore. It seemed to work before and perhaps I needed it just to stop me, but something odd happens when I am on Antabuse. I don't know how to explain this, but it is as if it occupies my mind all the time and I start making silly plans. There are so many small tricks you can play with it. As soon as I start taking it, I also start planning when I can stop taking it, and speculate about ways I can control myself again. Antabuse is a reminder. Now, when I don't take it, I know I can go down anytime and buy myself a beer – it takes no planning – and I feel good about that. Then I am in control. When I have taken Antabuse, I am so busy with thoughts about when I can start drinking again – as if I have to test it. I may try out with a light beer – that gives me a slightly unpleasant reaction, flushing and heartbeating – nothing serious. Then I know the Antabuse works. I wait a bit, then I take another, and perhaps one more of the light ones. If that works all right I'll try with the stronger ones – and step by step I can drink through it. Antabuse is a reminder – a challenge.

Since then, I have been struck by the number of stories told to me by patients and health care professionals about the challenges of taking Antabuse, and the games of control and cheating that are played in relation to the administration of the drug. That makes Antabuse a peculiar drug. Unlike most other medicines, it is not taken for its actual effect in alleviating ill health, but in order to control the patient's behaviour. With such an explicit moral purpose, and as a physical means of social control, Antabuse provides an interesting example in the ethnography of medical substances. While ritual therapies are normally seen as dramatic performances played out in public and addressing moral issues of general concern, medicines are considered more neutral and subject to discreet administration in private. But with Antabuse, public and private spheres are not easily separated, and external social control seems to be closely mirrored in individual struggles of willpower and self-control. Somehow, Antabuse is an embodied dramatisation of social control par excellence.

Antabuse is sometimes referred to as the family's tranquilizer. Everyday life is often unstable and unpredictable in families with alcohol problems and Antabuse may help to stabilise the condition. From the point of view of both the patients, the families, and the medical profession, Antabuse provides a fairly simple and discrete solution to a complicated problem, at least for a while. In spite of the good intentions, however, attempts to control the damaging personal and social effects of excessive drinking with Antabuse often seem to create new challenges and uncertainties rather than solve the problems.

In this chapter, I have been inspired by Gregory Bateson's theory of alcoholism, based on his analysis of the Alcoholics Anonymous (AA) programme for recovery. My main interest here, though, is not in the AA programme, but in Bateson's more general observations regarding control, challenge, and willpower. I have found these notions useful in reaching some understanding of the social mechanisms and inherent contradictions in trying to manage the uncertainties of excessive drinking with a control-oriented use of Antabuse.

Bateson and the cybernetics of self

Looking at anthropological contributions to research on alcoholism, Gregory Bateson's article on 'the cybernetics of self' stands out as a classic (Bateson 1973: 260-308). The article deals with the spiritual and organizational principles for recovery after alcoholism suggested by the fellowship, Alcoholics Anonymous[2]. Clearly enthusiastic over the logic of the programme, Bateson argues that the alcoholic's self-destructive behaviour is an accentuation of characteristic features in western culture, and that the ideas AA lays out for personal development and a sober life represent a more desirable way of being in the world, not only for alcoholics but for people in general. The argument is framed in Bateson's terms of epistemology, cybernetics and systems theory, and he states prophetically 'that a new epistemology must come out of cybernetics and systems theory, involving a new understanding of mind, self, human relationship, and power', and, furthermore, 'that the theology of AA coincides closely with an epistemology of cybernetics' (Bateson 1973: 280).

In his essay Bateson suggests that alcoholism may be seen as a kind of matching between sobriety and intoxication, so that the latter appears as an appropriate subjective correction of the former. Therefore, the causes of alcoholism must be sought in the person's sober life, and as a consequence it is not to be expected that any procedure which reinforces this particular style of sobriety will reduce the person's alcoholism. In other words, if the sober life of the alcoholic drives him or her to drink, then that style of life must contain an error, and intoxication must provide some sense of correction of this error. It is not quite clear in the AA literature, or in Bateson's essay, whether this error is to be sought in the person or in society, but Bateson reveals his own critical stand on society with this quotation from the AA literature: 'the [AA] member was never enslaved by alcohol. Alcohol simply served as an escape from personal enslavement to the false ideals of a materialistic society' (Bateson 1973: 282).

One example of such false ideals – or false epistemology, as Bateson would have it – is what in AA is called 'false pride' or even 'alcoholic pride'. False pride is not based on something accomplished, but is rather an obsessive acceptance of challenge, a pride in willpower as expressed in the proposition 'I can…'. When the alcoholic is confronted with his or her drinking, this principle of pride will be mobilised in the proposition 'I can stay sober'. However, success in this achievement destroys the challenge, since the contextual structure of sobriety changes with its achievement, and thus is no longer the appropriate context for pride. It is now the risk of the drink that is challenging and calls out for the 'I can drink', as illustrated by the example at the beginning of this chapter. Thus, the challenge component of alcoholic pride is linked with risk-taking, and the alcoholic is caught in a compulsive pattern of pride-in-risk.

False pride presumes a relationship to a real, or a fictive, 'other'. This other may be experienced as part of the alcoholic self or may be represented by the alcoholic's family, other important relations, or society in general. Bateson suggests that such relationships may be expressed in either symmetrical or complementary patterns. Symmetrical patterns are characterised by a type of behaviour that stimulates a similar intensified response from the other (as in the case of an armaments race), while complementary patterns are characterised by responses that intensify mutual differences (as in the case of sado-masochism). Western drinking habits tend to be symmetrical, in the sense that they are governed by rules of reciprocity, and often – especially among men in bars and pubs – rivalry and competition. Drinkers are impelled by convention to match each other drink by drink, and this pattern fits in with the challenging character of alcoholic pride. On the other hand, as the alcoholic deteriorates in his drinking, his family will often react in a complementary way by taking over responsibilities, exerting authority, and becoming protective, all of which only provoke rage and shame in the alcoholic.

The alcoholic's relationship to himself, as well as his relationship to the world around him, becomes a compulsory fight of challenges and defeats, and, since both symmetrical and complementary relationships are liable to escalate, the situation develops into what Bateson calls a schismogenetic pattern. Like the schizophrenic caught in a communication of double-binds, the alcoholic is caught in a game of challenges and control no matter whether he or she drinks or not. The AA programme breaks this pattern by providing another – and according to Bateson more correct and true – epistemology, initiated by surrender. Thus, the first step in the AA programme suggests that the alcoholic gives up the fight by admitting that he is powerless over alcohol – that his life has become unmanageable. The second and third steps, furthermore, call on the alcoholic to give up control and turn his will and life over to a Higher Power. These suggestions could hardly be more controversial than in a country, Denmark, where the controlling character of Antabuse has dominated alcoholism treatment for half a century.

Antabuse

While AA is relatively new in Denmark (Steffen 1993: 33), Antabuse has been widely used for more than fifty years (Thorsen 1993: 62). Not all Danes may have heard about AA, but surely every school child knows what Antabuse is. The effect of Antabuse was discovered in 1947 by two Danish researchers, Jens Hald and Erik Jacobsen, from the biological laboratories of Medicinalco in Copenhagen (Hald and Jacobsen 1948). The story goes that they were working on the potential of the drug disulfram for the treatment of worms, when, to test its toxicity, they ingested small amounts of the substance and discovered that it had serious adverse reactions in conjunction with alcohol[3]. Antabuse interferes with the breakdown of alcohol in the body, producing a toxic reaction between five and fifteen minutes after intake, and, according to Hald and Jacobsen's original *Lancet* article, the symptoms include:

> ... a feeling of heat in the face, followed by an intense flushing, located principally in the face but spreading in some cases to the neck and upper part of the chest and arm or even to the abdomen. A constant effect is dilatation of the scleral vessels, making the person look 'bull-eyed'. These are followed a little later by palpitations, and sometimes slight dyspnoea. After larger doses of alcohol nausea and vomiting often develop. If nausea is intense, blushing gives way to pallor. These symptoms, which are usually accompanied by headache, are very unpleasant. They disappear, however, within a few hours, generally leaving the person rather sleepy. (Hald and Jacobsen 1948: 1001-2)

Following Hald and Jacobsen's article, in the same volume of *The Lancet*, is an article by the Danish psychiatrist, Oluf Martensen-Larsen. He was at the time experimenting with the drug apomorphine in aversion treatment, and saw in the discovery of Antabuse new possibilities for developing a medical treatment for alcoholism. Concurrently with the examination of the pharmacological effects of the substance, he set out to study the clinical effects of Antabuse on alcoholics. From December 1947 to May 1948 Martensen-Larsen treated 83 patients with Antabuse. The general scheme of treatment was to call in the patient for an interview, give him 1-1.5 g. of Antabuse, and tell him to continue with 0.5 g. on a daily basis. The patient was told that he would become ill if he drank alcohol, and was asked to return for a second interview two or three days later. The night before or immediately before the interview the patient should take two or three drinks to show the effect of the treatment. Martensen-Larsen notes that sometimes the patients would already have taken alcohol before that time, often in larger amounts than recommended and with a violent reaction, but that this was only beneficial from a therapeutic point of view. Most patients would feel so uneasy after four or five drinks taken in one or two hours that they never wanted to repeat the experience. Some heavy drinkers, though, could take considerable amounts of alcohol before the effects appeared, but with continued medication, the tolerance for alcohol would be reduced, as described in this case story:

> … after taking Antabuse, 1.5 g. the previous day and 0.5 g. the same morning, a heavy drinker took nine drinks (under control) during an hour. He blushed and had a raised pulse-rate but nevertheless wanted to continue drinking. Five days later he was tested again and took twenty-six drinks before he had an explosive and copious vomiting. Like all serious cases he was admitted to hospital during the beginning of the treatment. After the second test he was discharged from hospital but continued the treatment. A few days later, after only two drinks, he had to break away from a lunch with his fiancée in a restaurant and take a taxi home. A few days later he became ill even after a single drink. (Martensen-Larsen 1948: 1004)

Martensen-Larsen was very optimistic about the treatment potential of Antabuse, and estimated that 74 of the 83 patients treated showed promising results. He admitted that the follow-up in his study was still too short to ascertain how long the results would last, and also concluded that the treatment with Antabuse should be only part of a more general treatment.

This addition was apparently overlooked in the first optimism sur-rounding the drug, but the enthusiasm soon faded when it became clear that Antabuse in itself did not solve the problem of addiction. In a field where the co-operation of the patient was considered a main problem, many physicians realised that it was no easier to convince alcoholics to take Antabuse everyday than to persuade them to stop drinking in the first place (Valverde 1998: 99). But the drug had other advantages: in the years following its introduction the criminal justice system explored the potentials of Antabuse to treat and monitor alcoholic offenders, and in some places it was made mandatory as a condition of probation or parole. The problem of compliance and control raised interest in a form of Antabuse that did not rely so heavily on the decision-making of the patient, and in France subcutaneous implants of Antabuse were developed in the 1950s (White 1998: 228). This technique is still offered by some Danish doctors.

Until the introduction in 1985 of Minnesota Model treatment in Denmark, and the subsequent spread of AA groups to all corners of the country, Antabuse totally dominated Danish alcoholism treatment. A few AA groups had been active since the late 1970s, but compared to other Scandinavian and European countries Danish attitudes towards the AA programme were very reluctant. Thus, when AA founder, Bill Wilson, visited Europe in 1950, he found the Danes more interested in the promising effects of Antabuse than in the spiritual message of the AA programme (AA 1985: 26). The somewhat rigid and controlling character of the Danish welfare system, stressing collectivity and sameness, combined with a cultural preference for 'controlled drinking' rather than abstinence, provided fertile soil for the use of Antabuse (Steffen 1997: 101). Outside Denmark the drug was never quite as popular. Already in 1948, it was brought to the US and advocated as an adjunct in treatment by the American doctor, Ruth Fox, but with little impact (White 1998: 226).

Controlled drunkenness

Antabuse is in Denmark routinely offered to anyone who gets in contact with the public health care system for problems with alcohol, whether this contact is through general practitioners, outpatient clinics or hospital wards. Research from 1988 shows that Antabuse was used in more than 90 per cent of all cases in the public outpatient wards, often under quite coercive circumstances, with one third of the patients claiming that it had no positive effects on their drinking problem (Skinhøj 1988: 23). A report from The Link organisation's outpatient clinics, based on data relating to 1736 users during 1992-93, states that 75 per cent of them were taking Antabuse at the beginning of treatment (Landsforeningen Lænken 1996). These findings are confirmed by a recent study showing that Antabuse medication still dominates Danish treatment for alcoholism (Järvinen 1998).

With all of the general emphasis on positive reinforcement being more effective than painful punishment, it is surprising how Antabuse treatment has been left out of that larger understanding. Most professionals agree, when asked, that Antabuse should only be used with the explicit consent of the patient and in combination with other forms of therapy. In practice, the prescription of Antabuse is seldom discussed and supportive activities are only utilized to a very limited extent, because the initiative depends a great deal on the individual patient.

One of the organisations in Denmark that offer treatment with Antabuse is The Link. The Link is a cooperative venture between *Landsforeningen Lænken* – the National Association of The Link, a fellowship of people with alcohol problems and their nearest relations – and The Link Outpatient Clinics in Denmark, a private foundation (though publicly funded) offering professional treatment for alcohol abuse. The aim of The Link fellowship is to help anyone, who wishes to gain control over his or her alcohol consumption. The Danish branch of The Link was founded in 1954 and was originally inspired by the AA concept of mutual self-help. However, The Link rejects the spiritual character of the AA programme and the principle of anonymity as a condition for their work. The history of the two organisations has led them in very different directions, but perhaps the most significant difference lies in their basic understanding of alcohol problems. While AA uses the concept 'alcoholic', indicating a special (internal) characteristic of the person, The Link insists on talking about 'people with alcohol problems', stressing a multi-factorial (external) approach. Consequently, while AA suggests a standard programme for all alcoholics, The Link offers individual treatment based, at least in principle, on each person's self-defined goals. It is also interesting to note that while AA suggests that the alcoholic surrenders and abandons the idea of control, The Link explicitly states that the aim is to help people gain control over their alcohol consumption.

The Link's strategy, however, seems to result in very diffuse treatment goals, or simply in Antabuse being prescribed as a standard treatment, with no plan at all. Only the most resourceful and highly-motivated patients manage to define clear goals for their own treatment, let alone ask for regular counselling or join group therapy of their own accord. Many seem to be content with a few kind words from the secretary in charge of handing out the medicine and controlling the intake, or they may take a cup of coffee and spend some time chatting with the other patients in the ward's lounge. Social activities such as pool, volunteering to make coffee, dinners, excursions, and holidays, which play a central role in The Link's notion of self-help, also require a degree of engagement and motivation which not all patients are able to mobilise. Since these therapeutic activities are not systematically related to Antabuse medication – Antabuse being prescribed by doctors, social activities attended to by social workers or volunteers – Antabuse often appears as a treatment in itself.

With such extensive use of Antabuse, one might expect some enthusiasm, or at least satisfaction, among the users of the drug. In fact, neither the patients who take the drug, nor the doctors who prescribe it, nor the medical secretaries who administer it, are very optimistic. Most of them would probably agree with the administrative director of The Link Outpatient Clinics in Denmark, who laconically calls Antabuse 'a chemical extention of good will' (Orbe 1996: 11). Usually, the effect of

Antabuse can be maintained by an intake of 600-800 mg. twice a week and the idea is, of course, that the fear of unpleasant reactions should prevent the person from drinking. According to this logic, the willpower to resist drinking only has to be mobilised twice a week, instead of every time the temptation of a drink comes up.

Thus, in contrast to most other medicines, Antabuse is meant to work by anticipation and serves its purpose best when the actual effect is left out, *i.e.* exclusively as a placebo. To some patients, Antabuse does indeed seem to have that effect: it provides provisional peace of mind and prevents sensations of craving (Pedersen and Markussen 2000: 11). Some actually manage to stay sober on Antabuse for many years. But more commonly, Antabuse medication falls into a periodic pattern of three to six months of abstinence, followed by rather dramatic binges of an escalating character, as described by this male teacher in his late forties. After a period of excessive drinking, he ended up at hospital for detoxification and treatment of his wounds. From there he was referred to an outpatient clinic and had Antabuse prescribed. He recalls the result of his treatment:

> Well, everything worked out as it should, I suppose. After six months on Antabuse I felt I could manage on my own and took a terrible relapse. When I had been drinking heavily for three weeks, I went back to the outpatient clinic. I had a consultation with a doctor, had Antabuse prescribed again and made sure to come there twice a week to take it. After another six months things repeated themselves: I decided on a relapse – or, at least I planned it to the extent that I didn't show up at the clinic on Friday to take my Antabuse.

Drinking periods may be more or less consciously planned and arranged with due respect to holidays and feasts, or they may be subject to more subtle and unconscious mechanisms. To some people relapses appear totally unpredictable and immune from personal control, and the uncertainties of the consequences are so incalculable that they seem to prefer any kind of control to prevent it from ever happening again.

Nevertheless, most patients first consult a clinic with a deeply-felt wish of being helped to achieve some level of moderate drinking, and they consider Antabuse a regulatory means in that direction. Professionals, in general, find moderate drinking an acceptable first goal for the person, but many think that abstinence is probably a more realistic goal in the long run. The attitude seems to be, that each individual should learn by his own personal experiences. Gradually, hopes of recovery in terms of moderate drinking fade or disappear with repeated experiences of relapse. Antabuse becomes a pragmatically installed mechanism of self-control, and regular binges an abreaction, perhaps triggered by the very constraints of control.

The charms of a medicine

Examining medicines and therapies as forms of social control is a common approach in medical anthropology (van der Geest and Whyte 1989). Periods of illness are occasions of dependency, when ideas of obligation and morality are mobilised, and therapy is always embedded in various forms of social relationships such as kinship, community, and social institutions. The sick role is associated with both privileges and obligations, just as the role of care-taker is embedded in certain moral demands. One of the primary obligations of the patient is to become well and therefore to comply with the treatment offered by professionals (Parsons 1951). In fact, one of the main purposes of taking Antabuse might be to confirm the patient's consent to the unspoken rules of compliance. In that sense, Antabuse may be better understood as a ritual treatment rather than a purely medical treatment. The ritual provides the professional with the symbolic power of controlling the patient's intake of the drug, and the patient demonstrates his will to comply with the rules of the game by accepting this external control (Orbe 1996: 12).

Normally, medicines are defined by their capacity to change the conditions of a living organism. They are expected to solve problems in undramatic ways and are valued for their effectiveness in alleviating ill health by removing the symptoms. Their concreteness as substances enhances the perception of illness as something tangible, and permits therapy to be separated from social relations. As such, medicines may be an attractive alternative to other kinds of therapy, a treatment that focuses on the individual body, which can be carried out privately, a fact that is particularly important when sickness is associated with shame and might reflect poorly on the patient or family. Thus, one of the charms of medicines is that they allow private individual treatment, and diminishing dependence on practitioners, experts, and kin (van der Geest *et al.* 1996: 154-6).

Antabuse, however, challenges these notions about medicines. On the one hand, it fits in very nicely with the need for discretion and privacy in relation to a problem that is considered highly stigmatising. On the other hand, the administration of the drug is embedded in a huge system of public institutions and social control. Firstly, Antabuse is a prescription drug and thus requires the interference of a doctor. Secondly, the drug is administered in ways that urge the patient to show up in public to take the medication. Finally, the actual intake is carefully surveyed and registered by representatives of the social system. Such public administration and strict surveillance prevent many, especially women, from seeking treatment at all. Here a former nurse tells how she secretly developed a substantial alcohol problem over a couple of years and then, desperately needing help, eventually went to see her general practitioner:

> I went up to my doctor and simply shouted to his face, that if he did not help me right here and now, I would drink myself to death! He instantly gave me some drugs for detox and suggested Antabuse treatment. But no, no – not for me, thank you! Showing up at the clinic twice a week to take my Antabuse, oh no – the secretary would soon find out, and in a small town like this people talk!

Submitting to the forms of surveillance and publicity involved in the administration of Antabuse is felt as shameful and humiliating by many patients. But then, Antabuse treatment can still be limited to the intake of a substance, in contrast to counselling and group therapy that involves other people and reveals more sensitive knowledge about the person. Using a medicine has the advantage of making the problem seem concrete and disease-like, it offers a mechanical solution and it clearly demonstrates the patient's compliance.

Cheating

Most patients end up accepting the control associated with Antabuse medication, and some will even claim that external control is exactly what they need. Nevertheless, cheating plays an important role. Innumerable stories about how to cheat with Antabuse are told, and although some professionals doubt that the stories are in accordance with reality, they do indeed reflect the patients' preoccupation with the subject.

Some stories focus on situations in which the patient is subjected to so-called 'voluntary coercion', a self-imposed constraint accepted due to the pressure of significant others. Although compulsory treatment with Antabuse is not allowed, various forms of motivational pressure certainly occur, particularly when the Prison Service or the Social Security authorities are involved. Agreement to enrol in controlled Antabuse medication can play a central role in negotiations about conditional release from prison, the commutation of sentences for drunk driving, parental access to children in cases of neglect, social security payments, or even participation in treatment programmes. Considerable pressure may also be put on the patient by family, friends or employers, and Antabuse may provide a visible and simple solution to such pressure. Under these conditions, the patient is often more influenced to take the medication by the pragmatic prospect of future gains, than by a genuine wish to stop drinking.

When possible, Antabuse is given under strict surveillance. Even when legal authorities are not involved, intake is noted down on a small yellow card carried by the patient as documentation of treatment (ironically referred to as a 'driver's licence' or 'the yellow card'). The medicine is preferably ingested as a tablet dissolved in water, which reduces the number of very simple methods of cheating available, such as hiding the tablet under the tongue and spitting it out later. Of course it does not eliminate the other common method, of sticking a finger in the throat and vomiting. Medical secretaries tell stories about patients pretending to drink the liquid, but instead, trying to let it flow unnoticed down their chin and into their jacket. Others try to chat with the secretary until the tablet settles at the bottom of the cup, in order to reduce the concentration of the drug, and then throwing the rest out (according to the secretary who revealed this trick, the tell-tale sign here is the sound of the plastic cup when it hits the bottom of the bin!). More inventive strategies include a patient who hid a wad of cotton in his mouth, to absorb the liquid so that he could spit it out afterwards. A more negotiable way of avoiding Antabuse is through complaints of side effects, though most doctors seem to doubt the seriousness of such complaints, or respond with medication that counters or reduces the effect of Antabuse.

Stories about cheating are, of course, well-known by patients as well as professionals. One wonders why they all engage in this game. In his classic study of play, Johan Huizinga notes that society is often more lenient to 'the cheat' than to the 'spoil-sport', because the cheat, by pretending to be playing the game, acknowledges the basic framework or the premises of the play, in contrast to the spoil-sport who threatens the very existence of the play-community by his non-compliance (Huizinga 1955: 11). Although the principle that rules should be kept lies at the heart of play, many examples from popular lore let the cheat win by fraud (Huizinga 1955: 52). Perhaps something similar is at stake in Antabuse treatment. A woman in her late fifties seemed to confirm such an interpretation, when she offered her point of view on Antabuse treatment. Like many others she was sentenced for drunk driving and offered 'controlled treatment', to reduce the length of the sentence. Consequently, she had to show up twice a week at the local outpatient clinic, to take Antabuse and have her yellow card signed:

I was offered an initial consultation with a doctor, but, apart from that, treatment consisted in socialising with the other clients. There was this room with a pool-table – just like in a bar – where people would spend their time telling stupid stories. Not so much about how to cheat with the Antabuse, but more about how to cheat the system with social security payment and things like that – how to swindle and live by your wits. That wasn't really me – I never liked bars anyway. It was grotesque, you could just cheat, I mean, throw up the Antabuse afterwards or, like some did, drink through it – but the coercion and the control of the system was so humiliating. I think the extensive use of Antabuse in Denmark is just due to thinking in grooves – we are in the homeland of Antabuse, you know[4] – and then it is about steering and control – everybody pretends that everything is under control.

Testing

According to the professionals, patients subjected to 'voluntary coercion' are a minority at the clinics and attempts to cheat with Antabuse are not that common. Listening to the patients, however, another sort of cheating, or rather 'testing', appears to be very widespread. This takes place among patients who have voluntarily agreed to take Antabuse, but who nevertheless engage in various forms of self-imposed testing or experimentation with the drug and its effects, not unlike the original aversion therapy trials carried out by Martensen-Larsen.

A man in his early fifties, working in graphics, recounts how he was escorted to an outpatients clinic by his neighbour, after a long period of time with a slowly escalating drinking problem. He had a consultation with a doctor and was prescribed Antabuse, which he willingly took. He actually liked coming to the clinic in the mornings and chatting with the other patients, and even went there on mornings when he did not have to take Antabuse. But, anyway:

... of course, I had to test it – just to see if it really worked. It was after a while in treatment. A couple of days after taking my Antabuse, I felt like having a beer at home. My wife was there, but she didn't say anything – or perhaps I thought it was none of her business – so I drank a plain lager at first. That was okay, nothing really happened. It was near Christmas, so I continued with one of these with a throttle, you know, a Christmas brew. That was it! I simply dropped out on the floor, fainted. My wife got terribly scared of course and called an ambulance, what else could she do? I got into the emergency unit and was checked for all sorts of ills – my heart, blood pressure, and whatever. At least I got a full check-up – usually that is reserved for the car – and fortunately, there was nothing wrong with me. That's nice to know, if I take the positive view on this whole event. Well, then I could say to myself, that at least I tried it. I guess, I am the kind of person that has to learn by his own experiences – and now I don't have to try that again! To be honest, it was quite scary, my eyes were swimming and I couldn't control my body – not least for my wife it was scary. I could have dropped dead, if I had had a weak heart for example.

Others have less dramatic experiences and simply manage to drink through the unpleasant effects by tolerating the symptoms until they eventually stop. For people with weak hearts this method is considered life-threatening, but it is not uncommon and often talked about with a touch of pride. A carpenter in his late thirties told me how he simply 'forgot' that he was on Antabuse after a detoxification and the next day went to the local bar, for a beer after work:

My heart started beating very fast and my face turned extremely red. It was scary for a while. But you know, it passes and then I don't care. The first time I drank on Antabuse the effects were much worse, but now I know that after a while it's over – it's no hindrance, if I want to drink, I drink!

An experienced professional supported the idea that some patients actually forget that they are on Antabuse, and considered it to be the most valid explanation for relapses of this kind. But among the patients, forgetting is just one factor on a wide scale, ranging from resistance and pride, via deliberate experimentation, to resignation and hopelesness. A retired worker in his late fifties pondered:

> I have been drinking on Antabuse many times, but it really is stupid. Not much happens, but it is of course rather unpleasant. I cannot say why I did it. Probably some kind of escape from reality. I can drink through Antabuse if I start with a light beer and then wait a bit, so I can just feel the effect of the drug. Then I take one more and then perhaps a plain lager, until everything works just as normal again and the malaise is over. But it is of course dangerous, at least for some people. I have gotten away with it unhurt even though it hasn't been nice. It is a stupid thing to do!

Finally, a retired secretary told how, years ago, her drinking problem developed into a self-destructive resignation, making Antabuse medication totally absurd:

> When I lost my job it just knocked me out and I lost control over my entire life. It is no excuse, I know, but it sort of made everything collapse, and in a couple of months I drank myself right to the bottom. I was just lying on the sofa terribly ill. A nurse came twice a week with my Antabuse, and when the neighbours asked what was wrong with me, I told them I was being given vitamin injections. In the end I was drinking snaps, although the only alcohol I liked was white wine. I also drank on Antabuse until I was removed to the hospital on the edge of dying. I couldn't have cared less.

The divided self

While few Danes explicitly agree with a disease model of alcoholism, and certainly very few professionals do, they do seem to embrace the idea that alcoholism is primarily a problem of control – or more precisely loss of control – which is in fact one of the basic premises of the classic disease model (Järvinen 1998: 66). Most people would rather stick to the idea that alcoholism is a consequence of poor social conditions, combined with psychological problems. This ambivalence is reflected in Antabuse treatment, which may appear as a logical choice if loss of control is considered to be the essential problem, but does not accord with the present understanding of alcoholism as primarily a psycho-social problem. Even when the wish for moderation instead of abstinence is taken seriously as a goal in Antabuse treatment, structured treatment programmes, working towards controlled drinking, are rarely offered. For most patients, Antabuse just works as a way to 'cork up the bottle' when the consequences of drinking become too heavy.

Antabuse may help install such a break and keep patients dry for a while, but then other mechanisms seem to set in. The combination of control and good will – whether control is externally-enforced or internally-motivated, and whether good will is demonstrated by taking Antabuse or not – means that the situation has to be challenged and the effects tested. The game takes on its own life and sometimes threatens to overshadow the original problem. This brings us back to Bateson and the concept of 'false pride'. After staying dry for a while, the alcoholic seems to have proved his ability to control the otherwise uncontrollable condition of drinking and, hence, to have eliminated the challenge of doing so. The alcoholic becomes 'cocksure' (Bateson 1973: 292). In the game of control, attention is turned back towards alcohol and the challenge of drinking.

This mechanism of pride and challenge does not depend on the use of Antabuse, as the next example will show, although the drug does seem to reinforce and elucidate the process. The case concerns a young man who has been through all sorts of treatments for addiction during the past decade, one of them a very costly stay at a private American treatment center. Although attention is directed to the effect of anti-depressive medication, I think the example also illustrates what Bateson and AA describe as becoming 'cocksure':

It was very exotic and exciting for me – I have never been to the States before – so of course that was an experience. I was treated by a psychiatrist and was instantly put on Prozac. She thought I was depressed and so I was – I really felt terrible. Well, the medication did help in the sense that I felt much better about myself and regained my self confidence. But it was a totally unrealistic kind of self-confidence – I thought I could rule the world! I spent five months at the center and had a great time, but only until I was going back, then things went wrong already at the airport. I don't know what got into me – I guess it was that feeling of unrealistic grandiosity – I behaved like a man of the world and thought that a drink would be no problem for me. All the way back on the plane I was being smart, flirting with the woman next to me, telling her all sorts of lies. Fortunately, I do not remember what happened, when I arrived home and met the welcome committee. That has totally been repressed. I know that I did do my best to walk out on my own feet, but apart from that…They were of course terribly disappointed with me…

According to Bateson, this specific kind of sobriety, in which grandiosity and pride drive the alcoholic to take risks and test himself, is characterised by an unusually disastrous variant of Cartesian dualism: a division between conscious will, or 'self', and the remainder of the personality (Bateson 1973: 284). Firstly, it blurs the fact that there is only one and the same person acting, and secondly, it sets the person in a seemingly symmetrical relationship to himself.

The idea of a divided self is, of course, not restricted to people with alcohol problems, but is a common notion in western societies, and basic to the concept of self control. Human reflexivity and the internalisation of collective norms involves a conversation with oneself, an inner dialogue between seemingly different parts of the mind. A short detour into the social interactionist perspective of self and selfhood developed by G. H. Mead in *Mind, Self and Society* (1934) may be helpful to understand the mechanisms here. Mead was concerned with the social origin and foundations of self on the one hand, and with the process of the emergence of individual selves on the other hand. In his model of selfhood he operated with a distinction between 'I' and 'me' as related parts of the self. While the 'I' represents the acting self, the 'me' represents the organized set of attitudes of others that the 'I' both reacts against and internalises. Mead's 'others' refer to a hypothesised 'generalised other' which represents the community to which an individual belongs. Thus the individual self emerges from an ongoing process in which the 'I' interacts with the 'generalised other' in accordance with the individual's ability to treat him- or herself as and object, and to take the attitude of the other towards him- or herself as an object. Thus, the self is partly constituted out of the interaction between 'I' and 'me', and partly out of the individual's interaction and dialogue with others. While most people live their lives with more or less unitary selves despite such inner conversations, when or if the sense of unity appears to be threatened it may lead to serious personal disorder (Jenkins 1996: 41-5).

This brings us back to the situation of the alcoholic, and the initial statement that 'false pride', in order to be activated, always implies a relationship to a fictive or a real other. The inner dialogue of the alcoholic assumes the character of a conversation between an 'I' and a 'me' with opposing interests, an internalised conflict, while the social control instigated in the patient by Antabuse becomes a physical manifestation of the 'generalised other'. Treatment takes on the character of a fight, splitting the self into two parts engaged in a symmetrical, schismogenetic pattern of control, challenge and compulsory risk-taking, to stay with Bateson's terminology (1973: 297). In this fight, the individual struggles not only against him- or herself, but also against significant others, against the institutions of society, and against cultural values and norms, norms that are medically incorporated and endowed with an automatic punishment in cases of disobeyance. And if Bateson was right that alcoholic pride, in particular, is activated by such patterns of control and challenge, as the examples used in this chapter seem to confirm, Antabuse only adds wood to the fire.

The challenge of control – transformation or return ticket?

In families dominated by alcohol abuse every day is a struggle to gain control over lives that have become unmanagable. With alcoholism basically understood as a loss of control in itself, a condition that seems immune to the exercise of personal willpower, quotidian life becomes unpredictable and full of uncertainties. In this situation, neither the alcoholic nor the family knows what to rely on or what to expect from day to day. They are also uncertain about how to solve the problem. For many people the prospect of giving up drinking altogether is almost unbearable, even when moderate drinking turns out to be extremely hard, or even impossible to manage.

The uncertainties and the ambiguities of the alcoholics about treatment options are, to a wide extent, shared by the medical profession. Both sides know very well, that the effort to control the intake of alcohol by inflicting a mechanical physical punishment, is an uncertain strategy in the long run. Antabuse is not the kind of drug that cures a disease, it hardly removes the symptoms. But at least it gives the impression that something is being done. It may even provide a placebo-like sense of control that can help both alcoholics, their families, and the professionals to manage the uncertainty for a while. Paradoxically, the attempt to control the situation by the prescription of Antabuse at the same time seems to create new uncertainties by challenging the very means of control itself. The various ways patients try to contest the effect of Antabuse by cheating, testing, and experimenting with the drug, show how control often results in strategies to counter the restraints of control. As originally pointed out by advocates of the labelling perspective in the sociology of deviance, it is not necessarily deviance that creates social control, but rather social control and its techniques that produce deviance (Jenkins 1996: 74). What is more, the way in which professionals tacitly accept the state of affairs shows that they are not too interested in giving up the impression that they are in control; they know what they are doing. Cheating does not spoil the game as such, but it blurs the outlines of the current state of play, apparently in the interest of many parties.

For most people in western societies drinking alcohol is a normal social and recreational activity. Although we tend to think of intoxication as a breakaway from more formal behaviour, alcohol researchers have argued that drinking patterns in general are governed by ritual rules leading towards feelings of transformation and redemption (Elmeland 1996). This suggests, that excessive drinking may be seen as a personal development process, an effort to break out of a cramped living space. The effort is rarely successful, partly because the goal is too vague, and partly because the means are not appropriate. Antabuse, however, will hardly help the person in this effort, but will rather work as a return ticket, sending the person back empty-handed (Elmeland *et al.* 1990:74). Bateson stated, in one of the premises of his theory of alcoholism, that if the sober life of the alcoholic somehow contains an error, it makes no sense to send the person back to this previous condition. This is exactly what Antabuse seems to do. While Bateson acknowledged his debt to the alcoholic patients with whom he worked in the Veterans Administration Hospital, and humbly admitted that 'I fear that I helped them not at all', the Danish health care system still pretends that everything is under control with Antabuse treatment.

Notes

1. This chapter builds on data from my research on the role of reform movements, medicines and spontaneous remission in recovery from alcoholism (Steffen 1993, 1994, 1997, 2002), carried out in Denmark over the past ten years. Data are drawn from two related research projects, the first on Minnesota Model treatment carried out in 1990-93, the second on reform movements, medicines and spontaneous remission carried out in 2000. The research was financed by *Rusmiddelforskningsinitiativet* [the Drug Research Initiative], *Socialstyrelsens Udviklingsmidler* [Development Fund of the Agency for Social Affairs], *Sygekassernes Helsefond* [Fund of the Health Insurance

Societies], and *Sundhedsstyrelsens Alkoholpulje* [National Board of Health's Alcohol Pool], all of which I thank for their support. I would also like to thank the many people from the treatment centers involved, who willingly participated in these studies and shared their experiences with me: *Heliosfondens* [The Helios Foundation] *Skovgårdshus, Alfa Behandlingscenter* [Alfa Therapy Center], The Link in Copenhagen, and groups of Alcoholics Anonymous in Denmark.

2. Bateson's theory of alcoholism stems from his work in a research team that studied schizophrenia at the Veterans Administration Hospital in Palo Alto, California, in the years 1949-52. Among the schizophrenic patients Bateson met a smaller group of alcoholics, some of them members of AA, and by listening to their experiences he got interested in the fellowship and the programme as such. Thus, the theory of alcoholism parallels his theory of schizophrenia in many respects, especially the ideas on double-binds.

3. The chemical formula of Antabuse is tetra-ethyl-thiuram-disulphide. Actually, the effect of the chemical ingredient thiram, used in the manufacture of synthetic rubber, had already been recognized by the rubber industry, where it was common knowledge that people who drank alcohol after exposure to thiram would experience profound discomfort (White 1998: 226). But it was not until Hald and Jacobsen, as a result of their unpleasant experience, speculated that disulfram might have potential in the treatment of alcoholism, that the drug was marketed and sold most frequently under the trade name Antabuse (anti-abuse).

4. It is a common ironic remark among people engaged in alcohol treatment that the widespread use of Antabuse in Denmark is due to the product being Danish. However, according to the producers, Dumex-Alpharma, no special effort has been made to market Antabuse for many years.

NINE

BECOMING MENTALLY ILL: EXISTENTIAL CRISIS AND THE SOCIAL NEGOTIATION OF IDENTITY

John Aggergaard Larsen

My name is Per and I was born in 1974 in Køge. My Mum, Dad, and I moved to Hvidovre in 1982. In the end of 1998 I was diagnosed schizophrenic, it gave an answer to many things[1].

With these words, a twenty-six year old man from Copenhagen began his account of his experiences of having severe mental health problems: becoming psychotic, being hospitalised in a psychiatric ward, struggling to find the right neuroleptic medication, and, during a two-year period after the hospitalisation, having continuous contact with a mental health team offering psychosocial support in combination with the medical treatment. When Per first heard that the psychiatrist had diagnosed him as schizophrenic he was frightened and unhappy. He thought that his life was ruined for good. Today, about two years later, he no longer thinks much about his diagnosis, he has accepted it. Furthermore, the diagnosis of schizophrenia now helps him to explain many things: not only his present situation and symptoms of mental illness, but also experiences and problems that he had in the past.

Per describes how during early puberty he experienced mild symptoms of his mental illness, such as anger, fantasies, and introversion. With time, the symptoms became worse. In 1991 his parents separated, and when Per went to visit his father in December of that year he found him dead. Over the previous months Per had worried for his father. Now his worst fears had become true: he had taken his own life. After that Per over a five month period saw a psychologist for bereavement counselling. In the following years, despite feeling depressed, he managed to complete his training as a toolmaker. Finally, in 1998, he realised that there was something wrong and he found the courage to talk to his general practitioner about his feeling of depression and debilitation. The GP referred Per to a psychiatrist who, after two months of treatment without any improvement, recommended that he should be admitted to a psychiatric ward. However, the hospital psychiatrist didn't think that Per was suffering from a serious mental disorder and he was not admitted.

Over the following weeks Per increasingly had paranoid thoughts, of people saying bad things about him, and he began to isolate himself. About five or six months later he felt that his thoughts were out of control, and he went to the community mental health centre [*distrikts-psykiatrisk center*] and requested to talk to a psychologist. Per thought that his problems were related to his father's suicide; his psychologist agreed, believing that he was repressing emotions that he needed to express openly. However, the more they excavated the issues during the therapeutic sessions, the worse he felt. In the end he felt that his head was going to explode. After not sleeping for some days he went with his mother to his psychologist and requested to be admitted to a psychiatric ward. He felt that he couldn't control his emotions or deal with anything. This time his request was met.

The moment after the door of the psychiatric ward was closed, Per regretted his decision, he wanted to get out. However, the staff wouldn't let him go, and soon he understood why: there was a conspiracy against him. The secret police were going to come and get him; along with his mother, his grandmother, the Danish prime minister, Bill Clinton, and the CIA, they formed a secret Satanist cartel. He was the Son of God, about to be sacrificed, cut open and chopped to pieces. However, he had to be careful what he thought, since there were secret agents at the ward; the guy who slept in the bed to the left of him was going to dope him and the guy from the secret police to the right was watching him to make sure that he didn't escape. Psychotic and paranoid thoughts like these would continue even after he reluctantly began to take the medication prescribed for him. But he felt somewhat better when, after a week, he was transferred to a special ward for young people and sufferers of first-time psychosis, where the door was open. However, only slowly did he feel better and find himself again [*kom til sig selv*]. Per stayed on this ward for seven months.

This chapter sets out to understand the situation in which Per and other first-time mental health patients find themselves, with particular regard to their compliance with psychiatric explanations of their situation and what this means for notions of individual identity. I will discuss how a psychiatric diagnosis can help people like Per to explain past experiences and problems, and what this new explanation means to their self-understanding and future orientation. They have to reconsider their lives and futures, and they are often still suffering from severe mental health problems and anxiety about the possibility of further psychotic episodes. Questions of their individual identities, and their adoption – or rejection – of mental illness, as an identity marker ascribed by mental health services, will be the focus of the discussion. I will suggest that the uncertainty experienced by young people becoming mentally ill can be illuminated by the concept of identity and will introduce a model of the social negotiation of individual identity, focusing on the experiential continuity of self.

In the same way as Per, some mental health patients think that diagnosis, and a psychiatric explanation of their condition, helps them to understand themselves and their difficulties better and gives them a feeling of certainty. On the other hand, some other first-time mental health patients maintain a more sceptical attitude to the explanations, concepts and theories presented by the mental health service and seek different ways of understanding themselves, their experiences, and their situations (Larsen n.d.). In this chapter, I will focus on the positive adaptations to, and uses of, the explanations and categories of mental health services. Understanding these can add much to our anthropological and sociological understanding of mental illness[2] and identity.

Mental illness and identity

Questions of identity are an established theme in the anthropology and sociology of mental illness[3]. Drawing on labelling theory, Thomas Scheff (1966) pointed out that the label, or social identity, 'mentally ill' has severe negative consequences for individuals. In particular, after an individual has been thus labelled their further actions and sentiments will be under-stood by other actors in relation to, and as confirmation of, their status as mentally ill. In a famous experiment to test this theory (Rosenhan 1973), nine researchers falsely claimed to have symptoms of mental ill-ness – hearing voices – and were admitted to psychiatric wards around the United States. When they resumed their normal behaviour, however, their actions were recorded by the nursing staff as signs and symptoms of their assumed mentally disturbed state. Even the writing of notes by the undercover fieldworkers was seen as pathological behaviour: 'Patient engages in writing behaviour' (*ibid.*: 253). Although the lessons of this study can be contested (Bowers 1995), the labelling model remains sig-nificant in pointing out the danger within the field of mental health of understanding individuals within a narrow and one-dimensional frame of reference: their status as mentally ill.

Thoits (1985) developed labelling theory further, pointing out the self-labelling processes that are involved when a person becomes involved in mental health care. She looked at the initial labelling of individuals as mentally ill, observing that patients under mental health care most often seek help and treatment voluntarily: at some point before actively seeking help they have thus identified their own difficulties as a 'mental health problem'. The concept of self-labelling refers to this process. Draw-ing on symbolic interactionism and Mead's notion of 'the generalised other' (1934), Thoits argues that individuals can look at themselves 'from outside'. In this process of self-analysis or -reflection, individuals apply cultural norms about emotions and behaviour that they have learned during socialisation. Thus individuals can conclude that their feelings and the difficulties they are experiencing deviate from the norm, and are possible indicators of mental illness, a concept which is also generally known within society, even if only one-dimensionally and stereotypically. To alleviate the difficult situation they have identified, individuals can seek help and treatment through the institutions of mental health care.

Thoits highlighted the possibility that this self-labelling can provide the opportunity for individuals to start to deal with their psychological or emotional difficulties through various types of 'emotion work'. She does, however differentiate between different types of labelling: talking about 'informal labelling', and distinguishing between 'supportive labelling' and 'coercive labelling' (1985: 239). Informal labelling is when lay people in the social environment interpret and characterise an individual's difficulties or behaviour as relevant to mental health treatment. She explains that this can in general be seen as a supportive labelling, depending on the thus-labelled individual's accepting the labelling, and his or her perceptions of the intentions behind the interpretation. If the labelled individual rejects the relevance of the label but people in the social environment anyway insist that it is applicable, the interpretation can be characterised as co-ercive labelling.

The relationship of self-labelling to individual understandings of the nature, cause and course of mental illness has been examined in a longi-tudinal qualitative and quantitative study among 169 people diagnosed as having major psychiatric disorders (Estroff *et al.* 1991). This study, carried out in the United States, examined the character and inter-relation of the ways in which the people studied talked about and understood the self and mental illness, and introduced the concepts of 'illness-identity work' and 'illness-identity talk'. In agreement with earlier research (Doherty 1975), Estroff and her colleagues showed that over time mental health patients often changed their statements about whether or not they saw themselves as mentally ill: over time individuals can attach many differ-ent meanings to the notion of mental illness (Estroff *et al.* 1991: 339). It is thus necessary to examine not only whether a person sees him- or herself as mentally ill, but also which meanings attach to this label, and whether these variables change over time.

The participants in Estroff's research produced five types of accounts of their mental illness – 'medical/clinical', 'emotional/developmental', 'social/situational', 'no problem', and 'religious/spiritual' – in addition to instances where the person could not or would not give any account. Statistical analysis showed that those who presented a medical/clinical, or a combined medical/clinical and emotional/developmental, explanation of their difficulties were most likely to say that they were 'mentally ill'. This only accounted for half of this sample, however, so a simple connection between the two variables cannot be claimed (Estroff et al. 1991: 359). The study also suggested a general tendency for participants to un-label themselves (as 'mentally ill') over the two years that the study was conducted. One year after the first interview was conducted, 43 per cent had changed their self-label. Estroff and colleagues speculated that the hospital context could have played an important role in the self-labelling as 'mentally ill' during the first interviews, and that a change of physical and social environment might account for some of the change in attitude (ibid.: 359).

A similar study examined mental health in-patients' own explanations of their situations, having been or being psychotic and hospitalised (Sayre 2000), exploring the seeming paradox that previous research has shown that patients' acceptance of the label of mental illness proved to result in better clinical outcome, despite most studies concluding that 'attributing one's problems to mental illness is associated with a reduced quality of life among people with schizophrenia because of perceived stigma' (ibid.: 79). Sayre argued that because of the decline in social status resulting from 'being mentally ill', the person thus labelled may experience loss of self-worth, which can add to their psychiatric symptoms by causing emotional disturbances such as anxiety, despair, and feelings of unworthiness. Among the thirty-five people in her study, all of whom were diagnosed as suffering from schizophrenia, Sayre identified six different types of explanation for their situation: 'problem', 'disease', 'crisis', 'punishment', 'ordination', and 'violation'. Compared to Estroff's study, Sayre found explanations – particularly 'punishment', 'ordination', and 'violation' – which are not part of the discourse of illness and care of mental health institutions. This is, however, not surprising, since the individual's situation was defined more narrowly by Estroff and her colleagues, as to do with 'illness'. Sayre argued that the different explanations or 'attribution accounts' can function positively, offering alternative explanations and protecting individuals and their self-perceptions and self-esteem against the negative stereotypes associated with mental illness.

Thoits (1985: 240-1) argued that the sometimes apparently 'irrational' explanations and beliefs subscribed to by mental health patients are a way to give meaning to experiences and emotions that are difficult for individuals to grasp. In Estroff's exploration of identity among people diagnosed as schizophrenic (1993), she argued that schizophrenia is an 'I am illness'. Unlike cancer or multiple sclerosis, for example, it is not 'just' something you 'have'. Mental illness is unusual in that it can be referred to both as something you *have*, an object, or as something you *are*, part of the subject. For example, one *is* 'a schizophrenic' or 'a psychotic'. To Estroff, these statements indicated how individuals locate themselves in relation to illness or diagnosis, and are aspects of 'illness talk' which reveal a person's self-labelled identification and illness explanation. Leaning towards Goffman's (1961) study of mental illness as a 'moral career', Estroff has shown in an earlier ethnographic study of a mental health day-centre in the United States (1981), that the individual identity 'mentally ill' can also be used strategically, as a resource: to manipulate social situations, to make a 'career' offering the possibility to 'be somebody', and to make a living from the economic support offered to the 'disabled' in western welfare societies. Similar conclusions have since been drawn by other research (Angrosino 1998; Barham and Hayward 1990; Braathen 1994).

However, there is more to mental illness than the social construction of identities. Barham and Hayward (1998) argued that part of the problem for mental health patients is that because of psychiatric theory and practice they are no longer thought of as persons:

To have undergone a schizophrenic breakdown is to have been dispossessed of one's right to think about oneself as a person. Instead, the person's concerns about himself or herself as person have been made subordinate to an identity as a schizophrenic. (1998: 165)

Barham and Hayward suggested that this picture is, if not directly due to, then at least upheld by, mental health research: the focus of most psychiatric and sociological studies in this field is the research subjects' identities as 'mentally ill'. They argued that a different picture of these people appears when we listen to what is being said by the people themselves. In one detailed case-study, Barham and Hayward showed how Ben, a 'chronic schizophrenic patient', has passed through many stages in his life, adopting different attitudes and strategies towards assuming, rejecting, concealing, and accepting his identity as 'mentally ill'. Depending on context, for example when he acts as an advocate for mental patients, Ben is sometimes identified solely as 'mentally ill'. In the church where he plays the organ, however, he is 'a musician' and 'a Catholic' and his identity as 'mentally ill' is 'a silent part of the self' (*ibid.*: 169).

As the introduction to this collection points out, there is generally increasing research interest in individual agency and subjectivity and the ways in which actors come to terms with uncertainty. In studies of mental illness this has marked a shift away from studying individuals solely because of their identity as 'mentally ill', towards their experiences, understandings and lives. Key issues involve the meaning to individuals of understanding their situations as 'mental illness', how individual self-understanding is transformed, and what this means to notions of identity.

The OPUS project: an innovative Danish mental health initiative

This chapter is based on an ethnographic study[4] of young, first-time mental health patients in Copenhagen, Denmark, receiving treatment following psychosis or other extreme and overwhelming mental experiences[5]. The treatment is offered within the OPUS project, which offers integrated community-based mental health care[6]. This treatment is following principles of early intervention in psychosis (Birchwood *et al.* 2000a) and based on models developed in the United States of 'assertive community treatment' and 'individual case management', which seem to offer better treatment and a better quality of life for mental health patients[7]. This out-going approach to treatment has been introduced in order to support the individual in the community, a need that has been heightened by the decline in referrals to psychiatric hospitals as part of de-institutionalisation[8].

The OPUS project introduced into Denmark these new principles of treatment and support for young people who are first-time users of mental health services. While assertive community treatment and individual case management were originally developed to assist long-time 'chronic' mental health patients, in OPUS the target-group is different: the aim is to assess and initiate intervention early in the treatment of schizophrenia, with the aim of improving individual prognoses. The project has from the start been political, trying to push the frontiers of mental health treatment in Denmark.

On inclusion in OPUS, most, although not all, of the participants are hospitalised during and subsequent to a psychotic episode. When their condition has improved and stabilised they are discharged from hospital and the project provides continuous treatment and support to the individual in the community. The participants stay in the project for approximately two years, with some flexibility for individual situations[9]. Participants have an individual case manager (or key worker) who is part of a small multi-professional team (psychiatrist, nurse, psychologist, social worker and occupational therapist). Case managers meet weekly with each of their participants – up to thirteen in total – meetings which can take place in the participant's home or the project office. Case managers offer participants personal supportive conversations as well as help with problems concerning housing, finding jobs, contact with relatives, and contact with social services.

Case managers also monitor the mental state of participants, suggesting alterations in medication to avoid relapse and new psychotic episodes. The ideology of treatment in OPUS is that if relapse can be avoided within the sensitive period following the first psychotic episode, then there is a better chance to avoid a further deteriorating prognosis and 'chronic mental illness'. Based on psychiatric assessments participants are

offered free neuroleptic medication while in the project. As part of the
'standard-package', participants are invited to join multiple-family psycho-
educational groups[10]. If it is considered beneficial, individuals can also
participate in social skills training groups[11], based on psycho-educational
and cognitive therapeutic principles. In rare cases, participants are offered
a series of twelve therapeutic meetings with their team psychologist.

OPUS offers more than medical treatment to relieve the symptoms
of mental illness or psychosocial support during the crises following
the onset of severe mental difficulties. In psycho-education, it also provides a system of explanation – a language or a discourse – which gives
meaning to the sensations and difficulties experienced by participants. In
contemporary psychiatry – as in OPUS – it is recognised that the active
understanding of patients can support their treatment and motivate them
to comply with it. The notion of 'insight into illness' [sygdomsindsigt] is
therefore an important aspect of the treatment, with regard to patients'
understandings of their difficulties (Birchwood et al. 2000b: 99; Estroff
et al. 1991: 339ff.). 'Psycho-education' has been introduced by the professionals to educate the patients, and sometimes also their relatives, about
their illnesses and their symptoms (McGorry 1995). The 'discourse of psychiatry' is no longer merely a technical means for professionals to control
the treatment of the (passive and objectified) patient. For patients this
means that they are considered as thinking subjects who act in accordance
with their knowledge and understandings. But it also means that their
knowledge and understandings are affected and changed (the attempt is
made to change them, anyway). This affects how they understand their
personal difficulties and situations, and their motivations for receiving and
complying with treatment, but it also affects how they see themselves:
who they are, who they used to be, who they are going to be, and what
they can manage in the future. Thus with the de-institutionalisation of
psychiatry, and the recent emphasis on introducing psycho-education
as an integrated part of treatment, new dimensions have been added to
issues of mental illness and identity.

These issues will now be investigated by looking at how two young
people in OPUS, Per and Eva, use psychiatric explanations to understand

their situations, and how this affects their understanding of themselves. It has been through considering their situations and stories that my theoretical argument has been developed. The argument has wider implications, however, because of the general nature of the situations in which they find themselves.

Per: reconnecting with pre-psychosis identities

The quotation from Per at the beginning of this chapter comes from a collaborative book project that was initiated in the early spring of 2000[12]. During our conversations, and in his written account, Per recounted that a few months after leaving the psychiatric ward he started in a special workplace where he could use his skills as trained toolmaker, working with machines and constructing tools. He hoped soon to be able to work full time at the workplace and then start looking for a 'real job' without subsidies.

Even though Per was supervised weekly by the staff in OPUS, and persistently drugged, he experienced one more psychotic episode and hospitalisation. On this occasion he was discharged from hospital sooner than the first time, but the experience depressed his expectations and he was granted a state early retirement pension [førtidspension]. He continued at the workplace, and is happy to have the opportunity to use his skills and to meet other people at the workplace. Two years after the first psychotic episode he feels better, confident that the new combination of drugs is helping him. With the assistance of the job consultant in OPUS he is trying to find a company where he can start working in a special supported arrangement for people receiving a pension from the state [støttejob]. If it goes well, he hopes that he can get a flexible job in a commercial company, supported financially by the municipality [fleksjob]. Maybe he can then get a 'real job'. For Per it is important to show himself and others that he can do the work he used to do. That even if the breakdown has changed his life in many ways – experiencing emotional and psychological difficulties, having to take medication, and receiving a pension – some things are still the same. Per has suggested to me that it has to do with his identity.

Per feels that he has changed in other ways. Before he used to hang out with some 'wild guys'. Now he doesn't see them any longer. Recently he saw some of them in a restaurant. For half an hour he was uncomfortable, but then he pulled himself together and went over to them and said hello. They were nice and one said to Per that he should call soon, so that they could meet. Per was happy with a positive response, and in a way he wants to call the old friend, since they used to have a laugh together. But, on the other hand, he doesn't want to, because it can never be the same as before. Per feels that, compared to his friend, he has, in a way, stopped. The friend has a job, a girlfriend, and he knows a lot of people. Per feels different now: he is isolating himself, it is difficult for him to keep a job, and he doesn't see so many people any more. Per has found a few new friends, who are more like himself, now. A problem with regard to his old friends is also that they appeared in his psychotic hallucinations and delusions: he thought they were laughing at him and trying to put him down. This still lingers. Even in the first interview I had with Per, when he was still in the psychiatric ward, he told me that he would dump his old friends and find some new.

Per is happy with the words he has learnt through the psycho-education in OPUS. They help him to explain thoughts and feelings that he sometimes still has. In social situations he sometimes still feels that people are thinking badly about him, but now he tells himself that he is having compulsive ideas [tvangstanker], which helps to alleviate the paranoia. If it continues, he can talk with the psychiatrist and get a higher dose of medication. On days when he feels bad, and has difficulties concentrating he can see it as racing thoughts [tankemylder] which he has learnt to see as a symptom of his illness, treatable with medication. Per says that thinking about his problems as symptoms of illness encourages him not to tell himself 'just to pull himself together' (and then feel bad when he can't). It reduces his feelings of guilt about the problems and difficulties he experiences. Instead he has learnt to see difficult situations as something he can practice and become better at. This makes it easier to handle.

The new bio-medical and cognitive psychological concepts and explanations Per has been taught in OPUS relieve his sense of guilt – and the pressure he felt, due to his difficulties – and also give him a new understanding of his earlier experiences. In particular, these are the difficulties he experienced before his psychosis: the anger, introversion, and the fantasies he endured through his adolescence. Now the experiences make sense to him, he understands them as symptoms of his developing mental illness.

Eva: the social challenge of preconceptions

One day I was sitting in my office in OPUS when Eva, another of my key informants, came in. She told me that lots of things were happening at that moment and it could be interesting to talk about it. Since she was early for a meeting with her case manager, we talked for a while.

Recently she had talked to her cousin, who had told her that she should not tell her friends and people that she met that she had a mental illness and had been in a psychiatric ward. Her cousin said that it was especially a bad idea to tell it to men, since it would put them off. Eva and I agreed that it, of course, is not something you mention when you first meet new people. However, it could be okay when you have got to know them a bit better. Probably there would be some who would be scared by it, and disappear, but we agreed that these people are, anyway, not too interesting to keep contact with. Eva told me that she also thinks that it is important to try to influence the preconceptions about mental illness which exist in Danish society. Eva thinks that her studies at the Politics Department at the University, as well as her membership of a user organisation for young people with mental health problems, have made her more critically aware of these problems. She thinks that it is important to try to work against preconceptions. If people like herself, who manage a university education, cannot stand up and speak openly about their experiences of mental illness, who can?

Through the user organisation Eva had met people who have described how they try to conceal their mental illness. One woman told Eva about an experience where, at a meeting for the parents in her child's school, she was asked by one of the other parents whether she was a lawyer or something, since she was so active in the discussions and so good at arguing. The woman didn't know what to say: she was ashamed to say that she has a mental illness and is receiving a *førtidspension*. Eva has discovered that she herself had preconceptions, for example towards people in receipt of this early retirement pension. She used to think that they all were miserable, doing nothing and just hanging around, often alcoholics or drug addicts. Now she has found out that while receiving a pension you can have a job, be active in different organisations, or study. It does not mean that you are 'lost'.

Eva explained how important it had been to get back to her former education after her psychosis and hospitalisation. She started up again taking only a single course, and without having to do exams. After two years she is now studying full time again. She said that it has been very important since it established some contact with who she was before she became ill. It was as if everything had fallen apart and all her dreams and ideas about her future had been destroyed. This was a terrible experience, and it was vital for her to cling on to the hope that she could resume at least part of the life she had before, and the future she was aiming for.

For Eva, her mental illness, psychosis and hospitalisation meant that her self-image, and the expectations and dreams she had for her future, had been scattered. Per and Eva are struggling to find, or reconstruct, dreams for their lives. For both it has been important to establish a connection to the life they had had before their psychosis. Per is trying to find employment where he can use the trade in which he was trained, and he hopes, over time, to be able to work full-time and without state subsidies in this trade, even if in the meantime he receives a state pension. Eva has resumed the studies she started before her mental breakdown, and even if it has been difficult for her, she feels that it has been important to re-create in this way her connection to what she used to do before, and the aspirations for the future that she used to have.

Negotiating identity

After a first episode of psychosis, and following mental health treatment, Per and Eva have to reorient their positions in life: who they are and where they are going. In this process they also have to rediscover who they were before, and in this way make sense of themselves as persons with a continuous identity. The psychoses were for them a personal breakdown, both mental and existential, and the integrity and continuity of their existence and identity were challenged by their experiences. Following psychosis they have been struggling not only to overcome that overwhelming experience and find a way to live with symptoms of mental illness, but also to see a continuity in their life and existence. They have to recreate individual 'ontological security', to take a concept from the controversial psychiatrist and critical social thinker R.D. Laing.

In *The Divided Self* (1990, first published 1959), Laing used the term 'ontological insecurity' to describe the existential situation of the person suffering from schizophrenia. He is concerned with situations where ontological security is partly or almost completely absent, looking at individual experiences of anxiety and danger which produce 'primary ontological insecurity' and consequent attempts to deal with this (*ibid.*: 39). He describes primary ontological insecurity thus:

> The individual in the ordinary circumstances of living may feel more unreal than real; in a literal sense, more dead than alive; precariously differentiated from the rest of the world, so that his identity and autonomy are always in question. He may lack the experience of his own temporal continuity. He may not possess an over-riding sense of personal consistency or cohesiveness. He may feel more insubstantial than substantial, and unable to assume that the stuff he is made of is genuine, good, valuable. And he may feel his self as partially divorced from his body. (*ibid.*: 42)

In contrast, Laing describes the situation and experience of the onto-logically secure person thus:

> A man may have a sense of his presence in the world as a real, alive, whole, and, in a temporal sense, a continuous person. As such, he can live out into the world and meet others: a world and others experienced as equally real, alive, whole, and continuous.
>
> Such a basically *ontologically* secure person will encounter all the hazards of life, social, ethical, spiritual, biological, from a centrally firm sense of his own and other people's reality and identity. (*ibid.*: 39, emphasis in the original)

Laing's assumption is that ontological insecurity is a defining characteristic of the person diagnosed with schizophrenia. It is, in other words, a static and primordial characterisation. Per and Eva, however, show us that even if their subjective feelings might accurately be described as ontological insecurity, this cannot be assumed to be static. On the contrary, it is contested and negotiated in social interaction.

From a position of ontological insecurity, Per and Eva are redefining their identities by seeking to establish direct lines of continuity with the life they lived and the dreams they had before psychosis: Per by working with his trade and seeking to get 'a real job', and Eva by returning to university and pursuing the plans she had of a student life and a job where she can use her academic training. But Per and Eva are also trying to integrate into this redefined identity an acceptance of their mental illness and the difficulties which they experience because of it. Per is using the language of psychiatry to redefine experiences he had before his psychosis, and Eva is beginning to engage in political work in organisations that try to influence public ideas about mental illness. Thus they have a double strategy for their redefined identities: first, to establish *biographical continuity with their former identities* by holding on to former dreams for the future and re-entering their previous social roles, and second, to establish *a new explanation of their situation* by conceptualising their lives and experiences before psychosis in the language of psychiatry.

The examples of Per and Eva indicate that in understanding the experiences of people who are labelled as 'mentally ill' and become users of mental health services we must consider identity as something more than a new social role and a stigmatising label. It is important to look at how individuals are challenged by, and reject or come to terms with, this role and identity, and how that relates to the extreme mental experience that was the initial reason for the labelling. This requires the integration into the discussion of theoretical developments with regard to the notion of identity. Existing anthropological and sociological studies of mental illness use the concept of identity to describe the categorisation of the individual as 'mentally ill', 'psychiatric patient', or 'user of mental health services'. However, recent sociological models of identity have addressed the changeability, fluctuation and negotiability of individual identity. As the examples of Per and Eva show, this is more in accord with the nature of the situation after an experience of mental illness.

The notion that an identity such as 'mentally ill' or 'schizophrenic' describes *the* identity of the individual is possibly a culturally specific emic understanding, as suggested by Estroff (1993). Within the sociology of identity, however, it can also be related to the work of Goffman, who has been highly influential within the field of mental illness with respect to the role adaptation or 'mortification' of in-patients in a psychiatric hospital (1961) and the concept of stigma (1963). Goffman studied the expressive techniques used by individuals to achieve and maintain social order: the continuous reproduction of everyday life is at the centre of his performance theory. In these studies Goffman concentrates on the expressive ability through which individuals develop their capacity to manage the impressions others receive of them, their *techniques of impression management* (Burkitt 1991: 58).

Central to Goffman's thinking on identity is the distinction between the inner and the outer self, a dualism that is reflected in the idea of a *personal identity* as distinct from a *social identity*. Goffman also distinguishes between the self as a character and as a performer: 'he makes it appear as though there are two selves: the self who is a mask and the residual self that it hides' (Burkitt 1991: 70). By thus stressing the meanings that individual actors give to situations and the impressions they foster of themselves, Goffman's interactionism tends toward subjectivism (*ibid.*: 69). At the same time, and paradoxically, his dramaturgical model has the serious limitation that human life may appear as an illusion, without real consequences:

> And while professional actors can leave their mask in the theatre at night before they go home – along with their make-up and costume – the selves that we create in everyday life are bound into a long-term identity, which becomes what we truly are. (Burkitt 1991: 71)

Thus 'who we are' is not only a role we play towards others, it also involves how we perceive and feel about ourselves. This is central to the distinction between *nominal identity*, the name of the identity, and *virtual identity*, what it means to bear and experience it (Jenkins 1996: 24). This conceptual distinction highlights the difference between being diagnosed as mentally ill, and what this diagnosis means to the person thus named. The identity ascribed by others, or otherwise achieved by the individual in social interaction, *does* have a meaning for the individual in question.

Jenkins' theory of the *internal-external dialectic of social identification* (1996) draws on these notions of nominal and virtual identity to clarify that identity is, first, social and cultural by being connected to a name – a concept which is related to a specific social and cultural context – and, second, experienced: felt and given meaning by the person who is bearing it. These two dimensions are parallel, two sides of the same coin. In this way Jenkins supports his argument for the intrinsically social and cultural character of identity and the self. As he writes:

> If identity is a necessary prerequisite for social life, the reverse is also true. Individual identity – embodied in selfhood – is not meaningful in isolation from the social world of other people. Individuals are unique and variable, but selfhood is thoroughly socially constructed: in the processes of primary and subsequent socialisation, and in the ongoing processes of social interaction within which individuals define

and redefine themselves and others throughout their lives. (Jenkins 1996: 20)

Jenkins argues that identity is created during two processes, one external and one internal, which are related dialectically:

> The self is, therefore, altogether individual and intrinsically social. It arises within social interaction. It is constructed within the internal-external dialectic of social identification. It draws upon the external social environment of people and things for its content. Even though it is the most individualised of identities – we might call it customised – selfhood is absolutely social. It depends for its ongoing security upon the validation of others, in its initial emergence and in the dialect of continuing social identification. (*ibid.*: 50)

The need to acknowledge both what is going on inside the person – their thoughts, doubts, feelings and aspirations – and the social situation and context in general, is thus crucial to the theorisation of identity. Craib criticises conventional sociological theories for not taking the experience, feelings, and thoughts of the individual sufficiently into account:

> sociological approaches to identity or the self tend to assume that the world is peopled by normotic personalities, by people who have no subjective or inner experience. (Craib 1998: 9)

Craib is stressing the need to focus on the process of internal negotiation involved in individual identity, and on the individual experience of an identity that is stable, in the sense that it is continuous.

> Social identities can come and go but my identity goes on as something which unites all the social identities I ever had, have or will have. My identity always overflows, adds to, transforms the social identities that are attached to me. ... My identity is not the same as my *social* identities. (*ibid.*: 4, emphasis in original)

Identity, social role, and discourse

In experiencing and struggling with fundamental personal uncertainty – ontological insecurity – Per and Eva are representative of the persons receiving mental health treatment who I have been in contact with in OPUS. But in other ways they are more particular than representative. For example, unlike Per and Eva, not everyone uses a combination of strategies to redefine their identities and create a continuity in their experience of who they are, were, and will be. To Per and Eva the combination of strategies allow them both come to terms with their experiences of mental illness and to create a continuity in their perception of themselves.

My data suggest that it is those who before their contact with mental health treatment had already established an occupational role (in a specific job, or as a student of a certain subject) to which they related positively, who can re-establish this social role as central to their identity and future position in society. Those without such a occupational role on which to fall back seem to be more inclined to base their social identity on their status as mentally ill and a recipient of mental health services. This highlights the importance to the individual of continuity between past and future social roles in the present manifestation of individual identity. It also affirms that it is positively important for the individual to take an active role in the development of a 'functional sense of self' during recovery from severe mental illness (Davidson and Strauss 1992).

Furthermore, Per and Eva both generally accept that psychiatric concepts and theories explain their experiences and situation. This is not always the case. When the individuals in OPUS avoid the psychiatric explanations of their situation, in some cases it is because, due to their prevailing and overwhelming psychotic experiences, they are in a situation where they are unable to start the process of redefining their identity. In other cases, people actively refuse the psychiatric concepts and theories, which they feel do not provide a satisfactory explanation of their experiences. Instead, they creatively replace or combine the psychiatric concepts and theories with alternative systems of explanation available in the cultural repertoire of society, for example psychodynamic or religious explanations (Larsen n.d.). Scared by the stigmatisation attached to being a mental health patient, some attempt to hold on to their existing self-understanding by distancing themselves from mental health treatment and its language and system of explanation. They prefer to see themselves as free agents and not dependent on the biomedical treatment of their bodies.

Mental health and social institutions present a certain discourse, a particular understanding and explanation of the situation and life of the people with whom I am concerned. This system of explanation is one of many possible in the social world of these young people, and it can be rejected in favour of another (cf. Estroff 1991; Larsen n.d.; Sayre 2000). The strength of the system of explanation or discourse offered during psycho-education is that it offers ways to deal with the mental problems and social difficulties that the individuals experience, and relieves them of the pressure of guilt. Psychiatric understandings and explanations can help people who, after a mental breakdown, often need a break from psychologically demanding pressures to initiate change and action.

Teaching psychiatric discourses to mental health patients can be seen as an attempt to overcome the ideological dualism of mind and body which still prevails in western medicine and psychiatry (Luhrmann 2000). Along these lines, it can also be understood as an introduction of 'symbolic healing' (Dow 1986) to modern psychiatry. In psycho-education it is acknowledged that it is important for the healing process that individual patients should give meaning to their situation and recovery by using concepts and systems of explanation. The discourse of psychiatry can be understood as a 'particularised mythic world' which will be shared during psycho-education by the therapist and the patient, enabling the therapist to attach the emotions of the patient to the shared symbols – the concepts and system of explanation – and manipulate these: hence symbolic healing (Larsen 2002a: 181-225, 2002c). As is suggested in the introduction to this collection, the attempt by modern biomedicine to impose 'particular cultural scripts' is powerful, since it is backed by the legitimate authority of science and the professional status and power of experts.

Recreation of individual continuity

The cases of Per and Eva suggest that George Herbert Mead's notion that consciousness cannot become an object to itself can be contested. Mead (1913) developed the notion of 'I' and 'me' to designate two different sides of the individual, the agent part and the self-aware, reflective part. The 'I' is the acting presence of the self within the group, which acts as a stimulus to others, and the 'me' is the attitude of self-reflection, which treats as an object the body's responses to others during interaction:

> The two faces of the social self are difficult to describe because, as Mead points out, consciousness cannot become an object to itself, and so the 'I' can never appear as an object of contemplation…as soon as an impulse or an object enters consciousness and is articulated through the inner conversation as an idea, wish or desire, it becomes an object in contemplation and therefore part of the 'me'. (Burkitt 1991: 38)

However, since it is possible for the individual to recollect what or how he or she felt and experienced in a specific situation in the past, it is possible for the individual consciousness to reflect on the thoughts and feelings – or consciousness – of itself. Central to this argument is the dimension of time. The individual consciousness can be an object to itself insofar as the individual experiences himself or herself in time and can think back to feelings and thoughts he or she had in the past. Even if the sense of a core individual identity – as suggested by Craib above – does not change under normal situations, the actual content of the core can be changed without the experiential core identity being lost.

However, in situations of major personal crisis such as a mental breakdown, that sense of a core identity can be lost, resulting in ontological insecurity, to use Laing's concept. The sense of a constant identity core, giving stability in self-image is lost. The sense of biographical continuity is broken, the life is disrupted (Becker 1997). This is an existential crisis: a crisis of identity. After experiencing a psychosis the individual's world no longer fits together as it used to do, it is falling apart. Escaping the hallucinations, delusions and compulsive ideas [*tvangstanker*], does not mean that life can easily be resumed as it was. The person concerned becomes aware about possibilities in their own imagination, that their senses and thoughts can delude them. Whether they see this as a special ability, or a personal weakness, or a malfunctioning of your cognition, or a bio-chemical illness, the experience of mental breakdown has changed their sense of themselves. They are no longer the person they thought they were. They are in a state of uncertainty.

My material shows that the mental breakdowns experienced by the young people in OPUS are also existential crises. The mental breakdown questions the integrity of their individual identity. The psychosis or severe psychological difficulties undermines their sense of continuity with their former self-creation-project[13]. The ambitions they had before are scattered by the mental and psychological difficulties they experience. Some try to re-create or re-establish continuity by fastening on to aspects of the image that they used to have of themselves. For others this endeavour is, for the time being, anyway, too dificult.

Giddens' characterisation (1991) of the individual lifespan as 'internally referential' is right, in that individuals do strive to establish biographical continuity, in two senses: presenting a consistent life project and directing their life choices. But, as Giddens has observed (*ibid.*: 55), many potential stories could be told about the development of an individual's selfhood. It is, therefore, important to be aware that this internal referentiality is a *narrative construct*, consisting of happenings in the life of the individual that can be retold as significant events using another 'master plot' when other circumstances prevail. This is not to say, however, that the continuity in life is an illusion, as Becker (1997: 190ff.) has suggested. As an element in narrative constructs, 'continuity' is used to create order in the life story when highlighting life events and dreams for the future within culturally specific discursive frameworks. Individual identity is thus based in a sense of continuity of self, of some central core of self that persists over time. At the same time self-understanding is dynamic, it can change with circumstances, changing its perspective on the core of individuality, creating continuity over time by tracing basic aspects of 'Who I am' in 'Who I was before', 'Who I am going to be' and 'What I am going to do in the future'. Individual identity is also context-sensitive and influenced by powerful external discourses. In these ways identity can be, and is, negotiated socially.

With a newly gained dominant self-understanding individuals can re-interpret earlier experiences. Per, for example, used to think that he wasn't able to pull himself together in social situations that he found difficult. Now he feels relieved from the pressure of guilt, because, equipped with the explanations he has been taught in OPUS, he can see the difficulties that he has experienced, and for which he used to blame himself, as symptoms of his illness.

Conclusion

To an individual identity means both 'being distinctive' and 'remaining the same', it entails both difference and similarity (Jenkins 1996: 4). Identity is also experienced, felt, and thought, and thus subjective. It therefore makes no sense to talk about objective, fixed identity: it is always situational, relational, and placed within a context. As such it can be negotiated. New perspectives and new experiences – as well as new social roles – can cause identity to change, to be seen in another way. What is important, if not crucial, to the maintenance of identity, is that the individual manages to uphold the sense that he or she remains the same and is distinctive from others.

This is where discourse is important. By changing discourse, and seeing oneself with a fresh perspective, it is possible for a person to see – or rather discover – aspects of their self, and their past experiences and actions, which can make visible a continuity of their identity which was not apparent before. So even if, through social interaction and negotiation, an individual assumes a new identity he will be able to experience this as authentic: his 'true identity', the one he always was, but just never before was able to see clearly. Discourse, social interaction, and the individual experience of continuity of self thus play together in the social negotiation of individual identity.

I have argued that in the individual uncertainty that follows a mental breakdown, and psychiatric treatment and psychosocial support, there are two basic moves that may re-establish a sense of continuity of identity. One is to *establish biographical continuity*, by trying to recreate the life the individual had before, the things they used to do, and to continue following the dreams and plans for the future that they used to have. This involves fundamental reconstruction work, since the mental breakdown has made the person, often painfully, aware that they have limits that they cannot transgress. This may make it difficult for them to manage stressful situations. Some people have also great difficulties engaging in social interaction and basic communication with other people.

The second move that can be made to re-establish the sense of continuity of identity following a mental breakdown, is for the individual to establish *a new explanation of their situation* by fundamentally changing the perspective from which they see themselves. They can reconstruct their identity as 'being mentally ill'. This is not just a new layer to be added to their identity. It fundamentally changes the way they see their life, their future, and their past. The past has not the least importance because in order for the self-understanding 'being mentally ill' to be established, it is important that some sense of continuity in one's experience of identity can be constructed, as already discussed.

The young people accepting this new identity therefore feel that the psychiatric diagnosis, confirming their status as mentally ill, explains many things in their past, even before their actual breakdown. It makes sense of their former experiences, sensations and actions. With their newly gained self-understanding as 'mentally ill' they can thus see continuity: from the situation they are in now back to who they were, what they did, and what they experienced before their breakdown. As Per said, 'The diagnosis gave an answer to many things'.

The discourse of psychiatry, as presented and taught in psycho-education, offers the patient understandings and a system of explanation that can be used to recreate a sense of individual continuity during a social negotiation of identity. The discourse of psychiatry is not the only applicable explanation of the experiences and situations of mental health patients (Larsen n.d.) but it can be useful in providing explanations that can be communicated and understood by others. However, as Eva pointed out during an interview, OPUS and other mental health institutions do not constitute the whole society. Other perspectives can still be applied in other social situations, and 'mental illness' does not have to embrace her entire life.

Notes

1. This quotation, and the description that follows beneath, is taken from Per's own written narrative of what happened to him and what he experienced (Larsen 2002b: 65-85). In this chapter pseudonyms are used for all names and person-specific indications of place.

2. Due to diverse practice in the existing literature, the concepts of mental illness, psychiatry, and mental health care, service, and treatment, will be used interchangeably to designate the empirical field of investigation.

3. Along with the focus on identity, a dominant perspective within sociological studies has been a historically oriented critical perspective on the workings of the social institutions surrounding mental illness (Foucault 1973; Rosen 1968; Scull 1989). For recent discussions of sociological perspectives on mental illness see Bowers (1995) and Busfield (2000).

4. The ethnographic study involved two years of fieldwork over a three and a half year period from April 1998. My access to this field was made possible by my role as project evaluator, employed by the municipality of Copenhagen. The study provided empirical data for my Ph.D research at the Department of Sociological Studies, University of Sheffield (Larsen 2002a). The research was supported financially through a scholarship from the Danish Research Agency (Forskningsstyrelsen).

5. The people included are between 18 and 45 years old, and have received a psychiatric diagnosis within the schizophrenic spectrum, following the diagnostic classification system ICD-10, F2.

6. OPUS was introduced in 1998 as an experimental project financed partly from research funds from the Danish Medical Research Council, the Ministry of Health,

and the Ministry of Social Affairs. The medical research team concerned constructed it as a randomised controlled trial, allowing some individuals included in the project to receive the special treatment and others to function as part of a control-group receiving standard mental health treatment. The intensive treatment and support is provided to individuals over a two-year period after which they are referred to the relevant standard service. Originally, the project was time limited, but it is now made permanent.

7. The treatment in OPUS is based on a model originally developed in Madison, Wisconsin, in the United States, by psychiatrist Leonard Stein and psychologist Mary Ann Test (Stein and Santos 1998).

8. The de-institutionalisation of psychiatry was first initiated in Denmark in the late 1980s (Knudsen *et al.* 1992).

9. Until now, the length of stay has been 27.5 months on average, with a range between 24 and 37 months (Larsen 2001).

10. The multiple-family psycho-educational group is set up and run following the guidelines developed by American psychiatrist William McFarlane (McFarlane *et al.* 1991).

11. The social skills training groups are following guidelines in a Swedish adaptation of the principles developed by Robert Lieberman (Borell 1996).

12. I recruited participants for the book project among the 15 service users in OPUS who were key informants for my research. I interviewed them on a half-yearly basis over a two and a half year period (Larsen 2003). During my third round of interviews I asked if they would like to write about their situation and experiences of receiving mental health treatment for the first time. Eight have, on and off, participated in at least one of the sixteen meetings in the editorial board, and six contributed with their individual stories for the book which has been published by an independent Danish publisher (Larsen 2002b). Two of the contributors were not very experienced writers, so I arranged with each to meet four or five times and continue the writing on their first drafts. We were sitting together in front of the computer and I did the writing while we talked. The method is a combination of conducting an unstructured interview and functioning as a dictaphone.

13. See Davidson and Strauss (1992) for a similar observation.

TEN

MEDICALIZED EXPERIENCE AND THE ACTIVE USE OF BIOMEDICINE

Hanne O. Mogensen

I didn't reach here [the hospital] until today because my husband was not at home, and he had to ask his relatives for money, and he had to be there to take me and the child on his bike. And also, my mother-in-law went to a funeral and she had to come home and look after the other children while I was gone. (Mother, interviewed after consultation at the Out-Patients Department of a rural hospital, eastern Uganda)

He is a good father. He always leaves some medicine in the house when he goes so that at least we can manage while he is away. He buys them from Indians or maybe this Essential Drugs Program. I can't remember the names but you can see them on the bottles...It is not only for my daughter, but also for others in the family, like my mother-in-law if she needs something while he is gone. (Young mother, eastern Uganda)

Introducing an article with quotes such as these could signify the initiation of a discussion of various topics, *e.g.* patients' dependency on money, young mothers' incapacity to act on their own, irrational drug use, commercialization of health, or the misuse of donor assistance (Essential Drugs being sold on markets). My purpose, however, is different. I wish to use the mothers quoted above to draw attention to the communal effort and moral negotiations that are required to get access to biomedical health care in eastern Uganda. These mothers will, in the context of an exploration of the notions of biomedicine and medicalization, help me to explore the tenacious assumption in the medicalization debate, that the expansion of biomedicine brings with it processes of individualization and decontextualization (Gordon 1998).

The coercive impact of biomedicine entering people's life all over the world is a recurrent topic in medical anthropology, and is often called 'medicalization'. Medicalization has been discussed by many scholars since the term entered the social science literature in the 1970s (Conrad 1992; Conrad and Schneider 1980; Illich 1977; Kleinman 1995b; Nichter 1989; Scheper-Hughes 1992). Resistance towards the expansion of biomedicine has been discussed, in particular, in relation to women's health and the medicalization of reproductive health (Bell 1987; Gijsbergs van Wijk *et al.* 1996; Kaufert and Gilbert 1986). Among anthropologists another recurrent topic has been the consequences of medicalization in developing countries (Nichter 1989; Scheper-Hughes 1992). Besides the unfortunate health consequences that over- and uncontrolled medicalization may have, the concern with medicalization is centred on the processes of individualization and decontextualization that are assumed to accompany medicalization. But how exactly do tablets and stethoscopes do that? Are these processes, as Scheper-Hughes (1992) has phrased it, swallowed with a pill?

When basing our analysis on people's experience, it is difficult to identify the processes that are assumed to accompany the expansion of biomedicine. When trying to understand matters from the practical point of view of people employing biomedicine as one out of many treatment options, biomedicine provides opportunities and is not experienced as a system constraining practice. Biomedicine is, like any other treatment option, used to steer through troubled waters, to create possibilities and hopes. The choice to use it is not more rational than any other treatment choice. Biomedicine is, like anything else, employed to find a way through the uncertainties of health as well as the uncertainties of moral negotiations and social life. The dehumanizing effect that is often associated with bio-medicalization is difficult to identify in a Ugandan context. Obtaining access to biomedicine is a social process, and Uganda is still a country in which much sickness and death are due to insufficient medicalization, rather than over-medicalization.

Recent anthropological literature has been more interested in biomedicine as employed by social agents, than in biomedicine as a hegemonic system and ideology. In a book edited by Lock and Kaufert (1997) several examples are given of resistance, not to, but through, biomedicine. The contributors to the book, of whom some have long been actively participating in gender and/or medicalization debates, join some recent developments within anthropology. They wish to highlight the pragmatics of everyday life, in the way that women respond to and use knowledge and technology. They want to draw attention to these women's agency, and avoid portraying them as passive victims. Women, it is argued throughout this volume, are not passive recipients of technological innovations. They are actively and creatively responding to biomedicine, and their agency should be situated in the context of their lived experience. While not wishing to question the hegemonic impact biomedical technology and institutions may have, these authors draw attention to women as social agents. Biomedical technologies, they argue, create possibilities (*e.g.* in the form of pain relief, cure, or fertility) as well as new forms of illness and domination.

This discussion is but another expression of the classical debate in anthropology over structure and agency. Does biomedicine as a system do something to people, or do people do something with biomedicine? The pendulum has swung towards agency in my discussion too. In the following I use my experience from field research in Uganda to look at what people do with biomedicine. In 1995-96 I did 12 months fieldwork among the Jop'Adhola in southeastern Uganda. I will also draw briefly upon material from Zambia, where I did 10 months fieldwork in 1993. While neither of the studies was from the outset a study of biomedicine as such (one being a study of people's experience of AIDS, the other of mothers' interpretations of symptoms and household negotiations over health care choices), they have provided insight into biomedicine as part of everyday life. When trying to relate my material to the medicalization debate I have had difficulties employing the terms: difficulties in grasping what we mean by 'medicalization' and 'biomedicine.' This article is, therefore, an attempt to employ my experience from the two field settings to scrutinize these terms. First I will outline how they are used in anthropological literature and then I will turn to Uganda.

The '-zations' of medicalization

There is no essential medicine, independent of time and space, says Kleinman (1995b:23). We should talk about not one, but a plurality of biomedicines, suggests Good (1995). But in spite of all the heterogeneity, there is believed to be something special about biomedicine and its Western roots. Kleinman suggests that the term 'biomedicine' refers to the established institutional structure and its epistemological and ontological commitments (Kleinman 1995b:25). I would like to add to this the substances, the pharmaceuticals and biotechnology which people in non-Western settings often explicitly point to as characterizing 'Western medicine.' The epistemological and ontological commitments of biomedicine are expected to cause *individualization* and *decontextualization* through the institutional setting, the pills, and the technology.

Inspired by Charles Taylor, Gordon (1988) discusses these commitments and their origin in the Western traditions of 'naturalism' (also called science) and 'individualism.' On the one hand, biomedicine has grown out of naturalism, which asserts the autonomy of 'nature' from the supernatural, the moral, the cultural, and the social. Biomedicine approaches sickness as a 'natural' phenomenon taking place in nature's human representative, the body, which is seen as separate from the mind. The parts of nature, and therefore also of the body, are considered to be autonomous elements that are related to each other through causation. Each can be removed from the context without altering the identity of the part, i.e. they may be *decontextualized*. Simultaneously, biomedicine is founded in the constellation of values in Western culture that we may call individualism: the idea that society is constituted of autonomous distinct individuals who can distance themselves from their social and cultural constraints and rationally reflect upon nature and themselves (Gordon 1988).

Many concerns have been raised regarding what happens when naturalism and individualism enter new spheres of life all over the world. The fear is that they cause misery of all kinds to be defined as medical, considered to be soluble with technical fixes, and that they will result in the decontextualization and individualization of people and their problems. These concerns have been debated in the social science literature since the 1970s (Conrad 1992; Conrad and Schneider 1980; Illich 1976) and have also become central to studies of the Third World (Nichter 1989; Scheper-Hughes 1992).

Sociologists dealing with medicalization have often done so in relation to social control, and therefore many of these discussions centre on how societies, through *professionalization* and *institutionalization*, develop therapeutic styles of social control, which transfer deviance and deviant behaviour, such as madness, alcoholism, homosexuality, eating disorders, or compulsive gambling, into the sphere of medicine. In comparison, scholars working in other parts of the world draw attention to the decontextualization and individualization of broader social and political problems like suffering, hunger, and sickness. Kleinman discusses how medicalization can bring a misguided search for magic bullets for complex social problems, such as the social consequences of the Cultural Revolution in China. Various kinds of traumatic experience during the Cultural Revolution were transformed into a psychiatric disorder, neurasthenia, extensively diagnosed in China but rarely employed as a diagnosis by Western psychiatrists. Neurasthenia thereby became a tool for political control (Kleinman 1986, 1995b). Scheper-Hughes discusses how the medicalization of hunger and childhood malnutrition in north-eastern Brazil is the consequence of economic oppression and distorted political relations. Mothers' learn to treat their children's ailing with tablets, though the root of the problem is malnutrition, poor access to clean water, and, more generally, poverty. With every pill they swallow they are made to forget this connection to the politico-economic causes of their misery (Scheper-Hughes 1992). Nichter also raises the concern that, in India, medicalization, in the form of pharmaceuticalization and commercialization, decontextualizes and individualizes problems and people. The overwhelming availability of pharmaceuticals on the private market makes patients accustomed to treating even minor symptoms with many drugs. This prevents the development of a consciousness about the relationship of health, and ill-health, to the environment (Nichter 1989).

Medicalization is thus said to come about through many interlinked processes: individualization, decontextualization, professionalization, institutionalization, bureaucratization, pharmaceuticalization, and commercialization. Whereas professionalization, institutionalization, and bureaucratization are debated in studies of the Western world, there is a larger concern with pharmaceuticalization and the commercialization of health in the Third World. As discussed by Ferguson (1981), medicalization in these parts of the world is often only weakly linked to the presence of professional biomedical practitioners. Biomedical care has developed in response to the way in which pharmaceutical products are made available through the market economy.

Whether dealing with Western or non-Western societies, the concern is always, however, that medicalization will bring *decontextualization* and *individualization*. This concern is related to the understanding of biomedicine as deriving from a combination of, on the one side, naturalism and its notion of the natural physical *body* (where elements are not altered by their context), and, on the other, individualism and the rational *mind* (which can reflect upon itself and distance itself from its surroundings).

In the following I will show how people live with biomedicine in southeastern Uganda and then I explore what is at stake for them when the body/mind distinction is enacted in their everyday life.

Medicalization in Uganda and the recreation of biomedicine

Uganda has in the past decades experienced a vast expansion in the availability of biomedical health care. Prior to the years of political instability and civil war Uganda had one of the continent's best functioning public health care systems. Free health care reached a large proportion of the population. The services offered then were not as varied as those offered today, and the distance between health units was often longer than it is now. That time is nevertheless remembered by Ugandans with nostalgia. The public health care system deteriorated considerably during the 1970s and 1980s, but since Museveni came into power in 1986, Uganda has experienced goodwill from donors and renewed investments have been made in the health care system. In addition, an even more noticeable medicalization has taken place along more informal lines and through processes of commercialization and pharmaceuticalization (*cf.* Ferguson 1981). Pharmaceuticals are sold on every market and in numerous small shops in every trading centre (Whyte 1991, 1992). Anybody with a little capital can set up a business selling pharmaceuticals and combine this with various degrees of diagnostic technology and counselling. Most of them have no authorization and many have no formal medical training.

Even within the public sector we may talk about commercialization and pharmaceuticalization. Due to the appalling working conditions of the staff, informal fees have been part of service delivery for decades, and now fees have become formalized. People expect to purchase tangible goods for the money they pay, and pharmaceuticals are perceived to be essential to the quality of care. Health workers in the government health system are in competition with informal providers of pharmaceuticals, but they also cooperate closely with the private sphere, to which they often belong alongside their job in the public sector. There is thus no clear-cut division between public and private, nor between biomedical and other treatment options. As I have discussed elsewhere (Mogensen 2000) idioms of distress are developing which are dealt with outside the formal biomedical sphere, but which anyhow draw upon the symbols, substances and technology of the biomedical sector. Practitioners treating these ailments often have some connection to the formal health care system, though little or no formal training (e.g. nursing aides, gate keepers, etc.)

As discussed by Whyte (1997), the possibility of buying pharmaceuticals makes the more costly and time-consuming process of seeking answers from diviners, and performing complex healing rituals involving the extended family, something to be avoided. But as Whyte has also shown (1992) pharmaceuticals are not neutral objects, independent of the social and cultural context in which they are used. They move in and out of social relations and cultural interpretations. Furthermore, although the availability of pharmaceuticals may temporarily exempt a person from entering the social conflicts of the extended family, in a longer time perspective, decisions that lead to the choice of biomedicine are, as the following case will illustrate, also part of social negotiations.

While staying with the Jop'Adhola, one of several ethnic groups living in southeastern Uganda, I followed a number of small children closely. I regularly discussed them with their caretakers and accompanied them in their healthcare seeking behaviour. Often I recommended visits to the health unit and offered assistance in the form of transport and money. My involvement with the families provided insight into the many negotiations surrounding any health care choice, including those initiated by my presence and my suggestions. I was at one stage deeply involved in the heated discussions among the members of one family on how to interpret a mother's loss of her two children and what to do to ensure future children's survival. The following is primarily based on the mother's retrospective account of her own healthseeking behaviour, but it is also an account told with a view to future actions, in an attempt to involve me in decision making.

The Jop'Adhola are a Nilotic group closely related to the Luo of Western Kenya. Their patrilineal system implies that a woman upon marriage moves in with her husband, his parents and brothers and their wives. A man and his family are therefore often surrounded by the homesteads of his brothers and paternal cousins. Bridewealth, paid by the husband's family, is typically relatively high, but is usually not paid until after a couple of births. Often bridewealth is paid over many years, if ever fully paid at all. Marriage, thus, is an ongoing process and a young woman struggles to achieve a secure status as a properly married woman, with a family-in-law who will be responsible for her and her children, even if her husband fails to be so. Achieng, a young woman who was married to a son in the homestead next to my assistant's home, had trouble realizing this. She had lost both of her two children when they were only six and five months old. After I had made a number of regular visits to the family, she once came to my assistant's home, where I stayed, to seek advice from us. She was very puzzled, she said, about why she was losing her children and she would like our opinion on the matter.

The first one was sick for three days before she died. She was six months old. The other one died after only one day of sickness, at five months old. In both cases she took them for treatment to the health centre. Achieng and her husband went to the health centre on the second day of sickness and they were told that she did not have enough blood. But she had never been sick before and it had never been necessary to take her to a health centre before. Previously, they had bought a few tablets for her, chloroquine and aspirin, but she always got better after swallowing these. She was a healthy baby and she had just started crawling. The boy vomited one day and then died. She went to the health centre with him in the morning. Fortunately they live nearby so she could walk there, and her husband had left a bit of money with her. They gave him tablets, chloroquine and aspirin. He was sick, but not very sick, not to a death point. When he did not improve in the afternoon she went back to the health centre, but the health worker told her to go home and look for local medicine, because if the medicine she had been given in the morning had not worked, then it must be 'family affairs'. He died that same evening.

When people are quarrelling in the family Achieng hears them say that it is *juok* disturbing the home. *Juok* is a spiritual force that in various ways causes fortune or misfortune, *e.g.* through witchcraft, ancestors or transgressions of ritual proscriptions. The brother of the father-in-law did not recognize that *juok* had come to him. He did not respect it properly by building the shrine and doing the sacrifices he was supposed to. Therefore the *juok* was now annoyed — and when annoyed it can kill. If celebrated properly, it does not do the work of killing. But her father-in-law took it in a Christian manner, not minding about his own brother's neglect of *juok*. He joined in family conversations about it, but he did not take it seriously. Instead he blamed Achieng for being irresponsible, since her children had died when she had taken them to her parents' home to visit. He also blamed her for delaying in going to the health centre when they were sick. But she assured us that she had never delayed.

The mother-in-law had told us one day that she also thought it was a kind of *juok* killing Achieng's children. She herself lost her last born when she was five years old. She also died while outside the home. It was during the wars, when Museveni was taking over from Obote, so they had to run away. They never managed to collect the child's 'shade' (*i.e.* to ceremonially bring her back to the home), and, since then, children from the home had been dying when away from home. It was a disorderly death that was never brought back in order. A diviner had confirmed this and Achieng and her husband had been given medicine to protect future children, but maybe that just sent the *juok* to another family member until ceremonies would be done to reestablish order. On another day we heard her criticize all her daughters-in-law for not taking her grandchildren for immunization and treatment in time. 'But does she ever provide any assistance for us, so that we can go there?', one of them said to the others, after the mother-in-law had left.

After her long monologue Achieng ended by saying that now we knew her story, and since she was pregnant again she would like to know if we had any advice for her, because she would like to 'join hands' and do everything possible for her children to survive. My assistant emphasized that, even if she went on with this 'juok-business', she should not forget to bring her children to the health centre for immunization and check ups. Achieng nodded and listened carefully. 'My husband usually gives me money to go when he has some', she said.

We knew from our daily interaction with the family that the husband of

Achieng had given his parents much trouble. He had been stealing things and the parents had had to pay six cows for what he had stolen. Therefore they now refused to assist him economically and pay bridewealth for his wife. I also heard the mother-in-law complaining that Achieng was 'stubborn' (not respectful enough towards her parents-in-law). She thought she knew better than everybody else because she had been to school for six years — and still she did not succeed in keeping her children alive. Besides cooking and caring for children, a good mother should also have good manners and know how to show respect to other people. Once you are married to a family you have to be well disciplined and jolly when visitors from the husband's side come. They will consider your character in case of help with sickness. Caring for children can therefore never be seen as limited to the mother's interaction with her children.

What is obviously at stake in these negotiations is blame and responsibility. It is, however, not simply a question of placing guilt, but a matter of identifying how and by whom, action needs to be taken so that life can continue in a desirable direction.

Achieng and her husband adhered to the explanation about some kind of *juok*, which, however, did not get in the way of visits to the health unit. *Juok* not only removed the blame from them, it also highlighted existing conflicts within the family, between the cousins of her husband, and between fathers and sons. It also highlighted Achieng's, and her children's, membership of the family, even though no bridewealth had been paid for her. The father-in-law had no interest in highlighting these conflicts between his own and his brother's family. If he initiated the ceremonies to 'finish the *juok*', he, furthermore, would indirectly acknowledge Achieng as a daughter-in-law, and would also be obliged to pay the bridewealth for her. On the one hand, he said that her children's sickness 'just came', and nobody should be blamed, while simultaneously he drew upon a public health discourse about the individual responsibility of the mother, Achieng. 'He takes it in a Christian manner', Achieng said, and by that she complained that he made her children's sickness a matter between her and God (hence, of an accident), not between her and the people around her. While Christianity is something that everybody would say they believe in, it can also signify withdrawal from family obligations through the refusal to participate in ceremonies concerned with *juok*. Notions of accident, something that just happens, and agency, something caused by an intentional agent, are, through these different diagnoses, played out against each other to challenge, call attention to, reshape or ignore social relations and mutual responsibilities among relatives.

As Whyte and Whyte (1981) have outlined, explanations of misfortune in Africa can generally be divided into two categories: as the result of an 'agent' (a witch, an ancestor, a relative cursing, etc.) and as the result of symbolic pollution, as in Mary Douglas's (1966) discussion of dirt as matter out of place. Pollution forces strike when rules are broken, when categories are mixed, when proper order is not maintained (Douglas 1966: 4-5). The power of symbolic pollution inheres in the structure of ideas, a power by which the structure is expected to protect itself, it is not a power vested in humans or other agents (Douglas 1966: 113). Pollution forces are anonymous and neutral. They are like laws of nature and beyond passion and conflict between people. The discourse on AIDS in southern Zambia that I encountered in the early 1990s presented AIDS as a result of symbolic pollution, as the consequence of the breach of laws of order and control. It was an accident. Nobody in particular was blamed. Regarding specific cases, AIDS was, however, often interpreted within the discourse of blame and human agency, *i.e.* people sending sickness to each other (Mogensen 1995). Hence notions of accident and willful action are in flux within interpretations of AIDS, as they are within most of the diagnoses employed by the people I lived among in Uganda (Mogensen 2000), as is also illustrated in discussions about *juok* in the above case. What is intriguing, however, is that this relationship is not only found in African explanations of misfortune but also within discourses about biomedicine. Achieng defended herself and her innocence by referring to her visits to the health centres, but her father-in-law used his references to this same health care system to point to her responsibility for the misfortune. Notions of agency and accident are as much at stake, and in flux, with respect to biomedicine as they are in relation to other explanations of misfortune. I will now show how this is exactly what the mind/body distinction, and notions of individualization and decontextualization, are expressions of.

Wilful action and accident

Medicalization scholars criticize biomedicine for its commitments to naturalism and individualism which have generated the distinction between a natural, physical and docile body, and a rational, individual mind that can distance itself from its social and cultural constraints. These ontological commitments are expected to become models for social interaction when biomedicine is employed.

From an external point of view it may seem that naturalism and individualism become models for societies, and for social interaction, through biomedicine. But when exploring everyday life, we may also catch sight of how different societies and social contexts influence how they are used. This replaces the question of what medicalization does to people, with the question of what people do with biomedicine, when reaching out to act upon the world. One way forward, I suggest, inspired by Kirmayer (1988), is to look at this through the notions of personhood and agency implicit in biomedicine and how not only tablets, but also these notions, are used in everyday social negotiations.

The terms decontextualization and individualization are sometimes used interchangeably, but they cover two different processes, which are at times contradictory and sometimes complementary. Whereas one attributes sickness to involuntary and *morally neutral* causes (decontextualization), the other *blames* the inappropriate behaviour of individuals (individualization). They thus imply different notions of personhood and agency, which are played out against other notions of personhood and agency when biomedicine is used to do something about concrete problems.

Naturalism, as Gordon (1988) further discusses, is founded on the principle that nature is physical matter obeying natural mechanistic laws, and is thus orderly and predictable. It is a reality that is omnipresent, universal, eternal and absolute — and therefore beyond time and space. It is thus assumed that sickness happens to people, that it is a mechanism; good, bad or righteous behaviour does not count. Instead of judging, medicine diagnoses, explains 'how' — but not 'why' (not the meaning of sickness) — and treats. The *cause* of sickness derives from mechanistic laws, and the *responsibility* to do something lies with the health care system and its technology. Nobody is *blamed*. Parallel to the notion of the docile mechanic body, and therefore of morally neutral sickness, is the notion of the rational mind mastering the body and being responsible for appropriate behaviour. The locus of human agency and subjective awareness is confined to the mind.

A view of the person as capable of withdrawing from their social and cultural context is predominant in public health models, and therefore also most health interventions in the Third World. Such models focus on individuals as rational agents, deciding — independently of their context — how to respond to recommendations made by health services. It is assumed that individuals rationally evaluate information and are free from outside constraints in taking action (Yoder 1997). Knowledge and culture are distinctive and autonomous parts of a person, and like any other part they may be removed to be replaced by something else, e.g. through health education. Consequently sickness, which is ideally morally neutral, simultaneously brings blame and responsibility to the individual, who through will, reason, and a healthy 'lifestyle', is believed to be able to prevent it or cure it (Gordon 1988:28). In general, health messages in preventive programmes boil down to messages about lifestyle changes for which the individual is responsible: keeping the house clean, filtering or boiling the drinking water, eating nourishing food, planning the family size, bringing the children for immunization, etc. (Mølsted 1995). The focus is on the wilful mind rather than the docile body and therefore it *blames* individuals who fail to avoid and to get rid of sickness. The *cause* of sickness is inappropriate behaviour and an irrational mind. The *responsibility* to do something is laid upon the individual.

In some situations, the docile body and ideas about decontextualiza-tion may seem opposed to the rational mind and the individualization of responsibility. However, sometimes they complement and reinforce each other. Kirmayer suggests that the voluntary mind can be used as a safety valve, in explaining the involuntary and mechanistic body. When technology fails to cure the morally neutral sickness, the voluntary mind can be blamed for not being cooperative, i.e. for causing inappropriate behaviour, or even for having a negative impact on the physical body, as in psychosomatic explanations (Kirmayer 1988). Sickness is something that just happens to bodies while the person is a helpless bystander. But to maintain this blameless posture, the patient must follow the physician's directives — be cooperative and compliant (Kirmayer 1988: 63). The relationship between 'wilful action' and 'something that just happens' is not static, but is in constant flux. Therefore sickness occupies a morally ambiguous realm, where the social context can exert a powerful effect on the legitimation of distress.

Negotiating responsibility

The relationship between 'wilful action' and 'something that just happens' is a dynamic relationship between two positions generally occurring in many contexts. It is found in biomedicine as well as in African explan-ations of misfortune. It is therefore not just notions of body and mind that are at stake for people employing biomedicine. It is, more generally, notions of 'wilful action', for which one is blamed, and 'accident', which has no blame attached to it. In any given context, these notions appear in dif-ferent ways with different emphases. It is not only a question of explaining misfortune, but also of engaging other people in the process of seeking health care. Social agents play out notions of willful action and accident, of blame and innocence, and of responsibility, to orient themselves in the social and moral space of their lives. If we look at these negotiations, we will discover that biomedicine, and its body/mind distinction, is not a hegemonic ideology swallowed with a pill. It is but one kind of experience of what brings suffering, of who should take action to do what, of whom or what should be blamed, if anything or anybody at all.

When life is interrupted by, for instance, the sickness of a child, a mother will attempt to mobilize other social agents to help get on with her life. Who she succeeds in getting involved depends on the negotiations about how the disruption of life happened, whether anybody should be blamed, and who should take action. A Ugandan father-in-law may refer to the public health discourse of individualism to blame his daughter-in-law for the neglect of her children. The daughter-in-law may respond by drawing attention to the father-in-law's responsibility. She can do so by raising the issue of ancestors disturbing the children, which only he as the head of the home can do something about. In another context, the daughter-in-law may herself use the biomedical view of accident to emphasize her lack of influence on the child's sickness. In that way, she draws attention to her husband's financial responsibility for her and her children.

The problem is not that one kind of treatment is more individualizing than another, but that resources always have to be mobilized. The question is how, and from whom, to mobilize resources, and therefore what relationships you have to the people around you, what part you play in their life. The ones with access to money are not necessarily the ones with access to knowledge about how to deal with the ancestors, or how to prepare herbs. But other people's responsibility is never absent from healthcare-seeking behaviour in eastern Uganda. The use of biomedicine can only be understood by following individual agents along the paths they take through the contexts of their life. When doing so, we will see that responsibility and morality are at the core of both biomedicine and other treatment options. We will see how notions of body and mind, of naturalism and individualism, are pitted against other notions, without necessarily causing a process of decontextualization and individualization. Biomedicine thus does not *a priori* convert suffering into technical problems, and replace moral goals of healing with narrow technical and bureaucratic objectives (Kleinman 1995b:35). It may be used to make a whole of a disrupted life, as may the other notions employed in struggles over responsibility for the body and for the suffering.

The larger context, of civil war devastating the country's economy, is not appropriate in the moment when there is a need to do something for a child who is seriously sick. What is sought at the health centre, or when using pharmaceuticals, is to a large extent symptomatic treatment. It that sense it may seem to be decontextualizing. But symptomatic treatment can also be part of the wider process of responding to the social, moral, and political context. Temperature, diarrhoea, vomiting, coughing, loss of appetite, loss of weight, etc., are part of all the conditions small children suffer from, which eventually develop into diagnoses that again develop and change over time. Engaging with a problem changes that same problem (Whyte 1998:13) and therefore treatment in itself contributes to the development of a diagnosis. Going to the health unit for help is part of this process of engaging with the problem's various symptoms. Going there again and again changes the problem and may raise a mother-in-law's or father-in-law's awareness about the severity of the situation. Each time diarrhoea occurs attempts may be made to treat it with pharmaceuticals or a visit to the health unit, but the more it happens the more attempts will be made to see the symptoms within a larger context, which is often what is done through local idioms of distress (cf. Mogensen 2000). Diarrhoea or loss of appetite is never an independent, isolated episode, and treating it with a tablet will not necessarily make it so. As long as biomedicine does not work more effectively than it does, as long as it does not release people from the problems of their everyday life — which medicine never will — people will not stop considering the larger context of their problems. If the diarrhoea keeps recurring, if the fever is on and off, it will create awareness that something ought to be done, that the sickness ought to be seen within a larger context. The more a mother has to look for tablets, the more eager she becomes to gain insight into the larger context of her problems. As one Ugandan mother said when recalling her child's death: 'It is just that with tablets and injections, the more you give, the less they work and you know you will have to look for other things to do also.'

Illness is a safe way to express anger and discontent without getting involved with political protest, or arguing with God about when we should die, according to Scheper-Hughes (1992:195). But sick bodies, I want to add, do not only *express*, they also act into the world. They also cry out for care and responsibility. Tablets call attention to symptoms and do not just pacify people. And biomedicine does not only consist of pharmaceuticals. Using biomedicine also means getting access to other notions of blame and responsibility within which to interpret sickness. Thus, it opens up different ways of linking events and trying out different things. Biomedicine does not necessarily imply handing over responsibility to an institution or a tablet. It is a way to interpret the past and project it into the future, a way of seeing events in one's life as linked, and of playing strategically with the ways in which they are linked. Maybe we could turn around the statement that, 'more and more forms of human discontent are filtered through ever-expanding categories of sickness, which are then treated, if not 'cured' pharmaceutically' (Scheper-Hughes 1992:196), and instead say that the ever-expanding categories of sickness and treatment options are used by people in eastern Uganda, to deal with various forms of discontent, drawing attention to suffering which may otherwise go unnoticed, and to children dying from infections, creating awareness among husbands and fathers-in-law who are being irresponsible, and maybe even, through repetitive use, contributing to an understanding of the larger context of things.

Conclusion

The expansion of biomedicine and the consequences of this for how problems are defined and dealt with, have for some time been much debated issues in medical anthropology. Biomedicine has often been assumed to have a hegemonic, universal and homogenizing influence, to be somehow anti-cultural and antisocial, and to have a destructive effect upon local ways of dealing with suffering and of giving meaning to life. At the same time another group of anthropologists has been involved in applied medical anthropology and public health work, and has worked on getting more, and 'more right', medicines to people. We should go beyond these oppositions, and show that is not a question of either one or the other.

Defining problems in medical terms may indeed result in the neglect of other problems, and inhibit the implementation of policies and activities dealing with these problems, for example, the focus upon condom use in relation to AIDS prevention ignores the social, political and economic contexts producing situations in which HIV is transmitted. But the solution is not to condemn the fact that people seize the opportunity to use a condom or swallow a pill. We should follow the paths they take through the biomedical system and its ontological commitments, look at how they practice biomedicine, and the way in which it becomes part of their social agency. This may help us gain insight into how to improve their opportunities for action so that a pill can be swallowed when life and death are at stake, and life and society be reflected and acted upon when the pill has had its effect.

ELEVEN

UNCERTAIN UNDERTAKINGS: PRACTICING HEALTH CARE IN THE SUBJUNCTIVE MOOD

Susan Reynolds Whyte

It is said that all anthropologists carry theoretical baggage on their journeys into the worlds they are trying to understand. In the late 1960s, when I was a novice traveller to Bunyole in Eastern Uganda,[1] Clifford Geertz had just published a paradigmatic article on religion and suffering. He wrote:

> As a religious problem, the problem of suffering is, paradoxically, not how to avoid suffering but how to suffer, how to make of physical pain, personal loss, worldly defeat, or the helpless contemplation of others' agony something bearable, supportable, something, as we say sufferable...The Problem of Meaning...is a matter of affirming, or at least recognizing, the inescapability of ignorance, pain, and injustice on the human plane, while simultaneously denying that these irrationalities are characteristic of the world as a whole. (Geertz 1966: 19, 24)

It is instructive to look back on Geertz's famous formulation as a milepost. Geertz was inspired by Max Weber in his discussion of the Problem of Meaning, which he saw as a threat to people's powers of conception. Chaos threatens when experience overwhelms man's analytic capacities, powers of endurance, and moral insight:

> Bafflement, suffering, and a sense of intractable ethical paradox are all, if they become intense enough or are sustained long enough, radical chal-

lenges to the proposition that life is comprehensible and that we can, by taking thought, orient ourselves effectively within it. (*ibid.*: 14)

For Geertz, religious conceptions of an ultimate reality offered meaning in the face of experiences of suffering and bewilderment. Adequate interpretation was the key to what was largely a cognitive problem.

For the people I met in Bunyole, however, the problem was not just how to suffer meaningfully. How to deal with misfortune once it afflicts you was, and is, the main issue. Disorders of mindful bodies, with their discomfort, anxiety, and prospects of death, are the most dramatic and demanding forms of suffering. With heavy loads of infectious diseases, and high rates of child mortality, every family experiences distress and loss. In the last decade, AIDS has become a burden too, and adults die after lingering and painful illness. The means at hand for dealing with these afflictions are many, though often insufficient. There are pharmaceutical products – capsules, tablets, and injections – as well as 'African medicines'. There are institutions and experts: health units and drug shops, biomedical professionals, and folk providers of advice and treatment. There are rituals for dealing with afflicting agents like spirits, shades, and offended kinsmen. There are ways of making meaning, sometimes by invoking symbols, forces and values that we might, with Geertz, call transcendent. But the confrontation with suffering is a practical more than intellectual exercise. Or better, intelligence lies in practical engagement, through which people come to know and understand. Rather than simply recognizing experience by assimilating it to lasting principles, people use meaningful modes of acting on the problem.

Many years after my first attempts to analyse Nyole dealings with misfortune, I came to read John Dewey's *The Quest for Certainty* (1929), which cast another light on Geertz's proposals for an anthropology of suffering and meaning. The pragmatic focus on doing rather than being, on consequences rather than antecedent truths, made of uncertainty something to be managed. In matters of suffering, undertaking was as important as undergoing. That fit with my experience of Nyole concerns. This orientation toward practice seemed to me to encompass rather than exclude Geertz's interest in interpretation; making meaning could be seen as a means to deal with life's uncertainties rather than an end in itself. Yet, as the editors of this volume point out in their introduction, casting matters in terms of uncertainty and control opens new analytical questions. It also requires, in my view, that we try to be as specific and explicit as possible, because uncertainty is a vague and slippery idea.

In this chapter I want to use ethnographic material from Eastern Uganda to discuss three different but interrelated issues in the anthropological study of sickness, uncertainty and control. The first has to do with the situated concern of people experiencing sickness and the subjunctivity with which they address their adversity. The unfolding of experience through time is important here, and the point is to appreciate actors as oriented toward a future they hope and fear for, using the means available to them to try to steer in the right direction. The second issue is about those means and the way they locate uncertainty as they are used to control it. It is not only the case that the means themselves may or may not be efficacious. Just attempting to deal with affliction through certain means sets out some kinds of uncertainties rather than others. Finally, there is the issue of the sociality of uncertainty and control: the means of dealing with uncertainty are accessible through social relations. Differentials in power and influence are relevant to people's experience of uncertainty and attempts to steer through it.

Situated concern and subjunctivity

There is a fundamental difference between uncertainty as a general characteristic of collective consciousness in an historical period and the uncertainty of situated actors faced with a particular adversity. Especially now in the era of AIDS in Africa, it is tempting to talk about 'the uncertainty of the times' just as sociologists speak of a risk society in Europe and North America. But the radically empirical point of departure is the world as lived and experienced and told by those involved. That requires that we concentrate on particularities first: somebody who is concerned about a certain matter over a time in their lives. Here is an example.

In April of 1999, when I was staying at our house in Bunyole, two of our neighbours, a father and his teenage son, came to tell their troubles and ask for help with the boy's school fees. The older man's wife, the mother of the boy Mahanga, had not yet been dead a year. She had left seven children, and now her firstborn son had died too, leaving a widow and three children. It was Mahanga who told the story about his mother and brother:

My mother had divorced and gone to Buganda. After two years she came back sick—with many sores on her body—and thin. She had a sister, whom she loved very much and she told her secretly that she had tested positive. That sister told us. My mother was staying with her brother near here, but my father was helping her, injecting her with penicillin and giving her drips. He's a sweeper at the hospital. Though they were divorced, she was the mother of his children so he still helped her. She was here sick for five months.

As you know, the traditional people can't believe someone is dying of AIDS or another disease. They think something is on the person. They went to the diviner and found that her dead father wanted a gift of food (ehing'ulo) – a goat and a hen.' ['Did you give it?'] 'We tried – plus some millet beer. But though they tried, there was no way of changing—the disease continued. They took her to the hospital. She was admitted and died from there.

Then it was my brother Patrick. He started to be sick in January. They tried a divination – some things came. It was the spirit Omuhyeno – of someone who died badly, who was pushed in the lake and drowned. It caught Patrick when he crossed the lake at Jinja. The spirit wanted a cock and a she-goat to be slaughtered by day, and a sheep by night. They did the ceremony at the end of January and he was possessed [by the spirit]. After that he was okay, walking around. But then the sickness came again. We took him to the hospital in March and he was admitted. They gave him a drip – two bottles – and tablets. He stayed there a week, and came home, finished two weeks, and died. He was thirty years old.

I asked what it was that killed Patrick. His brother said, 'That Omuhyeno.' But then he added doubtfully, 'We looked for the cause, but it refused to appear.' 'Could it be the same disease his mother had?' I asked. 'No,' replied the boy. 'Yes,' said his father, 'Because the body became thin and he was about to become mad. That disease affects the brain.'

Mahanga's story was familiar enough. It is not simply that many people are dying of AIDS these days. Even before AIDS, sickness and death, especially of children, were all too common experiences in Eastern Uganda. What is familiar is the process of attempting to control the uncertain outcome of affliction by trying out (*ohugeraga*) ideas – about the spirits of ancestors or the vengeful dead. People make a plan and they try rituals, even knowing they might fail, as did the family of Mahanga.

Mahanga's mother, unlike many others, went for an AIDS test – that fearsome digital mechanism that answers positive or negative. But the problem with an AIDS test is that it does not show any way forward – at least not for most people in rural areas far from AIDS support programs. Divination did suggest a plan of action for both mother and son. Though as the sickness unfolded, Mahanga came to doubt that the divination had shown the truth. Time will tell, we say, and time told that the cause had refused to appear. And now that they both had died, Mahanga's father could assert, with the authority of a hospital employee, that the symptoms had been like AIDS.

We could say that people in Eastern Uganda believe that AIDS has supernatural causes, or that some do and some do not. But such an indicative statement misses the element of situated concern and ignores the process of trying out. It neglects that unfolding of social experience in which people are intentional subjects. And it overlooks the uncertainties that so often attend undertakings.

As Richard Bernstein reminds us, one of the primary themes of 'the pragmatic ethos', which in many ways anticipated the concerns of what is loosely called post-modernism, is the recognition of contingency and chance (Bernstein 1988: 388-9). John Dewey (1929) wrote of the precarious nature of existence, and of chance as a fundamental property of experience with the world. His view was that certainty is an illusion – but we try for some measure of security. That is, we try to secure that which we value by confronting problems, recognizing the uncertainty of outcomes, reflecting on possible ways forward, and interacting to realize intentions.

There is an intriguing parallel between the classical pragmatist view of subjective experience in an indeterminate world and current theorizing about narrative. Stories have a structure in which intentional agents struggle towards an ending that is not yet certain. In narrative time, one thing leads to another; there is an unfolding of intention and consequence and a sense of moving towards outcomes which are imagined on the basis of what has happened so far. For the pragmatists this was the character of life, not only stories. Transitivity is the quality that William James emphasized – the directionality rather than the conclusion: '...reality is movement from terminus to terminus, a pursuing of goals, and arriving at conclusions. It is on its way to something' (Perry 1996: 371-2).

And just as Dewey saw problems as those which call forth intelligent action, so trouble is the 'engine of narrative' (Bruner 1996: 142). Conflict, difficulty, and suffering lend suspense and provide the counterpoint to human agency. 'Nothing is guaranteed in the realm of human action. We do what we can but – in the realm of narrative at least – there are always impediments' (Mattingly 1998a: 95).

There is one more commonality, that follows from the others: the mood in which intentional subjects address possible outcomes. Jerome Bruner drew attention to the subjunctivizing language of narrative[2] that 'highlights subjective states, attenuating circumstances, alternative possibilities...To make a *story* good, it would seem, you must make it somewhat uncertain, somehow open to variant readings, rather subject to the vagaries of intentional states, undetermined' (Bruner 1990: 53-4).

Subjunctivity, according to Webster's dictionary, is 'that mood of a verb used to express supposition, desire, hypothesis, possibility, etc. rather than to state an actual fact: distinguished from *indicative, imperative.*' The indicative is the voice of certainty, the imperative the voice of command, but the subjunctive is the mood of doubt, hope, will, and potential. Whether or not we accept the view that life itself has narrative structure (Mattingly 1998a), it seems to me that we can think of subjunctivity as a quality not just of narratives,[3] but of at least some aspects of life. Where people are negotiating uncertainty and possibility, subjunctivity is an aspect of subjectivity.

I understand subjunctivity in terms of *situated* concern; it is the mood of people who care about something in particular. Subjunctivity does not characterize systems of thought. It is not like Mary Douglas's danger and potential in the liminality between categories.[4] Nor is it like the ambiguity and uncertainty of postcolonial subjectivity – what Mbembe and Roitman, in their article on 'The Crisis of the Subject in the Post-colony', call the 'profoundly provisional and revisable character of things' (Mbembe and Roitman 1995: 342). When they talk about insecurity, and the uncertainty that flows from a confusing multiplicity of meanings, they describe a kind of generic subjectivity that informs everyone, a collective consciousness that is full of ambiguity, a shared cultural pattern abstracted from action. But making people cases of postcolonial subjectivity gives very little sense of what particular individuals are actually trying to do in the post-colony. Subjunctivity is not a characteristic of the times. It is about the specific uncertainty that particular actors experience as they try something that matters to them – as they undertake to deal with a problem. That is to say, it is a mood of the verb, it is about action, and especially interaction.

Locating uncertainty

So far I have discussed uncertainty and subjunctivity as existential issues for social actors, to which we should be sensitive as fieldworkers, analysts and writers. Now I turn to a second aspect of uncertainty, one that falls more in the realms of cultural analysis and social history. Here we ask how the available means of dealing with uncertainty formulate it in a certain way, directing attention and worry to some features of life rather than others.

That attempts to control uncertainty may have consequences in both focusing and increasing uncertainty has been an important theme in research on risk in late modern society:

> Risk meanings and strategies are attempts to tame uncertainty, but often have the paradoxical effect of increasing anxiety about risk through the intensity of their focus and concern (Lupton 1999:13).

In the same vein, medical sociologist Renée Fox describes an emerging 'uncertainty about uncertainty'. She sees a paradox in the expectation, on the one hand, that medicine should master problems, and the anxiety, on the other, about the unintended consequences of medicine's attempts to do so (Fox 1980: 44). In a later article, Fox (2000) attempts to specify the nature and sources of medical uncertainty: (consciousness of) changes in disease patterns; the increasing importance of prognoses; the organization of health care delivery; major advances in research that challenge the fundamental way of thought in biomedicine; and debates in bioethics. New and powerful diagnostic and therapeutic measures are seen to present new and unforeseeable hazards. New procedures in health care, such as obtaining informed consent for medical interventions, strengthen awareness of the uncertainty of the outcome.

Fox has concerned herself mainly with doctors and medical literature in the US and Europe. Her way of problematizing the relation between control and uncertainty is worth exploring in societies not generally characterized as 'late modern'. But it is important to shift the weight from the professional management of uncertainty and control to the use of control measures by lay people whose concerns may be very differently situated. In order to illustrate this approach, I will contrast two means of managing uncertainty in Eastern Uganda: divination and ritual measures aimed at the causes of sickness, and biomedical tests and pharmaceutical medicines.

In Bunyole, people resort to divination in order to find out how to manage grave or recalcitrant problems – usually sickness or reproductive disorders. Divination, whether by spirit possession or examination of Arabic books, identifies possible agents behind the suffering. The causal agents can be spirits of various kinds or living people; the point is to consider their motives for bringing affliction and to suggest a way of putting the relationship in order or counteracting the agent.

As a cultural form, divination has certain characteristic ways of formulating uncertainty. As I have described elsewhere (Whyte 1997: 60-83), uncertainty is asserted by both the diviner and the clients at the outset, during the consultation, and sometimes even at the end of the session. Clients declare their ignorance: 'The case is bad…because thoughts fail us – that is what we want you to tell us, where it comes from and where its source is, where it is going and where it ends.' The uncertainty of the clients is underscored by the esoteric sources of knowledge to which they do not have access: texts written in Arabic, a language they do not understand, and spirits speaking in indistinct voices. Diviners say that the potential agents appearing in the divination tell lies, or rush in without proper reasons. The diviner has the task of establishing conditional certainties in the form of a proposal that the client accepts as a reasonable explanation and plan of action.

Divination and the explanatory idiom of which it is a fundamental part construct uncertainty by emphasizing the agency of the spirit and human beings said to cause misfortune. Being implicated with a subject that acts upon you as you act upon it is an indeterminate business when you do not fully know that subject or what it is going to do. In that situation subjunctivity keeps possibilities open. At least that is how I understand the way people in Bunyole deal with the subjects that they suspect may be agents of misfortune. Those who bring affliction can be other living people, who invoke the ancestors in a curse or who use powerful substances to bring all kinds of ills. Cursers and sorcerers are almost always people with whom you are closely involved: senior relatives, co-wives, rivals, neighbours. You know them, but you do not know their hearts. Other sources of affliction are the shades of the dead or spirits of various kinds. Of those, people say, 'What you do not see though it looks askance at you – don't quarrel with it.'

This being implicated with what you do not really know helps explain why the language of ritual so often reveals doubt, conditionality, and possibility.[5] In divination the project is to identify and communicate with the agents of misfortune who come and speak when the diviner is possessed. Diviners can even seem to be talking to the spirits of living persons, who reveal why they cursed, for example, and what offerings and ceremonies are needed. But the diviners say that the agents sometimes lie. In one session that I tape-recorded, the mother's brother (a person often suspected of cursing) appeared first. The diviner said to his clients: 'This one has begun by giving us lies'; and he later remarked that some agents have quick heads – they rush into the divination for no reason, or quarrel without any grounds (Whyte 1997: 70-1). They are just deceiving.

In speaking to agents of misfortune, whether in divination or in a ritual of offering, the language expresses a lack of certainty about the agent. Prayers begin with *if*: 'Eeee Nalulima, if it is you, if you are in the house here on this little child...' (*ibid.*: 144). Doubt is there. Even a curser removing a curse, speaks to the ancestors and the cursed person with the words: 'If I am the one' (*ibid.*: 158-9). But more than that, the mood is subjunctive because it is full of conditionality and possibility, hope and desire. It acknowledges contingency but evokes possible futures.

Entreaties suggest visions about what the implicated parties could hope for. A spirit could get another bigger ceremony with a better offering if only the sick mother and child recovered. Listen to the words spoken to the little spirit Mukama, the invisible twin, suspected of sickening a mother and baby:

> Perhaps it's you who has been kicking that child of yours and your mother – you've been sitting in her chest, you prevent her from cultivating. Ah, we have wanted you to leave your mother, that one. A person digs before she gets the means of [helping her relative]. And if she does not dig, [what about] the goat you are demanding?...You leave that child, that child of yours. When tomorrow comes, it will be bouncing on its mother's breast. Let people say. 'So that's how it was, Mukama was the one who was beating this little child'. ... You may be

declaring and yet you are not Mukama. But if it is you Mukama, soon we will return here, and we'll eat those things. (*ibid.*: 142)

They beg Mukama to relent – if it is Mukama. They hope to see the baby lively and happy in the morning so that people will know by the consequences of the ceremony that it *was* Mukama. They want the mother to be well so that she can take her hoe to dig millet. Only then could she get the goat needed for the bigger ceremony for Mukama. So it is not just doubt, but hope for a better future that hangs on the ifs and maybes.

Time will tell. The prayer is spoken in the spirit of pragmatism which William James described as 'an attitude of looking away from first principles..supposed necessities and of looking towards ...fruits, consequences' (James 1974: 47). For James it followed that, 'The truth of an idea is not a stagnant property inherent in it. Truth *happens* to an idea. It *becomes* true, is *made* true by events' (*ibid.*: 133). The diviner suggests that truth might happen to the idea of Mukama. If the child recovers, then people will say, 'So that's how it was, it was Mukama.' But I have also heard diviners and clients say that one divination does not cure a person. The idea that emerges from a divination may turn out not to be true, and people may try another diviner and another proposal.

As means of controlling uncertainty, divination and rituals of affliction dramatically construct doubts about the causes of misfortune. Statements are made about the difficulty of knowing which agent caused the misfortune and whether that agent can be persuaded to lift the affliction. Uncertainty is focused on the Other who has acted upon you. In problematizing etiology, divination and rituals of affliction enact a diagnostics of relationships. Uncertainty is all about the underlying nature of the problem. The contrast with biomedical diagnostics is striking.

Much of the recent anthropological work on uncertainty and control in biomedicine is concerned with 'high tech' diagnostic techniques such as amniocentesis, various forms of genetic testing, and screening for early signs of cancer or cardiovascular disorders. Almost all of this research has been carried out in North America and Western Europe. The exceptions suggest how important it is to explore these issues in other settings. Mar-cia Inhorn's description of the 'dismal diagnostics' of infertility in Egyptian clinics shows that most physicians do not disclose to 'ignorant patients' the results of their investigations, much less explain the techniques they are using (Inhorn 1994: 272-85). How do techniques of control relate to the formulation of uncertainty in such situations?

In Eastern Uganda, much biomedical treatment is symptomatic and not based on examination of the body or testing of bodily substances. But that does not mean that people are uninterested in investigations that might provide guidelines for action. In fact many people value medical examinations, as we learned in a study on quality of care in six health facilities in the district (Nshakira *et al.* 1996). They noted how health workers touched them, looked at them, and whether they used any instruments like thermometers or stethoscopes. Laboratory examinations of blood, urine, stools, or sputum are appreciated by many – except for the fact that they cost extra. But I am not sure that examinations are valued because they identify a disease. In most cases the results are not discussed with the patient and often, as in the case of infertile Egyptian women, biomedical diagnoses are not explained to patients. Rather examinations suggest that care was taken and that the most modern technology was offered. Thus they enhance confidence in treatment and hope for a good outcome. They point towards possibilities and prospects.

In Uganda, laboratory tests do not have the kind of scientific truth status that they have in Denmark. Many health units do not have functioning labs, reagents are in short supply, technicians may not be well trained, they may be absent from their post, and microscopes tend to go missing. I have often heard doubts expressed about lab results, both by medical professionals and by educated lay people. People without schooling may not doubt the accuracy of lab work in the same way, but for them the measuring of body products by machine is more of a step on the way to treatment than a necessary basis for selecting correct treatment. So even though parasite counts or bacteria identification should be indicative, the way they are discussed and used is often subjunctive.

All of this has become increasingly poignant in the era of AIDS. The efforts put into informing the Ugandan public about HIV/AIDS, and the prevalence of the disease, insure that most people are aware of it (Schopper *et al.* 1995). The education campaign stresses that it is impossible to know by someone's appearance whether he or she is infected. But once the disease is well developed, many are aware of the symptoms: *herpes zoster* (*kissippi*, 'the belt') and other skin disorders, weight loss (slimming), and diarrhoea. That the condition is contracted through sexual contact is also well known, and when someone dies of suspected AIDS, it is a cause of great worry for his or her sexual partners. 'They have been screened,' is the ironic comment.[6] Most of all, AIDS is associated with suffering and death. Being a victim is stigmatized, not so much because of how you contracted it, but because of the prognosis.

In Bunyole, when people say that someone has AIDS, they imply that the person is mortally ill and unlikely to be cured. But to say that someone is affected by spirits or sorcery is to suggest that something can be done to help. Depending on how concern is situated, one idea or the other might be propounded. It is often seen as an unfriendly or hostile move to say that someone has AIDS, and health workers generally do not force people to confront that diagnosis if they do not want to know. Usually those closest to a sick person talk care-fully about the illness, not naming the death sentence. As I have described elsewhere (Whyte 1997: 213-9), they sometimes declare their uncertainty ('It's in God's hands, we don't know what will happen'). But I think such assertions of possibility are understood as preparations for the worst. More distant acquaintances talk more directly – although even here, the word AIDS, or 'Slim', is not necessarily pronounced. There are ways of saying things that make it clear enough.

But the situated concern with AIDS is not simply a matter of how close the speaker is to the sick person. It is also a question of timing. After someone has died, when there is no more trying, then it might be said that she died of AIDS. Hasahya and his son Mahanga were reaching that conclusion as they told about the recent death of Mahanga's brother. Retrospectively, AIDS explains why someone died; prospectively, it is difficult as a vision of how to live. The great accomplishment of The AIDS Support Organization, TASO, and some Christian communities, is that they have offered support for living positively towards a future no matter how long or short it might be.

Against this background, it is easier to understand the way AIDS tests are used. In Uganda, AIDS tests are mostly available in towns. Counselling is offered before and after the test, which makes it very different from other medical tests, where patients may not even be told their results. NGOs like TASO provide some social and limited material support to people who are found HIV positive and who are willing to accept their HIV status and join the organization. But many people do not take the step of openly identifying themselves as persons with AIDS. By not telling anyone the results of the test, you can keep possibilities open. If your health is good, you may recast the future hopefully. 'After all, it was only a lab test...' (Clarke 1993: 268).

In late 1997, AIDS testing was finally made available at Busolwe Hospital in the middle of rural Tororo District. Although many people welcomed the idea, few actually took the test. Only 83 people were tested in all of 1998, and of those, most were referred by TASO, which had opened a branch about 15 km. from hospital. The counsellor, Henry Mpambiro, explained that people saw no point in being tested:

'Now there is no drug, so why should I test? What help would I get?' they ask. We tell them the benefits—that it helps you to make plans, if you have children...With proper counselling, fears and suicide and depression decline...But there's a problem about telling spouses: a few agree, but many fear because the spouse will leave. For us here, it's still difficult, but in Kampala they have coped up with it. You are living with it. The period of dying is not known. You think you will die tomorrow – but you may live with it for ten years.

So much has been said about the way African people think about the causes of misfortune. Listening carefully to people in Eastern Uganda suggests that they are situating themselves more in relation to prospective than to retrospective concerns. Henry Mpambiro and his colleagues offer plans, and anticipate problems. At the same time, he mitigates the dreaded certainty with a note of subjunctivity: you may live with it for ten years.

Biomedical investigations do not necessarily focus uncertainty on the nature of bodily pathology or the risk of suffering pathology in the future. I am suggesting that for many lay people in eastern Uganda, they are of immediate interest as part of the treatment process. As long as health workers do not explain diagnoses, the most important uncertainty is outcome, not which disease you have. Tests are valued as indications of good treatment that will control the affliction. But AIDS tests are different because they may indicate that control is impossible.

Controlling the means of control

This overview of uncertainty and control of affliction in Eastern Uganda would be incomplete without a final consideration of practicalities. People act in the subjunctive mood to deal with the particular uncertainties of their situations. The means of controlling uncertainty formulate it in particular ways and point towards possible futures. But the practical issue for sufferers and their families is often how to get hold of the means of control. Dealing with uncertainty requires drawing on social relationships to mobilise resources. The problems of accessibility, as they are called in public health, can be considered in terms of costs, control, and contacts.

Costs are partly indirect—having to do with convenience, time, transport, and social relations. But they are very much a matter of money. For people with chronic shortages of cash, sacrificing a goat, buying injectable penicillin, or admitting a child to hospital are problems in themselves and not just means of solving problems. One of the reasons for the practice of 'trying out' treatments in eastern Uganda is a reluctance to make a large investment in a remedial strategy that may prove fruitless. Rituals in the explanatory idiom, addressed at the cause of misfortune, require the sacrifice of animals, and outlays of cash. When the need for such rituals was identified in divination, people often asked what they could do if they did not have the means. There was almost always a possibility of dedicating a rope in place of a bull, or cutting off the toe of a chick, with promises to sacrifice a 'huge cock' when the sickness cooled (Whyte 1997: 105-7).

Since user fees were introduced at public health facilities, and given the need to pay extra sometimes for 'tea' for health workers, people are concerned about how to get money to go for biomedical treatment. Although there is a fixed consultation fee, which is relatively modest, medicines, lab tests, and referrals to other facilities cost extra. Especially admission to hospital is very expensive in relation to local incomes. There is no way of knowing in advance whether these extra services and expenses will be required. Thus there is an element of uncertainty about the price of government health care. This is also true of other types of treatment, but it is my impression that people feel less able to negotiate with the providers of public biomedicine and less in control of the situation.

Control of the means of control is one way of understanding what is at stake in the balance between the formal and the informal sectors of the biomedical health care system in Eastern Uganda. Medicines, knowledge and skills are the resources set in against the uncertainties of sickness. In the government health care system, these are in the hands of gatekeepers, who dispense them to patients who are patient and willing to accept their role, pay the fees, and follow instructions. Government health workers tend to adopt a didactic, sometimes scolding tone, which implies that they, not their patients, are knowledgeable and competent. Many people find this set-up intimidating; others do not want to be dependent on a system that has deteriorated and failed them in the recent past.

For a person with few resources, being a customer at a small drug shop or storefront clinic allows a greater sense of control than being a patient in a formal health facility. Even when the person behind the counter is a trained para-medic (perhaps the same person who also works in the health centre), the customer is treated differently than the patient. The provider needs to please his customers, who are free not to buy or to take their custom elsewhere. Often shop attendants are not professionally qualified, and there is less social distance between them and their clients. If the provider recommends a course of treatment that is too dear, it is not embarrassing or awkward for the customer to buy fewer pills and try them out to see if they work.

In Uganda, as in many developing countries, the business of retailing pharmaceuticals is booming. As all kinds of medicines became common commodities, available to anyone with a little money, people were able to avoid the controls of the professional health system, which was functioning poorly in any case (Whyte 1991). Much as the ready access to drugs in the 'informal' economy is problematic from a public health viewpoint, customers seem to appreciate not having to depend on the formal system. Nevertheless, people do not relate directly and individually to an ideal free market in health care.

Access to the means of controlling affliction is always social in the sense that resources are differentially distributed in society. This sociality of control is particularly explicit in rural Uganda where kinship relations frame social and economic life, and where knowing the right people is assumed necessary for getting things done. The importance of having contacts is acknowledged in the ironic comment that 'it's not just a matter of technical know-how, but of technical know-who'. Connections are important when you need the knowledge, drugs and procedures that are widely available if not widely accessible.

Local shopkeepers are useful contacts when people need credit to buy medicines. A more educated or cosmopolitan neighbour can provide advice about symptoms and treatment possibilities. The importance of personal relations in Ugandan health care has been richly described in relation to the most valued of treatment procedures, the hypodermic injection. It is not only a question of knowing someone who can administer an injection, or teach you how to do it, but also of trusting the injectionist (Birungi 1998).

When it is necessary to use the formal health care system, contacts are extremely useful. The example above of our neighbour Hasahya is a case in point. As a cleaner in the hospital, he could facilitate the admission of his ex-wife and his son, and he could ensure a good standard of home treatment as well. Knowing someone who works or has worked in a medical facility is a great advantage to the family seeking health care. You gain access to their knowledge and skills, to the channels through which resources, especially medicines flow, and you may also be able to avoid having to pay for services. You will be treated with more consideration, because you are not just an anonymous patient, but a relative, friend, colleague, or neighbour.

What kind of control are people seeking in their attempts to deal with affliction? In a pragmatic and phenomenological view, subjects are trying to exert some degree of control, not necessarily as masters, but rather as helmsmen steering a course (Jackson 1998: 18-9). For people trying to steer through health problems, this kind of control involves interrelationships with institutions and practitioners. Drawing on pre-exiting personal connections, or trying to establish new ones, are ways of navigating. But there are other ways as well. Going to a little private clinic or a drug shop gives more leeway than going to an outpatient department that is more formalistic and impersonal. Being a customer rather than a patient gives steerage; you can decide what medicine you want, how much you can afford to pay; you can ask questions and expect to be treated with civility – since the provider is concerned with you in his business endeavour. The problem of technical know-who is one of leverage – the increased means of accomplishing some purpose. Being a customer, for some people at least, is also a form of leverage.

Conclusion

Geertz's seminal insight about the problem of suffering was that affliction gives rise to uncertainty as it challenges 'the proposition that life is comprehensible and that we can, by taking thought, orient ourselves effectively within it'. But whereas he emphasized the assurance that religion can offer in the face of chaos, I have wanted to highlight quite different aspects of the problem of suffering as it presents itself in Eastern Uganda. People do not just undergo suffering, but they undertake to steer through it. Here I have discussed their attempts to control affliction in three different lights.

Firstly, I wished to illuminate qualities of people as actors, trying to deal with problems. Analytically, it is important to situate them and their concerns in specific situations that are unfolding through time. The concept of subjunctivity alerts us to moods of action: explorative, worried, doubtful, hopeful. Starting this way allows us to appreciate how people use the means at hand to try to manage their uncertainties.

That led on to the second issue: how the means of dealing with uncertainty are used to formulate it in specific ways. Divination and rituals in the explanatory idiom problematize the social (relational) causes of affliction, rather than its symptoms. Uncertainty about outcome is linked to uncertainty about etiology. Biomedical examinations and tests are not parallel: as used in this rural area, they do not problematize the cause of symptoms nor are they effectively used to establish a diagnosis. Like ritual means, they focus hope on the uncertain outcome. The exceptions are tests for HIV/AIDS which can assert the certainty of death, with no accompanying hope for managing problems.

Finally, I wanted to light up the practicalities of access to the means of controlling uncertainties. The resources needed to deal with the uncertainties of sickness are unevenly distributed and socially embedded. The pressing concerns of most people are not problems of interpretation or existential issues of ontological certainty. They are worries about the money and supportive relationships that can give them steerage in getting through the uncertain passages of suffering.

Notes

1. This chapter is based on fieldwork with people in Bunyole County, Tororo District, from 1969-71, and at intervals since 1989. Since 1992, I have been working with researchers at Child Health and Development Centre and Makerere Institute of Social Research on two long term projects in Tororo District: the Tororo Community Health (TORCH) and Community Drug Use. Many thanks to colleagues in Uganda and to the Danish International Development Agency for continuing support.

2. A more technical discussion of how language subjunctivizes reality within narratives may be found in Bruner 1986:25-37.

3. Byron Good (1994) and Frode Jacobsen (1998) have followed Bruner in using the notion of subjunctivity to analyse narratives of illness. As ethnographers, however, both go beyond a narrow focus on stories to suggest the situational implications of subjunctivity for persons, families, and groups.

4. Good (1994: 205 n.20) refers to Victor Turner's use of the distinction between 'the indicative quotidian social structure' and the 'subjunctive antistructure of the liminal process'. This structural distinction differs from the positionality and directionality that I am emphasizing.

5. Heald (1991) makes a similar argument based on fieldwork among the Gisu of eastern Uganda. She suggests that skepticism and doubt are inherent in the institution and process of divination. The stereotypes of 'gullible savages' and sophisticated westerners are totally misleading. In fact, westerners may be more willing to accept the authority of their medical specialists than rural Ugandans who are accustomed to playing an important part in constructing knowledge about their own conditions.

6. The uncertainties and struggles for help associated with HIV/AIDS have been well described in Asera et al. 1996 and 1997.

BIBLIOGRAPHY

Aaby, P., Gomes, J., Høj, L. and Sandström, A. (1997), *Estudo de Saúde de Mulheres em Idade Fertil e os Seus Filhos: Dados de 1990-1995*, Bissau: UNICEF/Projecto de Saúde de Bandim.

Abiri, E. (2000), *The Securitisation of Migration: Towards an Understanding of Migration Policy Changes in the 1990s. The Case of Sweden*, Ph.D dissertation, Department of Peace and Development Research, University of Göteborg.

Adam, B. (1998), *Timescapes of Modernity: The Environment and Invisible Hazards*, London: Routledge.

Adelswärd, V. and Sachs, L. (1996), 'The Meaning of 6.8: Numeracy and Normality in Health Information Talks', *Social Science and Medicine*, vol. 43, pp. 1179-87.

Alcoholics Anonymous (1985), *Alcoholics Anonymous Comes of Age: A Brief History of A.A.*, New York: A.A. World Services Inc.

Alford, R. D. (1988), *Naming and Identity: A Cross-Cultural Study of Personal Naming Practices*, New Haven: HRAF Press.

Angrosino, M. V. (1998), 'Mental disability in the United States: An interactionist perspective', in R. Jenkins (ed.), *Questions of Competence: Culture, Classification and Intellectual Disability*, Cambridge: Cambridge University Press.

Armstrong, D. (1995), 'The Rise of Surveillance Medicine', *Sociology of Health and Illness*, vol. 17, pp. 393-404.

— (1988), 'Space and time in British General Practice', in M. Lock and D. Gordon (eds.), *Biomedicine Examined*, Dordrecht: Kluwer.

— Michie, S. and Marteau, T. (1998), 'Revealed identity: A study of the process of genetic counselling', *Social Science and Medicine*, vol. 47, pp. 1653-8.

Arnold, David (1993), *Colonizing the Body: State Medicine and Epidemic Disease in Nineteenth Century India*, Berkeley: University of California Press.

Asera, R. Bagarukayo, H. Shuey, D. and Barton, T. (1996) Searching for solutions: health concerns expressed in letters to an East African newspaper column. *Health Transition Review* 6 (2): 169-78.

— (1997) An epidemic of apprehension: questions about HIV/AIDS to an East African newspaper health advice column. *AIDS Care* 9 (1): 5-12.

Baer, H. A., Singer, M. and Susser, I. (1997), *Medical Anthropology and the World System*, New York: Bergin and Garvey.

Baker, E. C. (1946), 'Mumiani', *Tanganyika Notes and Records*, vol. 21, pp. 108-9.

Balandier, G. (1966), 'The colonial situation: a theoretical approach', in I. Wallerstein (ed.), *Social Change: The Colonial Situation*, New York: Wiley.

Ball, H. L. and Hill, C. M. (1996), 'Reevaluating twin infanticide', *Current Anthropology*, vol. 37, pp. 856-63.

Barbalet, J.M. (1998), *Emotion, Social Theory, and Social Structure. A Macrosociological Approach.* Cambridge: Cambridge University Press.

Barbosa, L. N. de H. (1995), 'The Brazilian *jeitinho*: an exercise in national identity', in D. Hess and R. DaMatta (eds.), *The Brazilian Puzzle*, New York: Columbia University Press.

Barfield, T. (ed.), 1997. *The Dictionary of Anthropology*, Oxford: Blackwell.

Barham, P. and Hayward, R. (1990), 'Schizophrenia as a life process', in R. P. Bentall (ed.), *Reconstructing schizophrenia*, London: Routledge.

Barham, P. and Hayward, R. (1998), 'In sickness and in health: Dilemmas of the person with severe mental illness', *Psychiatry*, vol. 61, pp. 163-70.

Barth, F. (1969), 'Introduction', in F. Barth (ed.) *Ethnic Groups and Boundaries: The Social Organisation of Culture Difference*, Oslo: Universitetsforlaget.

Bartlett, T. Q., Sussman, R. W. and Cheverud, J. M. (1993), 'Infant killing in primates: a review of observed cases with specific reference to the sexual selection hypothesis', *American Anthropologist*, vol. 94, pp. 958-90.

Bateson, G. (1973), *Steps to an Ecology of Mind*, St. Albans: Paladin.

Bauman, Z. (1990), 'Modernity and Ambivalence', in M. Featherstone (ed.), *Global Culture: Nationalism, Globalization and Modernity*, London: Sage.

Beck, U. (1992), *Risk Society: Towards a New Modernity*, London: Sage.

Becker, H. S. (1963), *Outsiders: Studies in the Sociology of Deviance*, New York: Free Press.

Becker, G. (1997) *Disrupted Lives: How People Create Meaning in a Chaotic World*, Berkeley: University of California Press.

Bell, S. E. (1987), 'Changing ideas: the medicalization of menopause', *Social Science and Medicine*, vol. 24, pp. 535-42.

Berglind, H. (1978), 'Pension or Work? A Growing Dilemma in the Nordic Welfare States', *Acta Sociologica*, vol. 21, pp. 181-91.

Bernstein, R. J. (1997), 'Pragmatism, pluralism and the healing of wounds', in L. Menand (ed.), *Pragmatism: A Reader*, New York: Vintage Books.

Birchwood, M., Fowler, D. and Jackson, C. (eds.) (2000a) *Early Intervention in Psychosis: A Guide to Concepts, Evidence and Interventions*, Chichester: John Wiley & Sons Ltd.

Spencer, E., and McGovern, D. (2000b) 'Schizophrenia: early warning signs', *Advances in Psychiatric Treatment* 6: 93-101.

Birdsell, J. B. (1993), *Microevolutionary Patterns in Aboriginal Australia: A Gradient Analysis of Clines*, Oxford: Oxford University Press.

Birungi, H. (1998), 'Injections and self-help: risk and trust in Ugandan health care', *Social Science and Medicine*, vol. 47, pp. 1455-62.

Boivan, J. and Takefman, J. E. (1996), 'Impact of the in-vitro fertilization process on emotional, physical and relational variables', *Human Reproduction*, vol. 11, pp. 903-7.

Borell, P. (1996), *Ett självständigt liv*, Värnamo: Psykologia. [Translated and edited from a manual by Robert Liberman, Clinical Research Centre for Schizophrenia & Psychiatric Rehabilitation, Los Angeles.]

Bourdieu, P. (2000) *Pascalian Meditations*, Stanford; Stanford University Press.

Bowers, L. A. C. (1995), *Mental illness as a social phenomenon*, Ph.D. thesis, University of Manchester.

Braathen, E. (1994), 'Galskap, makt og krop: Humor i en psykiatrisk institusjon', *Tidsskriftet Antropologi*, no. 29, pp. 71-88.

Braidotti, R. (1994), *Nomadic Subjects: Embodiments and Sexual Difference in Contemporary Feminist Theory*, New York: Columbia University Press.

Bringa, T. (1995), *Being Muslim the Bosnian Way: Identity and Community in a Central Bosnian Village*, Cambridge: Cambridge University Press.

Brubaker, R. (1984), *The Limits of Rationality: An Essay on the Social and Moral Thought of Max Weber*, London: George Allen and Unwin.

Bruner, J. (1986), *Actual Minds, Possible Worlds*, Cambridge, MA: Harvard University Press.

(1990), *Acts of Meaning*, Cambridge, MA: Harvard University Press.

(1996), *The Culture of Education*, Cambridge, MA: Harvard University Press.

Burkitt, I. (1991), *Social Selves: Theories of the Social Formation of Personality*, London: Sage.

Busfield, J. (2000), 'Introduction: Rethinking the sociology of mental health', *Sociology of Health and Illness*, vol. 22, pp. 543-58.

Cannel, F. (1990), 'Concepts of parenthood: The Warnock Report, The Gillick Debate and modern myths', *American Ethnologist*, vol. 17, pp. 667-86

Capps, L. and Ochs, E. (1995), *Constructing Panic: The Discourse of Agoraphobia*, Cambridge, Massachusetts: Harvard University Press.

Carreira, A. (1971), 'O infanticídio ritual em África', *Boletim Cultural da Guiné Portuguesa*, vol. 26, no. 101, pp. 149-216.

Carsten, J. (1997), *The Heat of the Hearth: The Process of Kinship in a Malay Fishing Community*, Oxford: Clarendon Press.

(2000) 'Introduction: cultures of relatedness', in J. Carsten (ed.), *Cultures of Relatedness: New Approaches to the Study of Kinship*, Cambridge: Cambridge University Press.

Carter, A. T. (1995). 'Agency and fertility: for an ethnography of practice.' In S. Greenhalgh (ed.) *Situating Fertility*. Cambridge: Cambridge University Press.

Ceyssens, R. (1975), 'Mutumbula: mythe d'opprimé', *Culture et Development*, vol. 7, pp. 483-550.

Clarke, I. (1993), *The Man With the Key Has Gone!*, Chichester: New Wine Press.

Cleland, J. and Wilson, C. (1987), 'Demand theories of the fertility transition: An iconoclastic view', *Population Studies*, vol. 41, pp. 5-30.

Cohen, D. W. and Odhiambo, E. S. A. (1989), *Siaya: The Historical Anthropology of an African Landscape*, Nairobi: Heineman Kenya.

Comaroff, J. and Comaroff, J. L. (1997), *Of Revelation and Revolution*, vol. 2, *The Dialectics of Modernity on a South African frontier*, Chicago: University of Chicago Press.

(1999a), 'Occult economies and the violence of abstraction: notes from the South African postcolony', *American Ethnologist*, vol. 26, pp. 279-303.

(1999b), 'Response to Moore: second thoughts', *American Ethnologist*, vol. 26, pp. 307-9.

Conrad, P. (1992), 'Medicalization and social control', *Annual Review of Sociology*, vol. 18, pp. 209-32.

and Schneider, J. W. (1980), *Deviance and Medicalization: From Badness to Sickness*, Philadelphia: Temple University Press.

Corlin, C. (1990), 'Chaos, Order and World View: Tibetan Refugees in Switzerland', *Disaster* vol. 15, no. 2, pp. 87-113.

Craib, I. (1998), *Experiencing Identity*, London: Sage.

Crowley, E. L. (1990), *Contracts with the Spirits: Religion, Asylum, and Ethnic Identity in the Cacheu Region of Guinea-Bissau*, Ph.D dissertation, Yale University.

Csordas, T. (ed.) (1994), *Embodiment and Experience: The existential ground of culture and self*, Cambridge: Cambridge University Press.

CTD [Centrum för Tortyr- och Traumaskadade] (1997), *Med livet i behåll: Om tortyr, överlevnad och återupprättelse*, Stockholm: Stockholms Läns Landsting.

Cussins, C. (1998), 'Producing Reproduction: Techniques of Normalization and Naturalisation in Infertility Clinics', in S. Franklin and H. Ragoné (eds.), *Reproducing Reproduction: Kinship Power and Technological Innovation*, Philadelphia: University of Pennsylvania Press.

Dalsgaard, A. L. (2004) *Matters of Life and Longing: Female Sterilisation in Northeast Brazil*, Copenhagen: Museum Tusculanum Press.

Daly, M. and Wilson, M. (1984), 'A sociobiological analysis of human infanticide', in G. Hausfater and S. B. Hrdy (eds.), *Infanticide: Comparative and Evolutionary Perspectives*, New York: Aldine.

(1988), 'Evolutionary social psychology and family homicide', *Science*, vol. 242, pp. 519-24.

DaMatta, R. (1997), *A Casa & a Rua: Espaço, Cidadania, Mulher e Morte no Brasil*, Rio de Janeiro: Editora Rocco.

Davidson, L. and Strauss, J. S. (1992), 'Sense of self in recovery from severe mental illness', *British Journal of Medical Psychology*, vol. 65, pp. 131-45.

Delaney, C. (1991), *The Seed and the Soil: Gender and Cosmology in Turkish Village Society*, Berkeley: University of California Press.

Desjarlais, R. (1997), *Shelter Blues: Sanity and Selfhood among the Homeless*, Philadelphia: University of Pennsylvania Press.

Dewey, J. (1929), *The Quest for Certainty: A Study of the Relation of Knowledge and Action*, New York: Minton, Balch and Company.

(1957), *Human Nature and Conduct: An Introduction to Social Psychology*, New York: The Modern Library.

di Leonardo, M. (1987), 'The female world of cards and holidays: women, families, and the work of kinship', *Signs*, vol. 12, pp. 440-53.

Diniz, S. G., de Mello e Souza, C. and Portella, A. P. (1998), 'Not like our Mothers: Reproductive choice and the emergence of citizenship among Brazilian rural workers, domestic workers and housewives', in Petchesky, R. P. and Judd, K. (eds.), *Negotiating Reproductive Rights*, London: Zed Books.

Doherty, E. G. (1975), 'Labeling effects in psychiatric hospitalization', *Archives of General Psychiatry*, vol. 32, pp. 562-68.

Douglas, M. (1966), *Purity and Danger: An Analysis of Concepts of Pollution and Taboo*, London: Routledge and Kegan Paul.

(1986), *Risk Acceptability According to the Social Sciences*, London: Routledge and Kegan Paul.

(1994), *Risk and Blame: Essays in Cultural Theory*, London: Routledge.

and Wildavsky, A. (1982), *Risk and Culture: An Essay on the Selection of Technological and Environmental Dangers*, Berkeley: University of California Press.

Dow, J. (1986), 'Universal aspects of symbolic healing: A theoretical synthesis', *American Anthropologist*, vol. 88, pp. 56-69.

Duden, B. (1993), *Disemboying Women: Perspectives on Pregnancy and the Unborn*, Cambridge: Harvard University Press.

Durkheim, E. (1964), *The Rules of the Sociological Method*, New York: Free Press.

Eastmond, M. (1989 [1997]), *The Dilemmas of Exile. Chilean Refugees in the USA*, Göteborg: Acta Universitatis Gothenburgensis.

(1998), 'Nationalist Discourses and the Construction of Difference: Bosnian Muslim Refugees in Sweden', *Journal of Refugee Studies*, vol. 11, pp. 161-81.

Ralphsson, L. and Alinder, B. (1994), 'The Impact of Violence and War: Bosnian Refugee Families and Coping Strategies', paper presented at 4th IRAP conference, Oxford, 5-9 January 1994.

Einarsdóttir, J. (2000), '*Tired of Weeping': Child Death and Mourning Among Papel Mothers in Guinea-Bissau*, Stockholm Studies in Social Anthropology no. 46, Stockholm: Almqvist and Wiksell.

(2004) *Tired of Weeping: Mother Love, Child Death and Poverty in Guinea-Bissau*, 2nd edition, Madison: University of Wisconsin Press.

Eisenbruch, M. (1991), 'From Post-Traumatic Stress Disorder to Cultural Bereavement: Diagnosis of South-East Asian Refugees', paper presented at 2nd IRAP conference, Oxford, 3-6 January 1991.

Ekberg, J. (1990), 'Invandrare på arbetsmarknaden', *Bilagor till arbetsmarknad och arbetsmarknadspolitik 1989*, Stockholm: Arbetsmarknadsdepartementet, Ds1990:35.

Ekblad, S. and Eriksson, N.-G. (1997), 'Ett hälsoblad som screening instrument för nyanlända flyktingar', *Del 1 Rapport*, Stockholm: Statens Institut för Psykosocial Miljömedicin.

EKT [Enheten för Krigs- och Tortyrskadade] (1997), *Tortyr och tystnad, tillit och tal: Dokumentation av projektet för krigs – och tortyrskadade flyktingar i Göteborg 1994-96*, Göteborg: Göteborgs Socialförvaltning.

Elmeland, K. (1996), *Dansk Alkoholkultur: Rus, Ritual og Regulering*, Holte: SocPol.

, Nygaard, P. and Sabroe, K.-E. (1990), 'Storbrugere: 12 fortællinger om alkoholbrug', *Psykologisk Skriftserie*, 15 (1).

Estroff, S. E. (1981), *Making it Crazy: An Ethnography of Psychiatric Clientsin an American Community*, Berkeley: University of California Press.

(1989), 'Self, identity and subjective experiences of schizophrenia: In search of the subject', *Schizophrenia Bulletin*, vol. 15, pp. 189-196.

(1993), 'Identity, disability, and schizophrenia: The problem of chronicity', In M. Lock and S. Lindenbaum (eds.), *Knowledge, power, and practice: Analysis in medical anthropology*, Berkeley: University of California Press.

Lachicotte, W. S., Illingworth, L. C. and Johnston, A. (1991), 'Everybody's got a little mental illness: Accounts of illness and self among people with severe, persistent mental illness', *Medical Anthropology Quarterly*, vol. 5, pp. 331-69.

Evans-Pritchard, E. E. (1937), *Witchcraft, Oracles and Magic Among the Azande*, Oxford: Clarendon Press.

Faria, V. E. (1997/1998), 'Government policy and fertility regulations: unintended consequences and perverse effects', *Brazilian Journal of Population Studies*, vol. 1, pp. 179-206.

Feist, T. (1995), *Social Citizenship for Whom?* Aldershot: Avebury.

Ferguson, A. E. (1981), 'Commercial pharmaceutical medicine and medicalization: A case study from El Salvador', *Culture, Medicine and Psychiatry*, vol. 5, pp. 105-34.

Fortes, M. (1936), 'Culture contact as a dynamic process: An investigation in the northern territories of the Gold Coast', *Africa*, vol. 9, pp. 24-56.

(1987), *Religion, Morality and the Person: Essays on Tallensi Religion*, Cambridge: Cambridge University Press.

Foster, G. M. (1987), 'Bureaucratic aspects of international health agencies', *Social Science and Medicine*, vol. 25: 1039-48.

Foucault, M. (1973), *Madness and Civilization*, New York: Vintage Books.

(1975), *The Birth of the Clinic*, New York: Vintage Books.

(1980), *Power/Knowledge: Selected Interviews and Other Writings 1972-77*, ed. C. Gordon, Brighton: Harvester.

(1988), 'Technologies of the Self', in L. H. Martin, H. Gutman and P. H. Hutton (eds.) *Technologies of the Self: A Seminar with Michel Foucault*, Amherst: University of Massachusetts Press/London: Tavistock.

Fox, R. (1980), 'The evolution of medical uncertainty', *Milbank Memorial Fund Quarterly/Health and Society*, vol. 58, pp. 1-49.

(2000), 'Medical Uncertainty Revisited', in G. L. Albrecht, R. Fitzpatrick, and S. C. Scrimshaw (eds.) *The Handbook of Social Studies in Health and Medicine*, London: Sage.

Frankenberg, R. (1993), 'Risk: Anthropological and epidemiological narratives of prevention', in S. Lindenbaum and M. Lock (eds.) *Knowledge, Power, and Practice*, Berkeley: University of California Press.

Franklin, S. (1992) 'Making Sense of Missed Conceptions: Anthropological Perspectives of Unexplained Infertility', in M. Stacey (ed.), *Changing Human Reproduction. Social Science Perspectives*, London: Sage Publications.

(1997), *Embodied Progress: A Cultural Account of Assisted Conception*, London: Routledge.

(2001) 'Biologization revisited: kinship theory in the context of the new biologies', in S. Franklin and S. McKinnon (eds.) *Relative Values: Reconfiguring Kinship Studies*, Durham: Duke University Press.

and Lock, M. (2003) 'Animation and Cessation: The Remaking of life and Death', in S. Franklin and M. Lock (eds.) *Remaking Life and Death: Towards an anthropology of the Biosciences*, Santa Fe: SAR Press.

Franzén, E. (1997), *Invandring och Arbetslöshet*, Lund: Studentlitteratur.

Friedman, K. E. (1994), *Den Magiske Världsbilden: Om Statens Frigörelse från Folket i Folkrepubliken Kongo*, Stockholm: Carlssons.

Geertz, C. (1966), 'Religion as a cultural system', in M. Banton (ed.), *Anthropological Approaches to the Study of Religion*, London: Tavistock.

Geissler, P.W., Harris, S., Prince, R.J., Olsen, A., Oketch, H., Nielsen, B.S., and Mølgård, P. (2002) 'Medicinal plants used by Luo mothers in Bondo District, Kenya', *Journal of Ethnopharmacology*, vol. 83, pp. 39-54.

Gerholm, L. (1992), 'Inavel och Galenskap: Folkligt tänkande kring schizofreni', *Socialmedicinsk Tidskrift*, no. 9-10, pp. 460-70.

Geschiere, P. (1995), *Sorcellerie et Politique: La Viande des Autres*, Paris: Karthala.

Giddens, A. (1990), *The Consequences of Modernity*, Cambridge: Polity.

(1991) *Modernity and Self-Identity: Self and Society in the Late Modern Age*, Stanford, California: Stanford University Press.

Gifford, S. (1986), 'The meaning of lumps: A case study of the ambiguities of risk', in C. Janes, R. Stall and S. Gifford (eds.), *Anthropology and Epidemiology: Interdisciplinary Approaches to the Study of Health and Disease*, Dordrecht: Reidel.

Gijsbergs van Wijk, C. M. T., *et al.* (1996), 'Gender perspectives and quality of care: Towards appropriate and adequate health care for women', *Social Science and Medicine*, vol. 43, pp. 707-20.

Goffman, E. (1961), *Asylums: Essays on the social situation of mental Patients and other inmates*, New York: Doubleday.

(1963), *Stigma: Notes on the management of a spoiled identity*, Englewood Cliffs: Prentice-Hall.

(1969), *The Presentation of Self in Everyday Life*, London: Allen Lane.

Good, B. (1994), *Medicine, Rationality, and Experience: An Anthropological Perspective*, Cambridge: Cambridge University Press.

and DelVecchio Good, M.-J. (1993), 'Learning Medicine: The Constructing of Medical Knowledge at Harvard Medical School', in S. Lindenbaum and M. Lock (eds.), *Knowledge, Power and Practice: The Anthropology of Medicine and Everyday Life*, Berkeley: University of California Press.

Good, M.-J. D. (1995), 'Cultural studies of biomedicine: An agenda for Research', *Social Science and Medicine*, vol. 41, pp. 461-73.

Gordon, D. (1988), 'Tenacious Assumptions in Western Medicine', in M. Lock and D. Gordon (eds.), *Biomedicine Examined*, Dordrecht: Reidel.

Greenhalgh, S. (ed.) (1995), *Situating Fertility: Anthropology and Demographic Inquiry*, Cambridge: Cambridge University Press.

Graham, M. (1999), *Classifications, Persons and Policies: Refugees and Swedish Welfare Bureaucracy*, Stockholm Studies in Social Anthropology, Stockholm: Almqvist and Wiksell..

Hacking, I (1990), *The Taming of Chance*, Cambridge: Cambridge University Press.

Hald, J. and Jacobsen, E. (1948), 'A Drug Sensitising the Organism to Ethyl Alcohol', *The Lancet*, vol. 255 no. 2, pp. 1001-4.

Handelman, D. (1976), 'Bureaucratic Transactions: The Development of Official-Client Relationships in Israel', in Kapferer, B. (ed), *Transaction and Meaning: Directions in the Anthropology of Exchange and Symbolic Behaviour*, Philadelphia: Institute for the Study of Human Issues.

(1978), 'Introduction: A recognition of bureaucracy', in D. Handelman and E. Leyton (eds.), *Bureaucracy and World View: Studies in the logic of official interpretation*, St. Johns: Institute of Social and Economic Research.

Hanson, F. A. (1993), *Testing, Testing: Social Consequences of the Examined Life*, Berkeley: University of California Press.

Harding, P. and Jenkins, R. (1989), *The Myth of the Hidden Economy: Towards a New Understanding of Informal Economic Activity*, Milton Keynes: Open University Press.

Harris, M. (1977), *Cannibals and Kings: The Origins of Cultures*, New York: Random House.

Hastrup, K. (1995), *A Passage to Anthropology: Between Experience and Theory*, London: Routledge.

Hausfater, G. and Hrdy, S. B. (eds.) (1984), *Infanticide: Comparative and Evolutionary Perspectives*, New York: Aldine.

Heald, S. (1991), 'Divinatory failure: the religious and social role of Gisu diviners', *Africa*, vol. 61, pp. 299-317.

Hecht, T. (1998), *At Home in the Street: Street Children of Northeast Brazil*, Cambridge: Cambridge University Press.

Helman, C. G. (2000), *Culture, Health and Illness*, 4th edition, Oxford: Butterworth-Heinemann.

Herman, J. (1992), *Trauma and Recovery*, New York: Basic Books.

Hjern, A. (1995), *Migrationsmedicinsk forskning: En översikt*, MFR-rapport 1, Stockholm: Medicinska Forskningsrådet.

Hodges, G. W. T. (1986), *The Carrier Corps: Military Labor in The East African Campaign, 1914-1918*, New York: Greenwood Press.

Horton, R. (1993), *Patterns of Thought in Africa and the West: Essays on Magic, Religion and Science*, Cambridge: Cambridge University Press.

Howell, N. (1979), *Demography of the Dobe!Kung*, New York: Academic Press.

Hrdy, S. B. (1990), 'Fitness tradeoffs in the history and evolution of delegated mothering with special reference to wet-nursing, abandonment and infanticide', in Parmigiani, S. and vom Saal, F. S. (eds.), *Infanticide and Parental Care*, Reading: Harwood Academic Publishers.

(1999), *Mother Nature: A History of Mothers, Infants, and Natural Selection*, New York: Pantheon Books.

Huizinga, J. (1955), *Homo Ludens: A Study of the Play-element in Culture*, Boston: The Beacon Press.

Iliffe, J. (1998), *East African Doctors: A History of the Modern Profession*, Cambridge: Cambridge University Press.

Illich, I. (1977), *Limits to Medicine: Medical Nemesis, The Expropriation of Health*, Aylesbury: Hazell Watson and Viney.

Ingold, T. (1997), 'Eight Themes in the Anthropology of Technology', *Social Analysis*, vol. 41, pp. 106-148.

Ingstad, B. and S. R. Whyte (1995), *Disability and Culture*, Berkeley: University of California Press.

Inhorn, M. (1994), *Quest for Conception: Gender, Infertility, and Egyptian Medical Traditions*, Philadelphia: University of Pennsylvania Press.

Jackson, M. (1989), *Paths towards a Clearing. Radical Empiricism and Ethnographic Inquiry*. Bloomington: Indiana University Press.

(1996). *Things as They Are: New Directions in Phenomenological Anthropology*, Bloomington: Indiana University Press.

(1998), *Minima Ethnographica: Intersubjectivity and the Anthropological Project*, Chicago: University of Chicago Press.

Jacobsen, F. F. (1998), *Theories of Sickness and Misfortune amongst the Handandowa Beja of the Sudan: Narratives as Points of Entry into Beja Cultural Knowledge*, London: Kegan Paul International.

James, W. (1974), *Pragmatism and four essays from The Meaning of Truth*, New York: New American Library [originally published 1907 and 1909].

Janzen, J. (1978), *The Quest for Therapy in Lower Zaire*, Berkeley: University of California Press.

Jao, M. (1995), *Estudo sobre o infanticídio nas etnias mancanha, manjaco e pepel*, Bissau: Instituto Nacional de Estudos e Pesquisas (INEP).

Jarosz, L. (1994), 'Agents of Power, Landscapes of Fear: The Vampires and Heart Thieves of Madagascar', *Society and Space*, vol. 12, pp. 421-35.

Järvinen, M. (1998), *Det Dårlige Selskab: Misbrug, Behandling, Omsorg*, Holte: SocPol.

Jenkins, R. (1996), *Social Identity*, London: Routledge.

(1998a),'From criminology to anthropology? Identity, morality, and normality in the social construction of deviance', in S. Holdaway and P. Rock (eds.), *Thinking About Criminology*, London: UCL Press.

(1998b),'Culture, classification and (in)competence', in R. Jenkins (ed.) *Questions of Competence: Culture, Classification and Intellectual Disability*, Cambridge: Cambridge University Press.

(2000),'Disenchantment, enchantment and re-enchantment: Max Weber at The Millennium', *Max Weber Studies*, vol. 1: 11-32.

Jessen, H. (1997),'En dialogisk fortælling om diagnose og død', in H. P. Hansen and P. Ramhøj (ed.) *Tværvidenskabelige perspektiver på sundhed og sygdom*, Copenhagen: Akademisk forlag.

Johannisson, K. (1994), *Den Mörka Kontinenten: Kvinnan, medicinen og fin de-siécle*, Stockholm: Nordstedts Förlag.

Kaufert, P. (2000),'Screening the Body: the Pap Smear and the Mammogram', in M. Lock, A. Young, and A. Cambrosio (eds.), *Living and Working with the New Medical Technologies: Intersections of Inquiry*, Cambridge: Cambridge University Press.

and Gilbert, P. (1986),'Women, menopause, and medicalization', *Culture, Medicine and Psychiatry*, vol. 19, pp. 7-21.

Kaufmann, G. (1998),'Gender and reproductive decision making: the contraceptive choice of women in a Brazilian favela', in G. Martine, M. Das Gupta, and L. C. Chen (eds.), *Reproductive Change in India and Brazil*, Delhi: Oxford University Press.

Kertzer, D. I. (1995),'Political-economic and cultural explanations of demographic behavior', in S. Greenhalgh (ed.), *Situating Fertility*, Cambridge: Cambridge University Press.

and Fricke, T. (eds.) (1997), *Anthropological Demography: Toward a New Synthesis*, Chicago: University of Chicago Press.

Kirmayer, L. J. (1988), 'Mind and body as metaphors: hidden values in biomedicine', in M. Lock and D.R. Gordon (eds.), *Biomedicine Examined*, Dordrecht: Kluwer.

Kleinman, A. (1986), *Social Origins of Distress and Disease: Depression, Neurasthenia, and Pain in Modern China*, New Haven: Yale University Press.

(1988), *The Illness Narratives: Suffering, Healing and the Human Condition*, New York: Basic Books.

(1995a),'Pitch, Picture, Power: The Globalization of Local Suffering and the Transformation of Social Experience', *Ethnos*, vol. 60, no. 3-4, pp. 181-91.

(1995b), *Writing at the Margin: Discourse Between Anthropology and Medicine*. Berkeley: University of California Press.

and Kleinman, J. (1991),'Suffering and Its Professional Transformation: Toward an Ethnography of Interpersonal Experience', *Culture, Medicine and Psychiatry*, vol. 15, pp. 275-301.

and Kleinman, J. (1997),'The appeal of experience; the dismay of images: Cultural appropriations of suffering in our times', in A. Kleinman, V. Das, V. and M. Lockwood (eds.), *Social Suffering*, Berkeley: University of California Press.

Koch, L. (2002)'The Government of Genetic Knowledge', in: S. Lundin and L. Åkesson (eds.) *Gene Technology and Economy*, Lund: Nordic Academic Press.

Koenig, B. A. (1988), 'The technological imperative in medical practice: the social creation of 'routine' treatment', in M. Lock and D. R. Gordon (eds.) *Biomedicine Examined*, Dordrecht: Reidel.

Knudsen, H. C. *et al.* (1992), *Distriktspsykiatri i København: En evaluering af de to første år*, Copenhagen: Institut for Social Medicin, Københavns Universitet/Københavns Sundhedsdirektorat.

Laing, R. D. (1990 [1959]), *The Divided Self: An Existential Study in Sanity and Madness*, London: Penguin Books.

Landsforeningen Lænken (1996), *Årsskrift*, København: Centralkontoret for Lænke ambulatorier.

Larsen, J. A. (2001), *Projekt Opus i København. Dokumentation og evaluering af et forsøg med 2-årig intensiv teambaseret psykosocial og medicinsk indsats for unge førstegangspsykotiske*, Copenhagen: Familie- og Arbejdsmarkedsforvaltningen, Københavns Kommune.

(2002a) *Experiences with Early Intervention in Schizophrenia: An ethnographic study of assertive community treatment in Denmark*, PhD Thesis, Department of Sociological Studies, University of Sheffield.

(2002b) (ed.) *Sindets Labyrinter – Seks beretninger fra mødet med psykiatrien*. Copenhagen: Hans Reitzels Forlag.

(2002c) 'Recovery og symbolsk helbredelse', *Socialpsykiatri*, vol. 3, pp. 26-28.

(2003) 'Identiteten: Dialog om forandring', in K. Hastrup (ed.) *Ind I Verden: En grundbog i antropologisk metode*, Copenhagen: Hans Reitzels Forlag, pp. 247-71.

(n.d.) 'Finding meaning in first episode psychosis: Experience, agency, and the cultural repertoire', forthcoming in *Medical Anthropology Quarterly*.

Last, M. and Chavunduka, G. L. (eds.) (1986), *The Professionalisation of African Medicine*, Manchester: Manchester University Press.

Layne, L. L. (1992), 'Of Fetuses and Angels: Fragmentation and Integration in Narrative of Pregnancy Loss', *Knowledge and Society: The Anthropology of Science and Technology*, vol. 9, pp. 29-5.

Leder, D. (1990), *The Absent Body*, Chicago: The University of Chicago Press.

Legesse, A. (1973), *Gada: Three Approaches to the Study of African Society*, New York: Free Press.

Lemert, E. M. (1972), *Human Deviance, Social Problems and Social Control*, 2nd ed., Englewood-Cliffs: Prentice Hall.

Lewis, G. (1981), 'Cultural influences on illness behaviour', in L. Eisenberg and A. Kleinman (eds.) *The Relevance of Social Science for Medicine*, Dordrecht: Reidel.

(1993), 'Some studies of social causes and cultural response to disease', in C. G. N. Mascie-Taylor (ed.), *The Anthropology of Disease*, Oxford: Oxford University Press.

Lewis, J. L. (2000), 'Sex and violence in Brazil: *carnaval, capoeira*, and the problem of everyday life', *American Ethnologist*, vol. 26, pp. 539-57.

Lindenbaum, S. and Lock, M. (1993), *Knowledge, Power, and Practice*, Berkeley: University of California Press.

Lindgren, A. (1995), *Bogen om Pippi Langstrømpe*, Portugal: Gyldendal.

Littlewood, R. (1990),'From Category to Context: A Decade of the New Cross-Cultural Psychiatry,' *British Journal of Psychiatry*, vol. 157, pp. 308-27.

Lock, M. and Kaufert, P. A. (eds) (1997), *Pragmatic Women and Body Politics*, Cambridge: Cambridge University Press.

Lock, M., Young, A., and Cambrosio, A. (eds.) (2000), *Living and Working with the New Medical Technologies: Intersections of Inquiry*, Cambridge: Cambridge University Press.

Low, S. M. (1994)'Embodied metaphors: Nerves as lived experience,' In T. Csordas (ed.), *Embodiment and Experience: The existential ground of culture and self*, Cambridge: Cambridge University Press.

Luhmann, N. (1997) *Iagttagelse og paradoks: Essays om autopoietiske systemer*, København: Gyldendal.

Luhrmann, T. M. (2000), *Of Two Minds: The growing disorder in American psychiatry*, New York: Alfred A. Knopf.

Lundin, S. (1996),'Longing for social and biological identity,' in J. Frykman and O. Löfgren (eds.), *Force of Habit: Exploring Everyday Life*, Lund: Lund University Press.

Lupton, D. (1996),'Your life in their hands,' in V. James and J. Gabe (eds.), *Health and the Sociology of Emotions*, Oxford: Blackwell.

(1999), *Risk*, London: Routledge.

Lyons, M. (1992), *The Colonial Disease: A Social History of Sleeping Sickness in Northern Zaire, 1900-1940*, Cambridge: Cambridge University Press.

MacIntyre, A. (1981), *After Virtue: A Study in Moral Theory*, Notre Dame: University of Notre Dame Press.

McFarlane, W. *et al.* (1991), *Multiple-family psycho-educational group treatment manual*, New York: New York State Psychiatric Institute.

McGorry, P. D. (1995)'Psychoeducation in first-episode psychosis: A therapeutic process,' *Psychiatry* vol. 58: 313-28.

Macek, I. (1997),'Negotiating normality in Sarajevo during the 1992-1995 war,' *Narodna Umjetnost*, vol. 34, pp. 25-58.

(2000), *War Within: Everyday Life in Sarajevo under Siege*. Ph.D dissertation, Department of Cultural Anthropology, University of Upsalla.

Malkki, L. (1995a),'Refugees and Exile: From 'Refugee Studies' to the National Order of Things,' *Annual Review of Anthropology*, vol. 24, pp. 495-523.

(1995b), *Purity and Exile: Violence, Memory and National Cosmology among Hutu Refugees in Tanzania*, Chicago: University of Chicago Press.

Marsh, M. and Ronner, W. (1996), *The Empty Cradle: Infertility in America from Colonial Times to the Present*, Baltimore: John Hopkins University Press.

Martensen-Larsen, O. (1948),'Treatment of Alcoholism with a Sensitising Drug,' *The Lancet*, vol. 255, no. 2, pp. 1004-5.

Martin, E. (1993) *The Woman in the Body*, Buckingham: Open University Press.

Martine, G. (1998), 'Brazil's fertility decline, 1965-95: a fresh look at key Factors', in G. Martine, M. Das Gupta, and L. C. Chen (eds.), *Reproductive Change in India and Brazil*, Delhi: Oxford University Press.

Das Gupta, M. and Chen, L. C. (eds.) (1998), *Reproductive Change in India and Brazil*, Delhi: Oxford University Press.

Mattingly, C. (1994), 'The Concept of Therapeutic 'Emplotment'', *Social Science and Medicine*, vol. 38, pp. 811-22.

(1998a), *Healing Dramas and Clinical Plots: The Narrative Structure of Experience*, Cambridge: Cambridge University Press.

(1998b), 'In search of the good: narrative reasoning in clinical practice', *Medical Anthropology Quarterly*, vol. 12, pp. 273-97.

Matza, D. (1969), *Becoming Deviant*, Englewood-Cliffs: Prentice Hall.

Mbembe, A. and Roitman, J. (1995), 'Figures of the subject in times of crisis', *Public Culture*, vol. 7, pp. 323-352.

Mead, G. H. (1913), 'The Social Self', in A. J. Reck (ed.), *Selected Writings: George Herbert Mead*, Chicago: Chicago University Press.

(1934), *Mind, Self, and Society from the Standpoint of a Social Behaviorist*, ed. C.W. Morris, Chicago: University of Chicago Press.

Miller, B. D. (1987), 'Female infanticide and child neglect in rural North India', in N. Scheper-Hughes (ed.), *Child Survival: Anthropological Perspectives on the Treatment and Maltreatment of Children*, Dordrecht: Reidel Publishing Company.

Mimica, J. (1997), 'Psychosocial projects: Evaluation issues derived from forced migrants' and helpers' point of view', paper presented at the conference, The Study of Forced Migration: Psychological, Legal, Humanitarian and Anthropological Interventions, Hvar, Croatia.

Mogensen, H. O. (1995), *AIDS is a Kind of Kahungo that Kills: The challenge of using local narratives when exploring AIDS among the Tonga of southern Zambia*, Oslo: Scandinavia University Press.

(1997), 'The Narrative of AIDS among the Tonga of Zambia', *Social Science and Medicine*, vol. 44, pp. 431-9.

(1998), *Mothers' Agency – Others' Responsibility: Striving for Children's Health in Eastern Uganda*, Ph.D. dissertation, Institute of Anthropology, University of Copenhagen.

(2000), 'False Teeth and Real Suffering: Child Care in Eastern Uganda', *Culture, Medicine and Psychiatry*, vol. 24, pp. 331-51.

Molin, J. (1998), 'Den nya svenska modellen', *Socialpolitik* no. 2, pp. 18-20. Moore, S. F. (1999), 'Reflections on the Comaroff lecture', *American Ethnologist*, vol. 26, pp. 304-6.

Murphy, R. *et al.* (1988), 'Physical Disability and Social Liminality: A Study in the Rituals of Adversity', *Social Science and Medicine*, vol. 26, pp. 235-42

Musambachime, M. C. (1987), 'The impact of rumor: the case of the banyama (vampire men) scare in Northern Rhodesia, 1930-1964,' *International Journal of African Historical Studies*, vol. 21, pp. 201-15.

Mølsted, H. (1995), *Contextualising vaccination: Balanta appropriation of preventive health measures in Guinea-Bissau*, Kandidats dissertation, Institute of Anthropology, University of Copenhagen.

Nichter, M. (1989), *Anthropology and International Health: South Asian Case Studies*, Dordrecht: Kluwer.

Nicolaisen, I. (1995), 'Persons and nonpersons: disability among the Punan Bah of Central Borneo,' in B. Ingstad and S. R. Whyte (eds.), *Disability and Culture*, Berkeley: University of California Press.

Novas, C. and Rose, N. (2000), 'Genetic risk and the birth of the somatic individual,' *Economy and society*, vol. 29, pp. 485-513.

Nshakira, N., Whyte, S. R., Jitta, J. and Busuulwa, G. (1996), *An Assessment of Quality of Out-Patient Clinical Care in District Health Facilities*, Tororo District, Kampala: Child Health and Development Centre Document.

Nyboe Andersen, A. *et al.* (1996), *Klar Besked om Barnløshed*, København: Aschehough Dansk Forlag.

Obeysekere, G. (1985), 'Depression, Buddhism, and the Work of Culture in Sri Lanka,' in A. Kleinmann and B. Good (eds,), *Culture and Depression: Studies in the Anthropology and Cross-Cultural Psychiatry of Affect and Disorder*, Berkeley: University of California Press.

Oboler, R. S. (1985), *Women, Power, and Economic Change: The Nandi of Kenya*, Stanford: Stanford University Press.

Ocholla-Ayayo, A. B. C. (1976), *Traditional Ideology and Ethics among the Southern Luo*, Uppsala: Scandinavian Institute of African Studies.

Ombongi, K. J. (2000), *Malaria in Colonial Kenya: A History of Disease Control Policy, 1897-1963*. Ph.D. thesis, Department of History, University of Cambridge.

Orbe, D. (1996), 'Antabus som ritual,' *Lænkens Årsskrift 1996*, pp. 11-13.

Parmigiani, S. and vom Saal, F. S. (eds.) (1990), *Infanticide and Parental Care*, Reading: Harwood Academic Publishers.

Parkin, D. 1985, 'Entitling evil: Muslim and non-Muslim in coastal Kenya,' in D. Parkin (ed.), *The Anthropology of Evil*, Oxford: Basil Blackwell.

Parsons, T. (1951), *The Social System*, London: Routledge and Kegan Paul.

Pedersen, V. and Markussen, O. (2000), *Drikkeadfærd: Trang eller Lyst? Evaluering af Kognitiv Alkoholbehandling*, København: Institute of Anthropology, University of Copenhagen.

Pels, P. (1992), 'Mumiani: The white vampire: A neo-diffusionist analysis of rumour,' *Etnofoor*, vol. 5, pp.165-187.

Perry, R. B. (1996), *The Thought and Character of William James*, Nashville: Vanderbilt University Press [originally published 1948].

Plummer, K. (1979), 'Misunderstanding labelling processes,' in D. Downes and P. Rock (eds.) *Deviant Interpretations*, London: Martin Robertson.

PNDS (1996), *Pesquisa National Sobre Demografia e Saúde*, Rio de Janeiro: BEMFAM, IBGE, DHS.

Price, L. (1987), 'Ecuadorian illness stories: cultural knowledge in natural discourse', in D. Holland and N. Quinn (eds.) *Cultural Models in Language and Thought*, Cambridge: Cambridge University Press.

Prince, R. J., Geissler, P. W., Nokes, K., Okatcha, F., Grigorenko, E.L., and Sternberg, R.J. (2001) 'Knowledge of herbal and pharmaceutical medicines among Luo schoolchildren in western Kenya', *Anthropology and Medicine*, vol. 8 (2/3), pp. 211-35.

Ragoné, H. (1999), 'The Gifts of Life', in L. L. Layne (ed.), *Transformative Motherhood: On Giving and Getting in a Consumer Culture*, New York: New York University Press

Rhodes, L. A. *et al.* (1999), 'The power of the visible: the meaning of diagnostic tests in chronic back pain', *Social Science and Medicine*, vol. 48, pp. 1189-1203

Rosen, G. (1968), *Madness in society: Chapters in the historical sociology of mental illness*, Chicago: The University of Chicago Press.

Rosenhan, D. L. (1973), 'On being sane in insane places', *Science*, vol. 179, pp. 250-8.

Roth, G. and Ekblad, S. (1993), 'Migration and Mental Health: Current Research Issues', *Nordic Journal of Psychiatry*, vol. 45 no 3, pp. 185-9.

Sachs, L. (1989), 'Misunderstanding as therapy: doctors, patients and medicines in a rural clinic in Sri Lanka', *Culture, Medicine and Psychiatry*, vol. 8: 49-70.

(1998), *Att leva med risk: Fem kvinnor, gentester och kunskapens frukter*, Värnamo: Gedins.

Samuelsen, H. and Steffen, V. (eds.) (2004) *The Relevance of Foucault and Bourdieu for Medical Anthropology: Exploring New Sites*, special edition of *Anthropology and Medicine*, vol. 11 no. 1.

Sandelowski, M. (1993), *With Child in Mind: Studies of the Personal Encounter with Infertility*, Philadelphia: University of Pennsylvania Press.

(1994), 'Separate but less unequal: fetal ultrasonography and the transformation of expectant mother/fatherhood, *Gender and Society*, vol. 8, no. 2, pp. 230-45.

Sayre, J. (2000), 'The patient's diagnosis: Explanatory models of mental illness', *Qualitative Health Research*, vol. 10, pp. 71-83.

Scheff, T. (1966), *Being mentally ill: A sociological theory*, New York: Aldine.

Scheper-Hughes, N. (1992), *Death Without Weeping. The Violence of Everyday Life in Brazil*, Berkeley: University of California Press.

Schneider, M. A. (1993), *Culture and Enchantment*, Chicago: University of Chicago Press.

Schopper, S. D., Ayiga, N., Ezatirale, G., Ido, W. J. and Homsy, J. (1995), 'Village-based AIDS prevention in a rural district in Uganda', *Health Policy and Planning*, vol. 10, pp. 171-80.

Scrimshaw, S. C. M. (1978), 'Infant mortality and behavior in the regulation of family size', *Population and Development Review*, vol. 4, pp. 383-403.

(1984), 'Infanticide in human populations: societal and individual concerns', in G. Hausfater and S. B. Hrdy (eds.), *Infanticide: Comparative and Evolutionary Perspective*, New York: Aldine.

Scull, A. (1989), *Social order/mental disorder: Anglo-American psychiatry in historical perspective*, London: Routledge.

Sennemark, E. (1997), *Möten, berättelser, betydelser: Bosniska flyktingfamiljers möte med svensk psykiatri*, M.A. thesis, Department of Social Anthropology, Göteborg University.

Serruya, S. (1996), *Mulheres Esterilizadas: Submissão e Desejo*, Belém: NAEA/UFPA/ Universidade do Estado do Pará.

SFR (1994), *Forskning om internationell migration och etniska relationer 1990/91-1994/95*, Stockholm: Socialvetenskapliga Forskningsrådet.

Simpson, Bob (1997),'Representations and the Re-presentation of Family. An Analysis of Divorce Narratives', in A. James, J. Hockey and A. Dawson (eds.), *After Writing Culture. Epistemology and Praxis in Contemporary Anthropology*, London: Routledge.

SIV (1995), *Statistik 1995*, Norrköping: Statens Invandrarverk.

Skinhøj, K. (1988), *Behandling for Alkoholmisbrug: ved Danske Alkoholambulatorier*, rapport 88: 5, København: Social Forsknings Instituttet.

Snowden, R. (1990), 'The Family and Artificial Reproduction', in D. R. Bromham, M. E. Dalton and J. C. Jackson (eds.), *Philosophical Ethics in Reproductive Medicine*, Manchester: Manchester University Press.

Stanworth, M. (1987), 'Reproductive Technologies and the Deconstruction of Motherhood', in M. Stanworth (ed.), *Reproductive Technologies: Gender and Motherhood and Medicine*, London: Routledge.

(1990),'Birth Pangs: Conceptive Technologies and the Threat to Motherhood', in M. Hirsch and E. F. Keller (eds.), *Conflicts in Feminism*, Routledge: London.

Stein, L. I. and Santos, A. B. (1998), *Assertive community treatment of persons with severe mental illness*, New York: W.W. Norton & Company.

Steffen, V. (1993), *Minnesota-modellen i Danmark: Mellem Tradition og Fornyelse*, Holte: SocPol.

(1994), 'Individualism and Welfare: Alcoholics Anonymous and the Minnesota Model in Denmark', *Nordic Alcohol Studies, English Supplement*, vol. 11, pp. 13-20.

(1997),'Life Stories and Shared Experience', *Social Science and Medicine*, vol. 45, pp. 99-111.

(2002), 'Nature or nurture: narratives of descent in Danish cases of alcoholism', *AM: Revista della Società italiana di antropologia medica*, nos. 13-14, pp. 27-45.

Stone, D. (1984), *The Disabled State*, London: Macmillan.

Strathern, M. (1992), *Reproducing the Future: Anthropology, Kinship and The New Reproductive Technologies*, Manchester: Manchester University Press.

(1993),'Introduction: A question of context', in J. Edwards, S. Franklin, E. Hirsch, F. Price, and M. Strathern, *Technologies of Procreation: Kinship in the age of assisted conception*, Manchester: Manchester University Press.

Stimson, G. V. (1974), 'Obeying doctor's orders: a view from the other side', *Social Science and Medicine*, vol. 8, pp. 97-104.

Tapp, N. (1988), 'The Reformation of Culture: Hmong Refugees from Laos', *Journal of Refugee Studies*, vol. 1:, pp. 20-37

Taussig, M. (1980), *The Devil and Commodity Fetishism in South America*, Chapel Hill: University of North Carolina Press.

Taylor, C. (1989), *Sources of the Self: The Making of Modern Identity*, Cambridge: Cambridge University Press.

Taylor, J. S. (1998), 'Image and Contradiction: Obsterial Ultrasound in American Culture', in S. Franklin and H. Ragoné (eds.), *Reproducing Reproduction. Kinship Power and Technological Innovation*, Philadelphia: University of Pennsylvania Press.

Thoits, P. A. (1985), 'Self-labeling Processes in Mental Illness: The Role of Emotional Deviance', *American Journal of Sociology*, vol. 91, pp. 221-49.

Thorsen, T. (1993), *Dansk alkoholpolitik efter 1950*, Holte: SocPol.

Tjørnhøj-Thomsen, T. (1999a), *Tilblivelseshistorier: Slægtskab, Forplantningsteknologi og Forplantningsteknologi i Danmark*, Ph.D. dissertation, Institute of Anthropolgy, University of Copenhagen.
(1999b), ''Det føles ikke mandigt på en måde': Mænd og infertilitet', *Kvinder, Køn og Forskning*, vol. 8, no. 3, pp. 71-89.

Trant, H. (1970), *Not Merrion Square: Andecdotes from a Woman's Medical Career in Africa*, East London: The Thornhill Press.

Tsing, A. L. (1993), 'Government Headhunters', in A. L. Tsing (ed.), *In The Realm of the Diamond Queen: Marginality in an Out-of-the-Way Place*, Princeton: Princeton University Press.

Turner, V. (1967), *The Forest of Symbols*, Ithaca: Cornell University Press.
(1968), *The Drums of Affliction*, Oxford: Clarendon Press.

UNDP [United Nations Development Programme] (2000), *Human Development Index 2000*, New York: Oxford University Press.

Unicef/IBGE (1991-1996) *Indicadores sobre criancas e adolescentes*. Brasilia and Rio de Janeiro: Unicef.

Valverde, M. (1998), *Diseases of the Will: Alcohol and the Dilemmas of Freedom*, Cambridge: Cambridge University Press.

van der Geest, S. and Whyte, S. R. (1989), 'The charm of medicines: metaphors and metonyms', *Medical Anthropology Quarterly*, vol. 3, pp. 345-67.
, Whyte, S. R. and Hardon, A. (1996), 'The anthropology of pharmaceuticals: a biographical approach', *Annual Review of Anthropology*, vol. 25, pp. 153-78.

van der Kolk, B. A., McFarlane, A. C. and Weisaeth, L. (1996) (eds.), *Traumatic Stress: The effects of Overwhelming Experience on Mind, Body and Society*, New York: Guilford.

Vuckovic, N. and M. Nichter (1997), 'Changing patterns of pharmaceutical practice in the United States', *Social Science and Medicine*, vol. 44, pp. 1285-1302.

Wachtel, N. (1994), *Gods and Vampires: Return to Chipaya*, Chicago: University of Chicago Press.

Weber, M. (1948) *From Max Weber: Essays in Sociology*, ed. H. H. Gerth And C. W. Mills, London: Routledge and Kegan Paul.

Weisaeth, L. and Mehlum, L. (eds), (1997), *Människor, Trauman och Kriser*, Stockholm: Natur och Kultur.

Weiss, B. (1996), *The Making and Unmaking of the Haya Lived World: Consumption, Commoditization, and Everyday Practice*, Durham: Duke University Press.

(1998), 'Electric vampires: Haya rumours of the commodified body,' in M. Lambeck and A. Strathern (eds.), *Bodies and Persons: Comparative Perspectives from Africa and Melanesia*, Cambridge: Cambridge University Press.

Weman, S. (1997), 'Expertkunskaper tryggar rätten till god vård', in CTD [Centrum för Tortyr- och Traumaskadade], *Med livet i behåll: Om tortyr, överlevnad och återupprättelse*, Stockholm: Stockholms Läns Landsting.

Weston, K. (1995). 'Forever is a Long Time: Romancing the Real in Gay Kinship Ideologies', in S. Yanagisako and C. Delaney (eds.), *Naturalizing Power: Essays In Feminist Cultural Analysis*, London: Routledge.

White, L. (1990), 'Bodily fluids and usufruct: Controlling property in Nairobi 1917-1939', *Canadian Journal of African Studies*, vol. 24, pp. 418-38.

(1993a), 'Vampire Priests of Central Africa: African Debates about Labour and Religion in Colonial Northern Zambia', *Comparative Studies in Sociology and History*, vol. 35, pp. 746-72.

(1993b), 'Cars out of place: vampires, technology, and labor in East and Central Africa', *Representations*, no. 43, pp. 27-50.

(1995a), "'They could make their victims dull': genders and genres, fantasies and cures in colonial southern Uganda', *American Historical Review*, vol. 100, pp. 1379-1402.

(1995b), 'Tsetse visions: narratives of blood and bugs in colonial Northern Rhodesia', *Journal of African History*, vol. 36, pp. 219-45.

White, W. (1998), *Slaying the Dragon: The History of Addiction Treatment and Recovery in America*, Bloomington: Chestnut Health Systems.

WHO (1992), *Female Sterilization: A Guide to Provision of Services*, Geneva: World Health Orgnization.

Whyte, S. R. (1991), 'Medicines and self-help: the privatization of health care in eastern Uganda', in H. B. Hansen and M. Twaddle (eds.), *Changing Uganda: Dilemmas of Structural Adjustment and Revolutionary Change*, London: James Currey.

(1992), 'Pharmaceuticals as folk medicine: transformations in the social relations of health care in Uganda', *Culture, Medicine and Psychiatry*, vol. 16, pp. 163-86.

(1997) *Questioning Misfortune: The Pragmatics of Uncertainty In Eastern Uganda*, Cambridge: Cambridge University Press.

(1998), 'Anthropology of Consequences: Problem and Practice in a Complex World', inaugural lecture, Institute of Anthropology, University of Copenhagen.

and Birungi, H. (2000), 'The business of medicines and the politics of knowledge in Uganda', L. M. Whiteford and L. Manderson (eds.), *Globalization, Health and Identity: The Fallacy of the Level Playing Field*, Boulder, CO: Lynne Rienner.

and Whyte, M. A. (1981), 'Cursing and pollution: supernatural styles in two Luyia-speaking groups', *Folk*, vol. 23, pp. 65-80.

Wikan, U. (1992), 'Beyond the Words: the Power of Resonance', *American Ethnologist*, vol. 19, pp. 460-82.

Wirtberg, I. (1992), *His and Her Childlessness*, Stockholm: Department of Psychiatry and Psychology, Karolinska Institutet.

Yoder, S. (1997), 'Negotiating Relevance: Belief, Knowledge, and Practice in International Health Projects', *Medical Anthropology Quarterly*, vol. 11, pp. 131-46.

Young, A. (1995), *The Harmony of Illusions: Inventing Post-Traumatic Stress Disorder*, Princeton: Princeton University Press.

CONTRIBUTORS

Anne Line Dalsgaard has a PhD and is Assistant Professor at the Department of Anthropology and Ethnography at Aarhus University. She has made several fieldwork visits to Recife, Northeast Brazil, since 1997. Her work combines a phenomenological approach to motherhood with an analysis of the historical, political, and economic factors shaping individual experience. She is the author of *Matters of Life and Longing: Female Sterilisation in Northeast Brazil* (Museum Tusculanum Press, 2004)

Marita Eastmond is Associate Professor of Social Anthropology at Göteborg University, Sweden. Her research interests comprise the politics of conflict and exile, violence, and discourses of suffering and normalisation. She has published on the Chilean left in exile, on repatriation and reconciliation in Cambodia, on ethno-nationalist conflict in Bosnia, and on the politics of trauma in Sweden as a host country. Her field work areas are Chile, Cambodia, U.S.A. and Sweden. She is the author of *The Dilemmas of Exile* (Acta Universitatis Gothenburgensis, 1997).

Jónína Einarsdóttir PhD, is Assistant Professor of Anthropology at the University of Iceland. She conducted fieldwork in Guinea-Bissau 1993-1998 and is currently doing research in Iceland on ethical questions concerning extremely premature children and their daily life. Her main areas of research are within the anthropology of children, development, reproduction, kinship, religion and ethics, as well as medical anthropology. She has published on children, breastfeeding and cholera and is the author of the book *'Tired of Weeping': Mother Love, Child Death and Poverty in Guinea-Bissau* (University of Wisconsin Press, 2004).

Paul Wenzel Geissler PhD, is a Senior Lecturer of Social Anthropology at London School of Hygiene and Tropical Medicin, University of London. His current research focuses on African ethnography, specifically (changing forms of) relatedness and time in the everyday life of people in western Kenya, and on the ethnography of science in Africa, particularly field research in a variety of medical field trial sites in sub-Saharan Africa.

Richard Jenkins is Professor of Sociology at the University of Sheffield, England. Trained as an anthropologist at Belfast and Cambridge, he has undertaken field research in Northern Ireland, England, Wales and Denmark. His current areas of interest include social identity in all its aspects, the cultural construction of competence, and the dis/re-enchantment of the world. He is the author of *Pierre Bourdieu* (Routledge, 2nd edition 2003), *Social Identity* (Routledge, 2nd edition 2004), *Rethinking Ethnicity* (Sage, 1997), and *Foundations of Sociology* (Palgrave, 2002), and editor of *Questions of Competence* (Cambridge University Press, 1998).

Hanne Jessen MSc, is a Research Assistant at the Medical Museion, University of Copenhagen. She has done fieldwork in different biomedical settings (hospitals, clinics, laboratories) in Denmark, with a focus on interaction between patients and professionals, particularly the processes by which different domains of experience and knowledge are represented and interpreted.

John Aggergaard Larsen PhD, is a Research Fellow at the European Institute of Health and Medical Sciences, University of Surrey. For his doctoral research he conducted ethnographic fieldwork as the evaluator of an experimental community mental health service in the Municipality of Copenhagen. His main areas of interest are the cultural phenomenology of mental health, participatory research, individual-society interaction and issues of identity and social inclusion in social and health intervention programmes.

Hanne O. Mogensen is Associate Professor at the Institute of Anthropology, University of Copenhagen, Denmark. She has conducted research on various topics in international health and medical anthropology, primarily in Zambia and Uganda. She is the author of the book *Aids is a Kind of Kahungo That Kills* (Scandinavia University Press, 1995).

Vibeke Steffen is Associate Professor at the Institute of Anthropology, University of Copenhagen, Denmark. She has conducted ethnographic fieldwork in Denmark on issues of health and illness over the past 15 years. Among her main research interests are problems of addiction, therapeutic processes, and narrative constructions of identity. She is the author of *Minnesota-modellen i Danmark* (SocPol, 1993).

Mette Nordahl Svendsen, PhD in Anthropology, is Project Manager at DSI Institute for Health Services Research in Copenhagen. Her research interests include: social implications of biotechnology, kinship studies, and the anthropology of knowledge.

Tine Tjørnhøj-Thomsen is Assistant Professor at the Institute of Anthropology, University of Copenhagen, Denmark. Her primary research area is kinship, infertility and reproductive technologies, and she has carried out ethnographic fieldwork in Denmark on these topics.

Susan Reynolds Whyte is Professor at the Institute of Anthropology, University of Copenhagen, Denmark. She has been engaged in field research on misfortune and health in eastern Uganda at intervals since 1969, and is involved in applied health research and research training in Uganda. She is the co-editor, with B. Ingstad, of *Disability and Culture* (University of California Press, 1995), author of *Questioning Misfortune: the Pragmatics of Uncertainty in Eastern Uganda* (Cambridge University Press, 1997) and co-author, with S. van der Geest and A. Hardon, of *Social Lives of Medicines* (Cambridge University Press, 2002).